Developing Language and Literacy 3–8

3rd Edition

Ann Browne

Los Angeles • London • New Delhi • Singapore • Washington DC

© Ann Browne 2009

First published 2009

Apart from any fair dealing for the purposes of
research or private study, or criticism or review, as
permitted under the Copyright, Designs and Patents Act
1988, this publication may be reproduced, stored or
transmitted in any form, or by any means, only with
the prior permission in writing of the publishers,
or in the case of reprographic reproduction, in accordance
with the terms of licences issued by the Copyright Licensing
Agency. Enquiries concerning reproduction outside those
terms should be sent to the publishers.

SAGE Publications Ltd
1 Oliver's Yard
55 City Road
London EC1Y 1SP

SAGE Publications Inc.
2455 Teller Road
Thousand Oaks, California 91320

SAGE Publications India Pvt Ltd
B 1/I 1 Mohan Cooperative Industrial Area
Mathura Road
New Delhi 110 044

SAGE Publications Asia-Pacific Pte Ltd
33 Pekin Street #02-01
Far East Square
Singapore 048763

Library of Congress Control Number: 2008938529

British Library Cataloguing in Publication data

A catalogue record for this book is available from the British Library

ISBN 978-1-84787-082-7
ISBN 978-1-84787-083-4 (pbk)

Typeset by C&M Digitals (P) Ltd, Chennai, India
Printed in Great Britain by CPI Antony Rowe, Chippenham, Wilts
Printed on paper from sustainable resources

Contents

The author   vi

Introduction   vii

1   Speaking and listening   1

2   Reading   25

3   Resources and activities for reading   57

4   Writing   91

5   Spelling, handwriting and punctuation   130

6   Bilingual learners   159

7   Language, literacy and gender   182

8   Special educational needs   202

9   Working with parents   229

10   Assessment   244

11   Planning for language and literacy   276

Appendix: A sample language and literacy policy   292

References and further reading   302

Companion website   310

Index   311

The author

Ann Browne's professional life has been as a teacher and lecturer in primary education. Throughout her career her main interests have been language and literacy and the education of young children. She is the author of a number of books about teaching and learning language and literacy.

Introduction

When I wrote the first edition of *Developing Language and Literacy 3–8* I wanted to provide an informative, up-to-date guide to good practice in teaching English for all those who work with young children. This continues to be my intention in this third edition.

This edition has been thoroughly updated to take account of developments in research, policy and practice. Many of the chapters have been rewritten and contain new examples of children and teachers at work. Each chapter contains a number of reflective activities and a list of annotated reading. The book now has a companion website which contains additional activities and links to sources of information. These features should enable readers to explore topics further. Visit http://www.sagepub. co.uk/Browne.

I know that teachers and children are both male and female but throughout this book when writing about teachers and children I have used 'she' and 'he' respectively. I have used this convention for the sake of simplicity. When writing about individuals I have referred to them as he or she as appropriate.

The children, students, teachers, researchers and writers whom I encounter in my work have provided me with many opportunities to reflect on learning and learners, to consider an appropriate language and literacy curriculum for young children, and have made it possible for me to collect the material that is included in this book. I would like to thank them.

I hope that this book recognises the expertise and importance of all who contribute to the education of young children and acknowledges the willingness and curiosity that children bring to learning, and that it can make a contribution to the quality of teaching and learning about language and literacy.

Ann Browne

1

Speaking and listening

Introduction

> **This chapter covers:**
>
> - how and why children learn to talk;
> - the connection between language and learning;
> - organising for speaking and listening;
> - drama;
> - speaking and listening across the curriculum;
> - standard English and received pronunciation.

Children learning language

Language acquisition

By the time that children are four or five almost all of them have achieved an amazing competence in at least one language. Studies of the vocabulary development of young children have shown that the average five-year-old knows at least 2,000 words and may know over 10,000 (Crystal, 1987). The number of words that a young child understands is thought to be far more than either of these figures. As part of the process of gathering this extensive vocabulary, most young children have mastered most of the phonemes or sound units of the speech used in their home or community. Research has shown that, by the time they go to school, children's speech is mostly grammatically correct and children from English-speaking homes use all the basic sentence patterns of English in their speech (Strickland, 1962; Loban, 1976). Although some children may make grammatical errors, saying, for example, 'she bringed it' rather than 'she brought it', such mistakes are usually the result of the overgeneralisation of a grammatical rule rather than a random mistake, in this case an awareness of how past-tense verbs are often formed. As well as being competent speakers young children are also expert listeners. It is their ability to listen that allows them to join in with the speech of adults from the time that they are a few months old. Listening gives them clues about the sounds and sound combinations which are used to form acceptable words and provides children with an understanding of how sentences are formed.

By the age of three or four months children are actively developing as participants in spoken communication. Babies respond to the talk of others with smiles, movements and sounds. They discover their own voices and gurgle with pleasure as adults speak to them. This stage in language development, known as babbling, gives very young children the opportunity to experiment with and imitate the sound patterns of their home language. As children experiment with producing sounds they gain greater control over their throat and mouth muscles and begin to engage in turn-taking behaviour, characteristic of spoken dialogue. For example, they wait for a pause in the speech of others before producing their own sounds. By about five or six months babies may begin intentionally to use their voices to attract attention and to initiate social exchanges. During the next few months babies start to establish a range of sounds, some of which are wordlike. These might include sounds such as 'baba', 'da-da' and 'ma-ma'. Adults are often delighted with the emergence of sounds that resemble familiar words and attribute meaning to them. They respond to children by repeating and expanding those words that they recognise, saying such things as, 'Da-da, yes, what a clever girl. Here's daddy now. Daddy is opening the door.' With encouragement such as this children gradually begin to attach meaning to particular groups of sounds and words, hearing, for example, that 'da-da' can become the word 'daddy'. Adult responses encourage babies to experiment more and provide examples which children use to build a vocabulary that sounds increasingly like that of adult speakers.

From the age of about 15 months onwards, children begin, with increasing accuracy, to imitate the sounds that they hear others use. They show that they want to join in communicative acts with others, signalling their intentions through their actions, gestures and the tone and nature of their utterances. Their communications increasingly resemble the words and phrases used by the adults around them. At about two years children's speech is characterised by abbreviated utterances that transmit meaning (Brown and Belugi, 1966). They produce correctly ordered groups of content words that can be understood by others. For example, a young child may say, 'Mummy gone shops'. The typical adult response to an utterance of this sort is to acknowledge the meaning, praise the utterance and expand what was said by giving the child the 'correct' adult version by replying 'Yes, that's right. Mummy has gone to the shops, hasn't she?' This kind of response provides children with models of the extended grammatical structure of language which they incorporate into their own speech. From about the age of three years most children begin to construct longer, more complex sentences and are able to use a number of tenses and styles. Their development as speakers and listeners continues until, by the time they start school, the majority of children are accomplished communicators with a large vocabulary, a command of a range of sentence types and a clear sense of grammatical correctness.

How and why children learn to speak

Most children develop their capacity to speak and to listen without any direct instruction or teaching. How children do this reveals a great deal about them as learners generally as well as about how they learn language. Adults can learn from this process. Understanding the way children develop speaking and listening provides teachers with an understanding of the conditions that support learning and strategies which help children to learn.

Babies are learners from the moment of their birth. The first cry that they utter as they are born, as with their later cries and sounds, results in attention and responses from those around them. From the start adults respond to children's facial expressions and the sounds that they make, with encouragement, praise and an expectation that the child's communication has meaning. At the same time as babies are learning that producing sounds enables their needs to be met, the adults who surround them are demonstrating the nature and use of speaking and listening. Care-givers assume that even very young babies are potential conversation partners and as they interact with babies they speak to them in a way that assumes that the baby is listening, may understand and has the potential to respond. Children overhear a great deal of conversation between those around them and are exposed to a great deal of conversation addressed directly to them. Adults interpret, repeat, support, extend and provide models of speech for children as they communicate with them. They do not limit their language or the child's learning but rather expose the child to the full range of language that is used in the child's environment. As children are exposed to more and more language and are supported in their production they become increasingly proficient in their language use.

At first babies use language for functional reasons; to express their needs and to get others to do things for them. At an early stage they may also see the social purposes of language. Because the attention of others is usually pleasurable babies soon discover that the production of sounds and language is one way for them to initiate and sustain interactions. Babies seem to enjoy producing sounds and at times produce long repetitions of similar sounds as they babble and gurgle and later experiment with real and nonsense words. Finally children seem to develop language because they are cognitive beings and active explorers of their worlds. Language is one method of finding out about the world that they live in. It enables them to widen their understanding by questioning, commenting, suggesting reasons, drawing upon previous experience and receiving information from others.

Language and learning

Being able to listen and to speak are essential if children are to succeed both inside and outside school. Speaking and listening occupy more time than reading and writing in the lives of most people. In school a developing facility with oral language is crucial for learning. In the early years a great deal of teaching and assessment is carried out through talk as the teacher explains, describes and questions children.

Learning to read and to write are founded upon children's oral language competence. As they learn to speak they discover that language contains meaning, follows a particular structure and consists of sentences, words and parts of words. They can apply this knowledge about language as they learn to read and write. As children progress through the education system knowledge and information are increasingly transmitted and recorded through reading and writing and their learning depends on a growing competence in a language mode that grows out of their ability to speak and listen.

From the start children's language development is associated with their exploration and growing understanding of the world they inhabit. Through listening, hypothesising, questioning and interpreting the responses they receive from others they learn a great deal. Language supports children's cognitive development by providing them with a tool to make discoveries and make sense of new experiences and offering them a means of making connections between the new and what is already known. All learning depends on the ability to question, reason, formulate ideas, pose hypotheses and exchange ideas with others. These are not just oral language skills, they are also thinking skills. We explore what we think and know through language. As we share events and describe our emotions to others and try to find the correct way of expressing these we often begin to discover what we really remember, feel or understand. Talk can help us to clarify and focus our thinking and deepen our understanding. As we struggle with expressing our ideas to others we often understand them more clearly ourselves. So perhaps the most important reason for developing children's oral language is the link between language development, learning and thinking. This kind of talk is not one where there are swift, short 'right answers'. It is often tentative. Words are changed and ideas expressed in a number of different ways. In order for the link between thinking and talking to be realised, children need time to think about what they know, time to think about how to express their thoughts and time to articulate and reformulate their ideas.

The extract in Figure 1.1 shows the potential language has to be a powerful tool for learning across and beyond the early years curriculum. Three Year 1 children, Suki, Martin and Thomas, were working together in the art area. They had been asked to print a large area of sky as part of a background for a display relating to the story *Charlie's House* (Schermbrucker, 1992). The teacher had asked the children to work together to complete the activity. They had to decide on the colour they would use for the sky and then decide what equipment they would use for the printing.

This extract shows children using talk to focus carefully on the activity and to do it well. They were using talk for a number of purposes and in a number of ways. Through their talk they were reflecting on a previous learning experience which occurred when they listened to the story, and integrating this with their own knowledge and understanding of hot countries. Although they had seen the pictures in the book, they had not realised the significance of the grey skies in relation to the climate. Martin's contribution is an excellent example of taking time to think and express his growing understanding

S:	Blue … This sky is blue.
M:	Like, like … the sky in the book.
T:	Is it? … I mean … just …
S:	Course it is … the sky in South Africa's always blue, like the sun is always shining.
M:	Doesn't.
S:	Does … What do you mean?
M:	Has to rain sometimes … that's why, that's how they got the mud … and in the winter …
S:	Yeah, I remember it rained.
T:	They got paint pots to get the water.
M:	But it's not in the book. [M goes to find the book and brings it to show the others] …
M:	Look … nowhere … nowhere blue.

Figure 1.1   Children learning through talk

through talk. At first he seems prepared to go along with Suki's suggestion but Thomas's question prompts his thinking. He then disagrees quite bluntly before being able to justify his new position. Thomas also gives reasons for his opinion after taking some time to think. As the children talk they listen carefully to one another and give each other time, and Suki seems happy to adjust her thinking in the light of what has been said and the evidence contained in the book. Exchanging ideas has given them the opportunity to re-evaluate what they assumed and to extend and amend their previous knowledge. Had the children been working at this task singly or with an adult who was directing them, it is unlikely that this learning and reflection would have taken place. In this extract the conversation emerging from a collaborative activity has been a valuable way of exchanging opinions, sharing knowledge, justifying ideas, reflecting on previous experiences and accepting new learning.

Concerns and solutions about teaching speaking and listening

For some time speaking and listening was a neglected element in the English curriculum. The publication of the National Literacy Strategy (DfEE, 1998) placed the emphasis for English teaching firmly on reading and writing and classroom practice reflected this. More recently the importance of teaching speaking and listening has been recognised. In 2003 new guidelines were developed by the DfES to support teachers and the Primary Framework for Literacy (DfES, 2006a) contains yearly objectives for oral language as well as for reading and writing. The review which preceded the framework (Rose, 2006) also recommended that the teaching of reading should be accompanied by teaching which develops children's abilities in speaking and listening.

These publications are doing a great deal to ensure that speaking and listening have a significant place in the English curriculum.

Classroom management

Routines and rules about quiet or silence while the teacher marks the register, when children move from the classroom for PE, lunch, playtime and assemblies and silent periods for reading, PE and stories reduce the time available for talk in the school day. Too many rules about times when children's talk is not allowed can also transmit negative messages about the importance of talking and listening.

Sometimes teachers think that the sound of children talking signals that children are not working and tell children to 'Be quiet' and 'Stop talking' so that they can get on with their work. They may fear that talk will develop into noisy and undisciplined behaviour. Teachers who do not understand the place of talk in learning and who feel insecure about noise in the classroom will influence their pupils' perceptions of talk. When children are taught by teachers who silence them or who suggest that talking is not work they learn that speaking and listening have little status at school. They will not see speaking and listening as a means of learning, and when they are given opportunities to speak often use talk to chat or gossip.

Teachers can find the prospect of organising collaborative activities for the whole class daunting. They may restrict opportunities for developing speaking and listening to whole-class discussion times or believe that allowing quiet talking when children work is sufficient. Whole-class discussions are rarely productive and their use needs to be limited. The majority of children are usually silent while one child or the adult speaks, very few children get the opportunity to contribute and interaction among the children is rare. Permitting quiet talking during an activity is not the same as children talking about an activity and using talk to exchange ideas, to question, to solve problems and to explain. Collaborative activities that demand pupil discussion need to be consciously organised by the teacher – productive talk does not just happen.

Teacher talk

The pressure to cover the statutory curriculum has encouraged some teachers to employ a more didactic style of teaching, a style that is concerned with the transmission of facts rather than the exploration of ideas (Moyles et al., 2001). This approach to teaching reduces the opportunities and necessity for discussion and the interaction that does occur is more likely to be concerned with eliciting and giving correct answers rather than using oral language for any of its other purposes.

When comparing children's language at home and at school, Wells (1986) found that at school children speak less with adults, get fewer turns, express a narrower range of meanings and use grammatically less complex utterances. They also ask fewer questions, make fewer requests and initiate a smaller proportion of conversations. In comparison with parents, teachers dominated conversational exchanges, giving children far fewer opportunities to speak in class than at home. He concluded that 'For no child was the language experience of the classroom richer than that of the home' (Wells, 1986: 87). This is dispiriting if we believe that school should present children with opportunities to broaden their experiences. A survey of classroom talk (Alexander, 2003) suggests that in school interactions between children and adults are brief rather than sustained, closed questions where children are expected to give brief correct answers predominate and there is little speculative talk. Both Alexander and Wells suggest that teachers need to see children's questions, explanations and comments as important and valuable. While listening may be an essential part of the speaking and listening curriculum, the opportunity for children to develop their own meanings through talk is a vital part of learning and language development.

Young children are strongly influenced by the models of talk presented to them by the adults who are important in their lives. Teachers are significant adults and as such can present a powerful model of language use to children. But how often do teachers present children with a model of talk used for speculation, enquiry or debate, or demonstrate that they too are exploratory users of language (NCC, 1989)? Very often the teacher's talk is perceived by children as being mainly expository or interrogatory. The teacher tells, commands or judges when she speaks to children and very often her questions give children too little time to respond and elicit only minimal answers (Mroz, et al., 2000). Wells (1986) suggested that in order to encourage children to use talk as a means of learning teachers need to be good listeners. When they listen to children they need to give them their full attention and let them see that what they are saying is valuable. They need to be supportive of and encouraging to children in their use of language and intervene in children's talk only when it is appropriate. Their questions should be real questions asked because they truly want to know the child's opinion or thoughts, not asked merely to check that children know what the teacher wants them to know.

Understanding the value of talk

It is easy for adults to place most emphasis on work that is regularly recorded, that can be seen and that can be assessed easily. Talk is none of these things. How do we tell if children have made a real effort to listen or to speak? How do we justify talk to others if there is no visible product? If teachers view talk as an inferior means of demonstrating learning and emphasise the more visible parts of the curriculum such as writing and recording, productive talk is unlikely to happen.

In this chapter I have tried to make a strong case for the learning potential of talk. By learning to speak children demonstrate that they are active learners and constructors of their own knowledge and as adults support the development and use of children's speech they enable children to articulate and satisfy their curiosity. The teacher's willingness to explore topics collaboratively with pupils, allowing them to negotiate meanings and extend their understanding through talk, is the key to developing children's learning. This means that teachers have to allow time for children to talk to adults and to each other about tasks that are undertaken and new ideas that they meet.

Respecting children

Children will feel confident and comfortable in speaking if the teacher shows a positive respect for and interest in their language and gives status to the different varieties of language they use. If this is not the case then they are less likely to contribute confidently and fluently to discussions and conversations. Confident talk develops when children's own language and way of talking and their right to be silent are respected. They also need to feel comfortable about making mistakes, being tentative and using language to think aloud. Children need to receive the message that talk is valued at school, that it is not second best to reading and writing as a measure of ability, but that it has a place in developing shared understandings, sorting out one's own thoughts and passing on information. Making time to praise good examples of talk in the classroom during the school day can help children to appreciate its importance.

Wells (1986) found that where teachers had high expectations they were more likely to encourage children to express their ideas at length, but that when they held low expectations of children as speakers and listeners, they gave children few opportunities to sustain a topic of conversation. Low expectations also led to teachers controlling discussions by asking simple questions which were answered briefly and quickly.

Teachers and children working collaboratively

The teacher can share her role as an organiser in the classroom with the pupils. She can involve members of working groups in decisions about the role to be assumed by each group member and the specific tasks that the group takes upon itself. For example, a group of children working on the class theme of 'Food' may decide that they want to make an information book about different kinds of bread. Will each child in the group research one type of bread, its ingredients, how it is made and where it is most commonly eaten? Will any of the children be able to bring different sorts of bread to school? Will the children ask the classroom assistant to help them make different sorts of bread? What will their information book look like? Who will make it? Who will illustrate it? What headings will they use to record their findings? How will they make all their decisions? The teacher can encourage the children to consult one another in order to plan their tasks and allocate roles.

The teacher can also share the role of expert. In the example given above the teacher could encourage the children to take as much responsibility as possible for their project. She may help them to establish some initial ground rules for their work but she will also help the children to identify each other as experts and to access information from other people or from books. As the task proceeds or once it has been completed the group may report their findings to the class. At this point the teacher could share the role of questioner with other members of the class rather than being the initiator of the questions and the focus for the group report.

There is now a great deal of interest in creating classrooms where teaching and learning are discursive and open, a style of working that has been termed dialogic (Alexander, 2006). In such classrooms teachers and children address learning together. Learning is a shared endeavour in which teachers and children build on each other's ideas. They listen to each other and discuss their ideas freely. Tentative talk, wrong answers and changing one's mind are all part of the learning process. In this context teachers treat what children have to say as worthy of attention and listen carefully to what they say. What the child says and means is the starting point for the teacher's response and her teaching. Dialogic teaching places speaking and learning at the centre of learning by harnessing the power of talk to stimulate and extend thinking, learning and understanding.

The teacher's role

Teachers and other adults in school, can play an important part in extending the oral language of young children. They are likely to do this well when they:

- attend to and support the child, only responding to what is said after having carefully listened to the child's words and meaning;
- create shared experiences and reasons for talk by engaging in dialogue during and about shared activities;
- create meaningful social, functional and communicative situations for talking in which speaking and listening can be used for a variety of purposes and with a genuine audience;
- spend time with children giving them experience and models of conversations;
- pose open questions and explore issues which are of interest to all the participants;
- extend children's vocabulary through demonstrating an interest in language and the way in which it is used and encouraging children's interest in the way words sound, are chosen, are interesting and are fun;
- assume that children have something important to say;
- view speaking and listening as an equal partnership and expect the child to contribute to this partnership; and
- provide an atmosphere of safety in which children feel confident enough to voice or rehearse opinions and ask questions.

Organising for speaking and listening

Productive talk can occur in a range of situations in the classroom. It can occur with the whole class, in specially created groups, during collaborative tasks and during independent work and play. Using a range of situations means that children get opportunities to use talk in different ways and engage with different speakers and models.

Whole-class opportunities

Story time

Introducing slightly different activities at story times and varying the way children listen to stories can be a productive way of encouraging listening. The teacher can announce that as she reads a story she is going to make a deliberate mistake and can ask the children to listen carefully and to put up their hands when they hear the mistake. The teacher can read a story containing a refrain such as 'but my cat likes to hide in boxes' (Sutton, 1973) and the class can be invited to join in with this. The class can be asked to listen out for particular words in stories, such as the children's names in *On the Way Home* (Murphy, 1982). After the story reading they might try to recall all the names of the children in the book. The teacher can ask the children to help her with a story-telling session. The teacher can begin the story and then ask the children to contribute sentences as the story develops. The teacher can keep the story focused by beginning sentences for the children using phrases such as 'One day ... On the way ... Then ... At last ...' Using a wordless picture book that the children are familiar with, at story time is an opportunity to invite the children to tell the story. Each child can be asked to volunteer a sentence as the pages are turned. This activity can be repeated and the class asked to identify the differences between each version. Games such as 'Simon Says' and word games such as 'Odd One Out' encourage children to listen and give them a reason for listening.

Circle time

During circle time children express their own thoughts and ideas. As the children sit together only the child or adult who is holding an object such as a ball or an imaginary microphone can speak. Circle times can become repetitive and children can get bored with them but, if used infrequently and to explore issues that are of importance to children, they provide a useful forum for children to express their opinions.

Talk partners

Talk partners is a way for all the children in the class to have an opportunity to talk and be listened to during whole-class discussions. The children work in twos. Very often the partnership is an established one but it can be varied by linking children's names on a large class list or asking children to pair up with the child sitting next to them. Pupils can use their talk partner to help them as they:

- try out ideas;
- formulate responses;

- discuss an issue;
- raise questions;
- explain a point;
- share an anecdote from their own experience.

Children can use their partner to remind themselves about what they were doing in an earlier session or to talk through the teacher's instructions before starting work. They can also consult their talk partner when they are working independently. They can discuss their work with their partner or ask them to act as a reviewer or editor when they are writing.

Plenary sessions

Children need to be given the opportunity to reflect on speaking and listening in order to improve as users of talk. By making talk the subject of a plenary session, commenting positively on the way in which children use talk and discussing ways of improving it, the teacher will be treating talk like other areas of the curriculum and raise its status in the eyes of the class.

Specially created groups

Specially constructed groups used during work in all areas of the curriculum provide opportunities for children to talk freely, creatively and clearly and to explain and clarify their thoughts. They allow children to experiment with ways of talking for different purposes and to a range of audiences. Group work also provides purposeful contexts for speaking and listening because when working collaboratively it is important to ask questions and to share ideas or knowledge.

The group structures that are described need to be clearly explained to children and may require a few trial runs before they work smoothly. However, it is well worth persevering with them since their value lies in the way in which they encourage children to communicate with one another rather than directing their thoughts and questions to the teacher. This is a much more natural way of speaking. They also provide all children with someone who will listen and respond to them straight away.

Snowball

This is an extension of the talk partners strategy and can be used for the same ends. Individuals' ideas are shared with partners, then shared in a group of four and finally reported to the whole class. In the process ideas change and grow. It can be used as an alternative to conventional news times. For example, four young children who have shared their news with each other can choose one child to tell their news to the whole class. The child who shares his news can then take questions about what he has said before handing back to the teacher.

Brainstorming

This can be done with talk partners, in small or large groups or with the whole class. The children contribute and record their ideas about an issue, topic or question. All contributions are listed quickly. This is a useful way of finding out what children know about a topic and opening up lines of enquiry for the class. If necessary the lists can be collated and the children can use these as a starting point for their work. If the children are not able to write easily the teacher can act as a scribe for whole-class contributions during this activity.

Visiting listener
One person – either the teacher or a child – visits each discussion group and notes good ideas or examples of supportive listening or speaking and reports these to the whole class during a whole-class discussion time, possibly a plenary. What is to be looked for can be discussed with the class before the listener begins his visits and used to construct a checklist. This draws everyone's attention to the good features of talking and listening.

Rainbow groups
After working on a topic, each member of each group is allocated a colour. All the children with the same colour meet together in new groups to share ideas, to report on their research or to compare what their original group did.

Jigsaw
The children work in groups on the class topic. Each member of the group is allocated one specific aspect of the topic to find out about and is designated as an expert on this. The next stage is for all those who were designated experts on the same topic to leave their original group and meet together to discuss what they discovered. The children then return to their original group and each child reports on their part of the group investigation. The original group then works together to finish its task or to plan a report incorporating all the information they have gained.

Envoys
If a group needs to check or obtain information, one child, who has previously been nominated as the envoy, can be sent to the teacher or to the book corner or library to find out what the group needs and then report back to the group. This is a very useful strategy for the teacher to use to prevent too many children asking for her attention at any one time.

Listening triads
The children work in threes and take on the roles of speaker, listener or recorder. The roles should change each time the group meets. The speaker explains or comments on an issue or activity. The questioner prompts and seeks clarification. The recorder gives a report of the conversation to the other two. This gives all children the opportunity to take on responsibility for supporting, sharing and summarising ideas. It helps children to evaluate and improve their use of spoken language.

Guided reading

The discussion that is the final part of a guided reading session provides an ideal opportunity for developing speaking and listening. The topics for the discussion can be set in the introduction to the session. The adult can ask the children to find something in the book that interested, surprised or disappointed them. The children should give reasons for their choices. The discussion should be free flowing as the children discuss the motives of characters or the author's message. For more ideas about discussions during guided reading see Chapter 2.

Independent activities

Resources

If the teacher is to plan experiences and create contexts for talk in the classroom, she needs to make sure that the classroom contains a number of resources that can be used by the children as they work together and that the environment is conducive to children talking together. Some resources may need to be purchased; others, such as masks and games, can be made by the children. The list that follows contains some suggestions about resources and the environment:

- tape recorders and tapes;
- telephones;
- dressing-up clothes;
- puppets;
- story props;
- a display board labelled 'Things We've Heard!';
- visitors who use various accents, dialects, languages;
- materials for practical activities;
- children's questions as starting points for investigations;
- magnet board and figures;
- games;
- masks;
- support for the use of home languages;
- role-play areas;
- role-play equipment;
- a listening area;
- interest areas and interactive displays;
- a carpeted meeting area.

Well chosen resources are important but the teacher also needs to demonstrate their use to the children. The following example shows the importance of not only providing children with the appropriate resources but also the need for the teacher to organise the activity, participate in the activity and support the activity in order to achieve the aims she has previously identified.

Classroom example: a teacher supporting children's role play

In the nursery the home corner had been transformed into a building site. The usual furniture and equipment had been stored elsewhere and replaced with large blocks and plastic bricks. There was also a selection of hard hats in the area. The preparation for building-site role play had included a display of tools and materials, reading *Miss Brick the Builder's Baby* (Ahlberg, 1981a) and *Charlie's House* (Schermbrucker, 1992) and a walk around the locality to look at small and large building projects and repairs that were taking place. The first group of children to work in the building site were asked to build a number of walls to divide the area into different rooms in a flat. Each child worked on his or her own wall and there was very little exchange of conversation except to negotiate the use of the materials for each individual project.

When the teacher observed this she decided to become one of the builders and accompany the next set of children into the building site. She modelled the language used by construction workers and organised the group of three children to work together and with her as they planned and built one wall. At the end of the day she reread *Miss Brick the Builder's Baby* to the class and discussed the work that had taken place in the construction site. The children described how they had worked and gave examples of the type of language they had used. Further examples of building workers' language and behaviour were considered and rehearsed. As the week continued the teacher provided more resources such as Wellingtons, mugs and milk bottles and at sharing times the children participated in short role plays associated with building sites. Some children made safety notices for the area and others made orange and white streamers to mark out the site. From time to time adults participated in the play and guided the children's language and actions.

By the end of the week not only had a set of walls containing windows and doors been constructed but the children had also really begun to experiment with the vocabulary and language forms that might be found on a building site, one of the original aims for the activity. After a disappointing beginning this became a very successful activity. The teacher's clear focus and the support she offered to the children enabled them to get into role and to widen their understanding and experience of language in a new situation.

Collaborative tasks

In order to support productive talk and cooperative learning between children when they are working independently tasks need to be carefully structured. Before children collect their resources for the task it might be helpful to build in a planning stage where the pupils discuss how they will go about the task and decide what equipment they will need. It might also help to limit the materials the pupils can use. For example, allowing one sheet of paper for every two children means that the children have to work in pairs to complete the task. Productive collaborative tasks include making or designing something together. Sequencing a set of photographs or pictures or lines from a poem or a picture book also generate talk that includes reasons, explanations and debate.

Collaborative tasks can be used to generate ideas for writing. For example, pairs of children can brainstorm ideas about how to take care of a pet, then group or prioritise their ideas, then select a limited number of their best ideas and finally write up their instructions. It is a good idea to embed speaking and listening tasks in normal classroom work which leads to a tangible outcome.

Working with individuals

It is common practice for teachers to work individually with children who seem to be finding their work difficult. In such cases it is easy for adults to tell the child what they have done wrong and to tell them how to correct their work or what to do next. Adults can do most of the talking and children most of the listening. If instead teachers choose to use a scaffolding approach the balance of talk is reversed as the teacher guides the child's thinking by asking well thought through questions and responding to their needs (Wood et al., 1976). The significant features of interacting with children in this way are to:

- believe that the child can work out the answer;
- listen to what the child says as he identifies the problem;
- summarise what the child has found out so far and what the difficulties now appear to be;
- orientate the child's attention to the significant aspects of the difficulty;
- help the child sequence his enquiry;
- give the child time to continue to grapple with the problem;
- ask a limited number of genuine questions about the problem or about the child's approach;
- respond as one would in a discussion with an equal;
- use tentative talk, such as 'I was wondering' or 'Perhaps if …';
- hold back and let the child do most of the talking as he continues to work out a solution;
- leave the child once he has resumed work but offer to provide support again if required.

This approach helps children to keep control of their learning and because the child remains actively involved, he is more likely to remember and understand what he has achieved. It also gives the child the opportunity to think about the difficulties and their approach and this may help them to solve the problem themselves.

Drama

Drama is an integral part of the curriculum for speaking and listening although it can, if based on a familiar book as many drama sessions in the early years are, develop children's understanding of a text and support their reading and writing as well. The use of drama techniques provides children with opportunities to develop speaking and listening skills when they speak as a character, plan scenes, use dialogue and evaluate their own performance and that of others.

Young children's first experiences of drama probably occur in the role-play area. The example of children using the role-play area as a building site given earlier in this chapter shows children speaking in role, planning scenes and dialogue and refining their play. Other early dramatic experiences which often occur independently include using story props to retell or create a story and using telephones. In these activities children are exploring characterisation and using dialogue appropriate to the character they are imitating or creating.

More structured drama can be planned and led by the teacher. The starting point for such work is often a story that the children know. It can also be a photograph, a drawing or a painting. For example the painting, *The Boyhood of Raleigh* by J. E. Millais (Tate Britain) could be a stimulus for deciding what the sailor is saying, creating the conversation between the sailor and the two boys, acting out what happens next, acting out what might happen ten years after the scene in the painting and role playing the events that led up to the boys' meeting with the sailor. Texts created by the teacher such as letters, diary extracts or secret messages can be introduced at any stage of a drama session to change the direction of the children's production. Texts can also be used to introduce historical source material or add authentic details about places. Carefully chosen artifacts such as a key or a lantern can support the imaginary context and sustain the drama. Items from history collections can be brought to life in this way.

Drama conventions

There are a number of techniques that can be used by teachers when using drama. Some of these are described below.

Paired improvisation

This strategy helps to get children quickly into character and into the story. Pairs are given roles. After a short period of thinking time they begin a dialogue, making up their conversation in role as the characters.

Hot-seating

Hot-seating focuses closely on a character and enables motivation to be explored. Individual pupils take on the role of a character from a book or someone with a particular viewpoint on an issue. In role they answer questions from the rest of the class. The questions can be improvised or prepared. Children working in pairs to generate ideas and prepare questions can provide another opportunity for speaking and listening.

Teacher in role

Here the teacher plays the part of a character. Working in role can be a way of challenging children's ideas, introducing new ideas and guiding children's involvement without stopping the drama.

Role on the wall

For this activity the children work in groups. Each group is given a character from the drama and draws an outline of the character on a large sheet of paper. Inside the outline they write about the character's thoughts and feelings. Outside the outline they write about the visible characteristics such as age and appearance. The children can also list what they would like to know about the character and this could be in the form of questions which could be used during hot-seating.

Freeze frame

Freeze frames are still pictures or silent tableaux used to illustrate a specific incident or event. They are useful for scrutinising an incident or situation. The children are asked to represent the characters at a significant moment in the drama. Positioning and body shape need to be considered carefully in order to represent ideas or emotions. Freeze frames can slow down the action to encourage thought and reflection and then move the drama on after considering this key moment. Freeze frames can be brought to life through adding dialogue or a caption for the image.

Thought tracking

This is a good technique for creating and then examining the private thoughts of characters. It can focus on the characters in a freeze frame, or a character from an ongoing drama when the action has been frozen. Participants are asked to say what their character is feeling or thinking. Thought tracking can act as a focus to move the action on and provide an opportunity to share and extend ideas.

Conscience alley

This is a means of exploring a character's mind at a moment of crisis and of investigating the complexity of the decision they are facing. The class creates two lines facing each other and one child in role walks between the lines. As the character passes by the children voice the character's thoughts both for and against a particular decision or action that the character is facing or they offer advice. When the child reaches the end of conscience alley he should make a decision about his course of action.

Meetings

The teacher in role, perhaps as an official, can call a meeting for the whole class to attend. Meetings enable information to be shared with the whole group and give the children an opportunity to discuss the situation before they make a decision about what to do next. Meetings used at the start of a drama can be an efficient way of creating roles or focusing on a problem.

Forum theatre

Forum theatre allows an incident or event to be seen from different points of view, making it a very useful strategy for examining alternative ideas or exploring how a dilemma might be solved. A small group acts out a scene while the rest of the class work as directors. They can ask the group to act or speak in a different way, suggest that a character might behave differently, question the characters in role or suggest an alternative course of action.

Classroom example: a drama sequence

What follows is an example of a drama based on *Six Dinner Sid* (Moore, 1990). To start with, the class, working in six groups, one for each of the residents of Aristotle Street, might undertake a role on the wall activity for one of the six neighbours. This could be followed by a hot-seating activity where one child from each group takes on the role of the resident they have been discussing. These two activities should add substance to the children's acting as they become the residents in the drama. Working individually the children might then imagine they are the resident they have investigated and then hold, stroke and feed Sid. This could be followed by a thought-tracking activity in which children could talk aloud to Sid and voice their thoughts about him and their relationship with him. Next the children could act out taking the cat to the vet. Again what might they say to Sid and what might they say to the vet? The next important event is the vet's phone calls. Working in pairs the children could improvise the conversation that takes place between the vet and one of the residents. Drawing on their knowledge of their character how would they react? What kind of words might they use? The final part of the drama could take the form of a meeting of the residents to discuss what to do about Sid. This could be chaired by the teacher and the children could discuss whether to act as the residents in the story do and only give Sid one meal each day or whether to be more understanding and continue to provide him with six dinners. If they decide to feed him just one meal the children could come together in groups consisting of the six residents talking to each other as they give Sid his one meal. This could be freeze framed and a caption added to the tableau. If they decide to continue sharing Sid they could, again working in groups of six residents, improvise their conversations as they get to know each other better.

Drama can be accompanied by other activities which can extend the children's understanding of the characters and events in their story. For example, during the work on *Six Dinner Sid* the children could each draw and paint one of the houses in Aristotle Street. This provides a further opportunity to get into role as one of the characters. The houses can also be used in the drama as scenery. At points in the drama characters can write a diary entry. It might be interesting to read Sid's diary for the evening that he left Aristotle Street and went to live with a more understanding set of neighbours. Digital cameras can be used to freeze frame an event in the drama and the pictures can be used later to evaluate the children's body language and physical interpretation of the scene or used as a stimulus for writing some dialogue.

Responding to and evaluating drama

The children's own drama sessions can provide them with opportunities to discuss performance and interpretation but giving them a broader experience of drama will give them more to think about as well as giving them ideas that can be incorporated into their own improvisations. There are a great many Theatre in Education companies which visit schools and some classes may be able to visit local theatres which put on productions suitable for young children. To get the most out of these experiences there should be preparation and follow-up.

Speaking and listening across the curriculum

English is never just a discrete subject area in the curriculum. It draws its content from other subject areas and is used as a tool in all aspects of life in and out of school. It is always cross-curricular in its application and can be developed in every area of the early years curriculum. Teaching and learning in all subjects depends a great deal on children's abilities to interpret and use oral language. Teachers explain, question, describe and evaluate and children listen, answer, discuss and work out ideas through talk. Work in each subject area will introduce children to subject-specific vocabulary and particular uses of language. In time this extends children's ability to convey exact meanings and complex ideas.

Speaking and listening take many forms and can support thinking and learning in many ways. The list that follows outlines some uses of spoken language:

analysis
argument
asking and answering questions
challenging
clarifying
collaborating
commenting
comparing
describing
developing ideas
disagreement
discussion
entertainment
evaluating
exchanging ideas
explaining
exploring understanding
expressing emotion
giving orders
hypothesising
imagining
initiating action or change
instructing
investigating

justifying
making oneself understood
negotiating
participating
persuasion
planning
prediction
reasoning
reflecting
rehearsing ideas, roles or
    experience
reporting
requesting
reshaping what is known or thought
sharing opinions, experiences
    and emotions
speculating
stating
suggesting
summarising
telling and listening to stories
thinking aloud
understanding ideas
understanding others.

Mathematics	Subject-specific vocabulary which may carry a different meaning to everyday usage, e.g. *table*, *point* Comparison, e.g. *longer than* Reasoning, *if ... then* Explaining
History	Reasoning, using *so* and *because* to explain cause and event Comparing and contrasting then and now Exploring feelings through empathising with others
Geography	Describing features of the environment Comparing and contrasting similar features in the environment
Science	Formulating questions and hypotheses, *I wonder if ...* Comparison Prediction, *I think ...* Describing a process or procedure Reasoning, linking cause and effect

Figure 1.2   Talk in different curriculum areas

Most activities at school offer children opportunities for speaking and listening, but only if teachers focus on their talk potential. As teachers plan their work they might ask themselves which activities can be organised in a way that encourages or necessitates speaking and listening for different purposes and different audiences. Activities such as problem-solving, maths investigations, technology, experiments and writing and telling stories can incorporate a talk dimension if carefully planned. When planning for speaking and listening and planning collaborative activities it is a good idea to identify the types of talk that are being covered and check that over the course of a term children will have had the opportunity to use the full range of types of talk. Figure 1.2 lists some forms of language that are used in different subject areas.

Investigating speaking and listening with children

Undertaking a project on speaking and listening can be a good starting point for raising the status of talk, for encouraging children to reflect on their own use of language and as a preparation for introducing collaborative group work. Such a project might start by making a collection of words to describe talk. In the example in Figure1.3 the words were contributed by the children over a period of a week. They consulted dictionaries and asked adults at home for their suggestions. All the words in Figure 1.3 were collected by the children and written on a large chart.

   Using this as a starting point, the children could undertake a number of activities which would be more productive if carried out in pairs as more talk would be generated. They could:

- match rhyming pairs of words, e.g. 'flatter' and 'natter';
- match opposites, e.g. 'whisper' and 'shout';

- write dictionary definitions for the words on the list;
- consider when they use different types of talk;
- act out different ways of using talk;
- illustrate different ways of using talk;
- look for examples of talk written in books;
- alphabetically order the talk words;
- add speech bubbles to illustrations;
- construct their own talk history for a day, for a week, for their lifetime;
- list the kinds of talk they find difficult and easy;
- use talk in different role-play settings, for example as a cafe owner and customer, TV interviewer and interviewee, adult and child;
- find words for talk in different languages;
- identify what they like to talk about;
- consider what makes a good speaker and a good listener.

These activities would provide children with the opportunity to become familiar with some of the knowledge, skills and understanding outlined in the Programme of Study for Speaking and Listening at Key Stage 1 (DfEE/QCA, 1999a). These include learning to:

- choose words with precision;
- take into account the needs of their listeners;
- identify and respond to sound patterns in language;
- create and sustain roles individually and when working with others

(DfEE/QCA, 1999a: 44).

In particular the project would help children to learn about language variation, especially how some words are more suited to formal situations and others to informal occasions. At Key Stage 2 children are expected to make a study of language and become more self-consciously aware of oral language. They can do this through reflecting on variations in vocabulary, exploring word choices and subtle variations in meaning and evaluating their own use of talk. These opportunities are present in a language project. The BBC website Voices http://www.bbc.co.uk/voices contains some helpful material for teachers planning a language project.

address, ad-lib, advise, agree, announce, answer, argue, ask, assert, babble, call out, challenge, chat, chatter, comment, communicate, converse, cry, declare, describe, disagree, discuss, drone, enquire, exclaim, explain, express, flatter, gab, gabble, garble, gossip, greet, groan, grumble, grunt, howl, inform, insist, instruct, interrupt, jabber, jeer, joke, lecture, lie, listen, mean, mention, mumble, murmur, mutter, name, natter, negotiate, observe, persuade, pronounce, question, rant, rap, recite, report, say, scream, share, shout, shriek, speak, speculate, state, suggest, swear, tell, think out loud, threaten, translate, utter, voice, waffle, whisper, yell.

Figure 1.3 Words to describe talk

Standard English and received pronunciation

Standard English

Standard English is one dialect of English. Like other dialects it is a systematic form of language that has accepted rules and conventions. 'In spoken Standard English significant features are standard forms of irregular verbs; agreement between person, case and number (especially with the verb "to be"); the correct use of pronouns.' In its written form, 'standard English comprises vocabulary as found in dictionaries, and agreed conventions of spelling and grammar' (NCC, 1993: 16). The difference between standard English and other dialect forms is that standard English is the form of language used for 'non-regional public communication' (Whitehead, 2004: 32). The public and official use of standard English, the term 'standard' and the association of the word 'correct' with the term can lead people to think that standard English is the most socially prestigious dialect form of English.

If standard English is seen as the 'best' form of English, dialects that differ from standard English may be rated as second class, careless and ineffective. As a result children who enter school fluent in the language spoken in their homes and communities but who are used to communicating in ways that are different from the language used and valued in school, often standard English, may be classed as having an impoverished form of language.

In the National Curriculum (DfEE/QCA, 1999a) standard English is given a significant mention in the programmes of study for speaking and listening and writing at Key Stage 1. The expectation is that children should be encouraged to use the oral and written forms of standard English in addition to other dialect forms of English. This continues earlier official advice (NCC, 1993: 16) which stated: 'The aim should be to equip young people with the ability to use Standard English when circumstances require it … It is important to encourage pupils' ability to extend their speaking … repertoires: to make their language "fit" the context.' Using the vocabulary and grammar of standard English with increasing fluency and proficiency in those circumstances that require it will, in the long term, help pupils meet the communicative requirements of education and employment. Standard English gives speakers of English access to a world language that is appropriate in formal or serious situations such as interviews, communicative situations beyond the home and with people outside one's immediate family or peer group. Young children, too, have the right to feel confident when speaking to a range of people and in a variety of circumstances. Consequently, as long as references to standard English are not interpreted as meaning that it is superior to any other dialect used by pupils, few would disagree that the teaching of standard English is both desirable and important.

It is important to remember that oral language is closely allied to one's identity. Consequently any denigration of a child's normal dialect may be seen as a criticism of the child, his family and his environment. It is not necessary to use standard English all the time. When communicating with friends or colleagues we can all use jargon and incomplete or irregularly constructed sentences. It is worth considering that, when they start school, the majority of children living in the twenty-first century are probably well aware of the standard dialect form of

English through exposure to the language used on television and radio broadcasts such as story telling, news and documentary programmes. They are also likely to be implicitly aware of numerous other dialect versions of English as viewers of and listeners to cartoons and films as well as TV programmes such as *Coronation Street*, *East-Enders* and *Neighbours*. They are well able to code switch as they listen to and understand these very different varieties of English and, as with the development of their early language, their ability to listen is the basis from which the production of language will emerge. It is likely that as children see the need to use different varities of English their language use will change and develop to meet new needs and audiences as long as they are exposed to different models and to situations which demand the use of different dialects. In this way they will be able to judge the power, use and limitations of standard English and set it alongside their home dialect as yet another speech option.

One way in which teachers can encourage all children to use standard English may be through reading and writing. Standard English is the dialect most commonly found in books and the one that we all need and aspire to when writing for others. Book language provides a model of complete and grammatically exact language for children to listen to and respond to. As children themselves begin to write for audiences beyond themselves they will come to see the need for extended and clear communication that draws on a vocabulary and grammar that is shared by all potential readers. Sensitive intervention in children's writing will lead to the discussion of the different varieties of English that exist and the reasons for their existence and provide opportunities for children to use standard English purposefully.

Received pronunciation

Standard English and received pronunciation are sometimes thought of as synonymous; this is not the case. Standard English is a dialect and a dialect is characterised by its grammatical patterns and vocabulary. Received pronunciation does not refer to grammar or vocabulary; instead it refers to pronunciation or accent. Most accents reveal the speaker's geographical origins, but received pronunciation is a regionless accent used by a minority of English speakers. It is not used as the model of English pronunciation in British schools and speakers should be 'rightly proud of their regional pronunciation which identifies where they come from' (DES, 1988a: 14). In short, 'spoken standard English is not the same as received pronunciation and can be expressed in a variety of accents' (DfE, 1995: 3).

Perhaps the role of the school in relation to accents should be to counter negative attitudes towards them, since these can affect self-esteem and identity. A distinctive regional accent may identify a new entrant to school as coming from a different place or as being an outsider and impede the child's acceptance as a member of a new local community. Some people manifest hostile attitudes to English spoken, for example, with an Asian accent. If this occurs the teacher, drawing on her own knowledge and awareness of language, should discuss this with the pupils, stressing the need to respect one's own language and that of others. Relationships in the classroom among adults and children and among the pupils themselves are often established through talk. Good relationships leading to feelings of self-worth and acceptance are essential for all learning and especially for the development of oral language. The teacher's own attitude to the language the children use is crucial for the development of children's personal confidence and their willingness to take the risks that will be necessary as they extend their language repertoire in response to new situations and new audiences.

Summary

When teaching speaking and listening we need to:

- understand the value of speaking and listening;
- select tasks that enable children to use talk to learn;
- plan carefully so that children use talk productively;
- create classrooms in which children do most of the talking.

Reflective activities

1. Observe a child's use of language at school in the classroom and in the playground. Does the child use language more confidently in some situations than in others? What conditions support or inhibit the child's talk?
2. Think about the conversations you have had in the past 24 hours. In which situations did you use language to learn or work something out? When and with whom did you use standard English and received pronunciation?
3. Observe a child's use of language at school. Does the child use language to learn? Can you give examples of what they were learning and how?
4. How could you use hot-seating, freeze frame and paired improvisation to develop children's understanding of and response to a narrative poem?

Suggestions for further reading

Alexander, R.J. (2006) *Towards Dialogic Teaching: Rethinking Classroom Talk*, 3rd edn. York: Dialogos (1st edn 2004). This booklet provides teachers with an introduction to the idea of learning through negotiation, discussion and questioning. It gives practical suggestions for encouraging dialogic teaching and learning.

DfES (2003) *Speaking, Listening and Learning: Working with Children in Key Stages 1 and 2*. London: HMSO. This pack contains advice about developing speaking and listening and practical examples of children using speaking and listening in all areas of the curriculum.

2

Reading

Introduction

This chapter covers:

- the reading process and the strategies readers use;
- how young children learn to read;
- the changing conceptualisation of literacy;
- creating an environment for reading;
- classroom resources;
- teaching methods.

The reading process

Reading is an active and complex process which draws on the application of a number of skills and knowledge about language and print. The skills that are needed include the ability to recognise letters and words, to match letters with sounds and to combine a series of sounds to create words. Reading also relies on the reader's ability to predict words in a text using knowledge about language such as sentence structure, word meanings and the meaning of the text. In applying skills and knowledge the reader is guided by the expectation that what is read should make sense. From the start children need to learn about and use a range of strategies in order to become successful readers. We need to make sure that they draw upon their knowledge of letters and words, apply their knowledge about oral communication to texts and understand that reading is a purposeful and meaning-making activity.

Knowledge about print and reading

Research into the pre-school language and literacy experiences of children who were able to read before going to school has revealed a number of factors that help children to make a successful start to reading (Clark, 1976; Clay, 1979; Wells, 1982; Brice-Heath, 1983). The findings indicated that it was the children's understanding of stories and books, their exposure to models of reading and being read to regularly which contributed to their success. These experiences helped them to understand:

- how a book is held and read;
- the directional rules of writing;
- that print, not illustrations, carry the unvarying message;
- that print is composed of words;
- that words contain letters;
- that punctuation helps the reader to understand what has been written;
- that stories usually have a particular structure;
- that people do read and that they read for different purposes.

Many of the out-of-school experiences that help children to learn to read have now been incorporated into the early reading curriculum of schools. As a part of the curriculum for communication, language and literacy (DfES, 2007a) children are expected to learn about the uses of written language and about how texts work. This knowledge does not need to be taught in a decontextualised way; it develops as stories and books are shared, discussed and used with children.

Phonological awareness

Phonological awareness is the understanding that language contains units of sound that are smaller than the word. For a number of years researchers have associated phonological awareness with success at learning to read in the early years (Bradley and Bryant, 1983; Goswami and Bryant, 1990). Being aware of the separate sounds in words is the foundation for learning phoneme–grapheme correspondences (Goswami, 2003).

Children's phonological development follows a clear pattern, from an awareness of syllables, to an awareness of onsets and rimes within syllables, to an awareness of individual sounds or phonemes (Treiman and Zukowski, 1996). Segmenting words into syllables is the easiest level of phonological awareness. During the Foundation Stage teachers help children to recognise syllables in words. They can do this through clapping games where children tap the beats in their names, join in with nursery rhymes and simple songs and think of new words to end lines in familiar rhymes.

Once children have the ability to recognise syllables they can start to distinguish the smaller units of sounds that are contained in syllables. These smaller units are known as onset and rime and apply to the units of sound that begin and end syllables (Goswami and Bryant, 1990). The onset is the consonant or consonant cluster at the beginning of the syllable and before the vowel. The rime is the vowel and any consonants that follow. In the word *dad*, the onset is *d* and the rime *ad*. In the word *play*, the onset is *pl* and the rime *ay*. Syllables beginning with a vowel such as, *ill* do not have an onset. Words of two syllables or more may contain two onsets and two rimes. For example, in the word *garden g* and *d* are onsets and *ar* and *en* are the rimes. But when introducing children to onset and rime it is best to work with words of one syllable.

Analogy is the ability to use what is known in order to decipher something that is unknown. When children can hear and see the onsets and rimes in syllables and words they can be encouraged to listen to and think of similar words. For example, if children know that *Jill* and *hill* have the same rime they can begin to compile a list of other words which also end in *ill*. Later, children can be shown how to recognise the written symbols for the rimes in words that they read. They can be encouraged to use the spelling pattern of a word that is known as a prompt as they read an unfamiliar word that contains the same rime and sequence of letters. Children can also use this strategy when writing. If they say words out loud to themselves as they write they can be encouraged to base their spelling on how they know similar sounding words are written. Analogy is a useful learning strategy when learning to read because:

- it encourages children to make use of and apply their existing knowledge;
- it is less abstract than depending on individual letter sounds and symbols;
- it encourages children to use their knowledge to solve word recognition and spelling problems;
- it reduces dependence on memory.

Phonics

Phonological awareness helps children to recognise how spoken and written language are related and gives them an awareness of phonemes and the alphabetic system of English. Once children can identify onsets and rimes and use analogy, they are in a good position to learn about phonics and how to analyse words and synthesise sounds in order to read words. During the Reception year and throughout Years 1 and 2 children embark on a systematic phonics programme which builds on their existing knowledge about sounds.

Children have been using phonics to learn to read since the middle of the nineteenth century and, although it became less significant during the 1950s, it has continued to influence practice in schools. In this method children learn about the relationship between letter shapes and letter sounds in order to read words. In English there are 44 sounds or phonemes and these are written using the 26 letters of the alphabet. The letter or combinations of letters that represent each sound are known as graphemes. The 44 phonemes in the English language and some of the graphemes used to represent them are shown in Figure 2.1. The graphemes are in bold.

Vowel sounds			
5 short vowel sounds	5 long vowel sounds	Further vowel sounds	Further vowel sounds
a cat	ai day, pain	oo pull, put	oi coin, boy
e pen	ee sweet, sea	ar cart	air fair, bear
i big	igh night, my	ur fern, burn	ear dear, here
o bog	oa boat, bone	or corn, saw	ure sure, poor
u nut	oo blue, moon	ow cow, out	er comer, picture
Consonant sounds			
b bag	k cat	s sit	th thumb
d dog	l leg	t top	th then
f fun	m man	v van	ch chip, watch
g got	n nut	w went	sh ship
h hat	p pet	y yes	zh treasure
j jam	r run	z zip	ng sing

Figure 2.1 The 44 phonemes in English

Phonic knowledge can be taught in many ways. *The Primary Framework for Literacy* (DfES, 2006a) outlines a progressive plan for the teaching of phonics. The stages are as follows:

- learning the sounds for each of the 26 letters of the alphabet;
- using this knowledge to read and write simple consonant-vowel-consonant (CVC) words;
- learning consonant blends such as *sp* and *cr* and blending and segmenting CCVC and CVCC words;
- learning sounds that are represented by more than one letter such as *sh* and *ay*;
- learning alternative grapheme–phoneme correspondences such as the *s* sound for *c* in *city* and the *j* sound for *g* in *gem*.

A great many programmes for teaching phonics exist, including *Letters and Sounds* (DfES, 2007b), the materials produced to accompany the literacy framework. A list of published schemes that are widely used in England together with the publishers' descriptions of what they offer can be found at http://www.standards.dfes.gov.uk/phonics/.

In the *Independent Review of Reading,* Rose (2006) suggested that phonic work is most effective when:

- it is part of a broad, rich curriculum;
- it starts by the age of 5;
- it is multisensory;
- it is time limited;
- it is systematic, carefully planned and progressive;
- it is taught daily at a brisk pace;
- it is reinforced and applied when children read; and
- progress is carefully assessed and monitored.

It is important that children learn to apply their phonic knowledge. Reinforcing phonic knowledge can take place during guided and shared reading and after individual reading sessions. Words, the letters they contain and the sounds of these letters can be discussed when they are relevant to the learner's needs and when they help with recognising the actual words that are being read. Teachers can also share texts with children which contain simple rhymes, repetition and word games. By drawing children's attention to the aural and visual patterns and play on words in books, teachers will be developing children's familiarity with the sounds of language. Texts such as *Dr Seuss's ABC* (Seuss, 1963), *Each Peach Pear Plum* (Ahlberg and Ahlberg, 1978) and nursery rhymes, action rhymes, alphabet books and advertising slogans all offer children lessons about phonics.

A totally phonic approach to reading would now be considered very limiting by most teachers. Instead, phonics is seen as one of a number of strategies that can be drawn upon by readers when they are confronted with an unfamiliar word. In a survey of reading in primary schools HMI wrote: 'Headteachers in the most effective schools recognized the importance of introducing pupils early to a broader range of reading strategies alongside phonics' (HMI, 2004: 11, para. 26). In the influential review into the teaching of early reading in England which had a particular focus on the teaching of phonics the author, Jim Rose, wrote; 'It is widely agreed that phonic work is an essential part, but not the whole picture of what it takes to become a fluent reader' (Rose, 2006: 16). His findings have been recognised in the current literacy framework which states that 'phonic work should be set within a broad and rich language curriculum that takes full account of developing the four independent strands of language – speaking, listening, reading and writing' (DfES, 2006a: 7).

Recognising whole words

Whole-word methods began to be used in the 1940s and 1950s. At this time children were expected to learn all the words contained in each reading-scheme book before the book was read. The words were often learned from a set of cards. Each card was looked at and the word written there was said aloud. The words that were selected for learning in this way were those that occurred most often in children's reading material and those that could be distinguished from one another easily because of their distinctive shape. It was thought that children would find learning complete words more motivating than learning letter sound correspondences and that scheme books containing interesting, rather than phonically regular, words would appeal to children.

It is true that some words are more easily remembered than others including those with distinctive shapes such as *bicycle*, those that are important to children such as their names or high interest words such as *dinosaur* or those that are seen frequently such as *street*. But many words that occur regularly in books for young children have similar visual features. Function words such as *there*, *their* and *here*, and *him*, *his*, *her* and *has* fall into this category. Function words are also unlikely to have an important meaning for individuals and this can make them difficult to remember out of context. Learning large numbers of words by rote can also place considerable strain on young children's memories. The reading materials that supported this approach often contained a limited number of frequently repeated words which constrained the interest and the development of stories in the early books. Although a pure whole-word approach is rare now, some people still think that it is important for children to memorise a reading vocabulary. Many of the books for beginning readers in modern reading schemes continue to reflect this belief and contain only a limited number of frequently repeated words.

The automatic recognition of words can be very helpful to readers. When they recognise words quickly they are free to concentrate on the meaning of the text. Mature readers build up a large sight vocabulary through their experiences with books and print and use automatic word recognition as one of their reading strategies (Stanovich, 1980; Raynor and Pollatsek, 1989). But beginning readers, who have had far fewer reading experiences than fluent readers, will not have had the opportunity to build up a large store of automatically recognisable words. Having a large sight vocabulary is as much the result of being a good reader as the cause. Practising with flash cards and words in word tins is more likely to produce boredom and misunderstandings about reading than to create fluent and enthusiastic readers. Children acquire a sight vocabulary of words that they recognise quickly through repeated encounters with common words in shared and individual reading and through their own writing. *I, like, and, went* and other high- and medium-frequency words occur frequently in reading material for young children and are words that children need to write. Teachers can draw children's attention to these words during shared and guided reading and children can play word recognition games to help to remember them.

Graphic knowledge

The visual appearance of words provides readers with information which they use when reading. Readers use initial letters, word endings, letter strings, word length and word roots to help them recognise words. They do this without necessarily translating these features into their oral equivalents. Graphic knowledge is particularly helpful when inexperienced readers need to distinguish between words that seem very similar. Readers need to look carefully to decide whether a word is *then* or *them* or *where* or *when*. Children need to be encouraged to develop the habit of looking carefully at words. This can be done during shared and guided reading and through activities such as sorting and matching groups of words.

Grammatical awareness

Grammar describes the way that language is organised and in particular word order. It is an important device in language. The order in which words are placed in sentences follows rules which all language users know and use when they construct and understand language. Applying this knowledge is of great assistance when reading as it often enables the reader to anticipate the sorts of words that follow the ones that have just been read. In English we expect sentences which are organised in a particular way. Look at the following sentences.

> The cat chased the mouse, not The chased cat the mouse.
> The black cat chased the grey mouse, not The cat black chased the mouse grey.

Reading the first sentence in each of these pairs is straightforward, but reading the second one, where the word order is muddled, is more difficult. Reading the following passage may help you to appreciate why word order is important in reading.

Nomral Reading

Nomral reading is a knid of high spede geussuing game, which explians why we find it difficult to proof raed. The raeding process is incredibly flexilbe and can cope with all kinds of worng infromation, such as revresed letters, missprimts, punchation errers and chainges in teip font, eny of witch wood compeltely fox a computre. But so long as sence is comming over the I bounds on. What does hold up the porcess is unfamiliar language constructions, as a when of juggled the about are all sentence words the brian gets into an awful staet tyring to recnocile a snesible anticipated messaeg and the ronsensical messaeg which was actually recived.

You may have found parts of this text difficult to read. It is not usually the distorted spelling in 'Nomral Reading' that distracts readers but the loss of meaning that occurs when the grammatical supports are taken away part way through the text.

Now try to read the following text and then answer the questions which follow.

'The Wuggen and the Tor'

Onz upon a pime a wuggen zonked into the grabbet. Ze was grolling for poft because ze was blongby.

The wuggen grolled and grolled until ze motte a tor.

Ze blind to the tor, 'Ik am blongby and grolling for poft. Do yum noff rem ik can gine some poft?'

'Kex,' glind ze tor, 'klom with ne, wuggen. Ik have lodz of poft in ni bove.'

1. Where did the wuggen zonk?
2. What was s/he grolling for?
3. Why was s/he grolling for poft?
4. Who did s/he meet?

You may never have seen many of these words before but you can probably work out the function of many of them. *Wuggen* and *tor* are nouns because they are preceded by *the* and *a*. We know that *zonked* is a verb because of its *ed* ending and its position and relation to the other words in the sentence. In order to answer the questions which followed the passage you were drawing on your grammatical knowledge to produce statements that were grammatically correct if somewhat nonsensical.

Goodman and Goodman (1977) and Smith (1971) demonstrated the significance of grammatical knowledge in fluent reading and suggested that young readers need to be encouraged to draw on their own knowledge of grammar when they are reading. Through their experience as speakers and listeners children are familiar with the syntactic constraints of language. They can, if they realise that written text communicates in similar ways to speaking, apply their existing knowledge in order to make informed predictions about unknown words. Read the following sentence and decide what word you would put in the space.

The boy w   to the shops.

You probably realised that what was needed was a verb and may have inserted *went* or *walked*. If the space had been a word that a child could not read they could have made an informed guess, based on their understanding of how language works, just as you did.

Contextual knowledge

Texts are a collection of one or more sentences that have a coherent theme. Each sentence in a text should reveal more of the author's meaning. Being aware of the subject matter and the meaning of a text is an important support when reading unfamiliar material or words. For example, the word *wind* means different things according to the context in which the word is found. It can be a feature of the weather or it can be a verb describing a turning movement. The context of the text determines which and the reader's understanding of the text affects his correct or incorrect reading of the word.

Readers expect to understand the meaning of words that they read and the sense of what is conveyed in a text. If they encounter words or passages which do not make sense to them, they hesitate and reread what has been read in order to help them understand. If what they are reading makes sense they will read more easily. Reading the following passage may help you to appreciate how meaning is at the forefront of our minds when we read.

From *The Turn of the Screw* by Henry James

The story had held us, round the fire, sufficiently breathless, but except the obvious remark that it was gruesome, as, on Christmas Eve in an old house, a strange tale should essentially be, I remember no comment uttered till somebody happened to say that it was the only case he had met in which such a visitation had fallen on a child.

You may have found this text hard to read because the way in which it is written makes it difficult to understand. The sentence unfolds slowly and is interrupted by the addition of a number of details. Experienced readers often have to read and reread this sentence as they pursue its meaning. As you read the next story consider how, despite the lack of letters and complete words you are able to read it.

'The Man Who Kept House'

Once upon a t – – – th – r – – – – – woodman who th – – ght
th – – no o – – w– rked – – h– rd – – – – did. O – –
ev – – – – – wh – – – – c – – – h – m – fr – – w – – k, – – s – – d to
h – – w – f –, 'Wh – – – – y – – d – all d – y wh – l – l
– – aw – y c – – – – – – w – – d?'
'I k – – p h – – se,' re – – – – – – – – w – f –, 'and k – – – – – –
h – – – – – – h – – d w – – k.'
'H – – – w – – – !' said the – – – – – – – –. 'Y – – d – – 't k – – w
w – – – h – – – w – – – – – ! Y – – sh – – – – tr – c – – – – – – w – – – !'
'–' – be glad to,' – – – – – – – w – – –.
'Why d – – 't y – – do m – w – – k s – – – d – y ? I' – – st – – – –
h – m – – – – k – – p h – – – –,' – – – – the – – – – – – – –.
'If y – – st – – h – – – – – – – do – – w – rk y – –'ll h – – – to
m – – – butt – r, c – rry w – t – r from – – – w – – –, w – sh – – –
cl – – – – –, cl – – – – – – h – – se, – – – l – – k aft – – – – – b – by,'
– – – – – – – w – f –.

As you prepared to read this passage you may have found that the title, the organisation of the text, the punctuation and your experience of stories and in particular traditional tales led you to have certain expectations about what the text might contain. This probably helped you to read and make sense of the story.

Readers make sense of texts by using their knowledge of language and books and their experience of the subject matter and of the world at the same time as they read the letters and words on the page. Attending to the meaning of the text and drawing on one's experience as a language user and on personal knowledge help readers to make informed predictions about any words that are unfamiliar. For this reason understanding is an important reading strategy.

If we want children to use understanding as a strategy to help them read, we need to teach them about the way written texts are structured and the way language is used in different genres of texts. We can show them that the title, the information on the cover, the layout and the illustrations tell us about the content of a book and how this provides clues about unfamiliar words.

Comprehension

Readers who can use the context to help them read unfamiliar words show that they are trying to make sense of what they read. They are aware of the literal meaning of the text. This is one aspect of comprehension but comprehension goes further than this. Comprehension means actively engaging with texts. It involves discovering hidden meanings as well as what is obvious. It means looking closely at how texts have been written. It involves deciding whether this is a book that I enjoyed reading and that I care about and being able to give reasons for that decision. Based on Barrett's (1968) work on reading, Guppy and Hughes (1999) identified three levels of comprehension:

- Reading the lines – using phonic, graphic, contextual and syntactical strategies to make literal meanings.
- Reading between the lines – understanding the author's intentions and implied meanings.
- Reading beyond the lines – reacting to the text, appreciating and valuing the author's meanings, understanding and evaluating the author's craft.

Even the simplest texts can be read at a level that allows the reader to read between the lines and beyond the lines. As an example read the following nursery rhyme:

Jack and Jill
Went up the hill
To fetch a pail of water.
Jack fell down
And broke his crown
And Jill came tumbling after.

At the literal level we can read this as a brief narrative about climbing up and falling down a hill. But as you read it how did you visualise Jack and Jill? Are they brother and sister, man and wife, old or young? What does the hill look like? What else is on the hill? Did Jack break a royal crown or the top of his head? Was Jill badly hurt or was she able to help Jack? Did you notice the rhymes and some of the more unusual words? Did you think this was just a nonsense rhyme or does it have some deeper significance? All readers of this rhyme are likely to visualise the scene in different ways and have their own interpretation of what happened. Their experience of the world and of other texts, possibly other nursery rhymes or their origins, will influence their interpretation. Young children can read in this way too. They might wonder why Jack and Jill had to fetch water from the hill or ask what happened next. They might comment on words such as *pail* or *tumbling*. By doing this they are going beyond the literal and trying to read between and beyond the lines.

Meek (1988) has written about young children's understanding of the conventions and subtleties of picture books and suggested that when reading or listening to books children go beyond the surface features of the text. They are able to understand meanings that are only implied. She gives the example of reading *Rosie's Walk* (Hutchins, 1970) where the literal meaning of the words only tell a fraction of the story. The reader has to infer what is happening as Rosie takes her walk. Part of the pleasure of reading this book comes from the reader knowing more than Rosie. It is the hidden story, the reader's empathy with the characters and the author's skill that makes this a classic picture book that children have enjoyed for many years. Understanding, evaluating and responding are integral to reading. They are what gives the reader pleasure and they are the reasons why we read. Discovering and discussing the possible meanings of texts invites children to explore the possibilities and pleasures of reading and should be part of any reading programme from the start.

Combining reading strategies

Reading involves the application of a number of strategies. Readers draw on their familiarity with the subject matter, their previous experience of written material, their knowledge about reading and their expectation of meaning as they read. They use their knowledge about letters, sounds, words, grammar and context to recognise words and reconstruct the text. They evaluate and respond to what they read. In a good reading programme children are given the tools to decode texts and are encouraged to make use of all the strategies that are available to readers. They also have opportunities to engage with and talk about texts and to enjoy and use what they read.

Young children learning to read

Building on oral language learning

Through their experience as speakers and listeners children are familiar with syntactic, semantic and aural strategies as ways of processing and producing oral language. They expect language to make sense and they expect to understand what they hear. If, when they are learning to read, children are aware that written language has some similarities to oral language they can be encouraged to apply their existing knowledge to the act of reading. By making the communicative aspects of reading clear to children, showing them that reading is about the recreation of meaning and providing them with experiences of books, stories and writing which allow them to see the connections, children can be introduced to reading positively and easily.

There are also lessons to be learned about the teaching of reading from the way that children learn oral language. They do not learn to speak by being taught sounds, or by being taught a predetermined set of words which they then practise. Their oral language learning takes place in a context of talk, where they witness demonstrations of the purpose and use of talk, where they receive responses and encouragement from experienced speakers, where they are treated as speakers and where there is every expectation of success. Children are not expected to speak perfectly from the start, nor do they have to wait until they have perfect control over spoken language before they are allowed to speak. Inexperienced speakers are permitted and encouraged to practise as they learn. Their utterances take place in real situations, have meaning from the start and concern things they are interested in.

Learning to read may be easier and more relevant to children if teachers work with children on reading in ways that are similar to those that have success-fully supported the development of oral language. Applying these favourable conditions for learning to speak to learning to read results in an approach where children are met, from the start, by positive expectations about their ability to read. They are placed in situations where they are surrounded by books and demonstrations of reading and the role of the adult is to support and extend what the child tries to do as complete texts are read together. This is an ideal context for encouraging learning.

Children as active learners

Early years educators know that young children bring a great deal of knowledge and a number of established and productive learning strategies to school. Through actively engaging with the world around them and generating and testing their hypotheses about their experiences and observations young children are accomplished learners. Young 'children do not sit passively waiting to be told what they should learn ... They learn by having a go, by trying things out. Early childhood is a continual process of experimentation, risk taking and negotiation, in purposeful, intentional ways' (Wray et al., 1989: 61). During their early learning about the world they inhabit children become aware of reading, writing and printed material. Although they may not be able to read or write in the ways that adults do, children understand a great deal about literacy, the purposes for reading and writing and how others read and write. As they grow up they see print in their homes, in their communities and even on their clothes and they observe others reading and reacting to print.

Older approaches to reading did not take account of how young children learn or of what they might know about literacy. They did not capitalise on their innate capacity for learning and their own learning strategies. Teachers can now do both of these. They can make learning to read part of a continuum of language learning when they work with what children can do and accept that each child will know different things about literacy. They can reject reading programmes and sequenced skills teaching that are based on the view of the child as a passive learner and necessitate giving every child the same experiences in the same way. Teachers can now decide to teach by reacting to the active learning that they see and responding 'to the problems that children face at crucial points in their development' (Ferreiro, 1986). This enables them to fit their teaching to the needs of children.

The purposes for reading

There are two reasons why it is important to think about the purposes reading can serve and why adults and children read. First, there is increasing concern about the number of children who can read but seem not to have any reason to read and so choose not to (HMI, 2004; Mullis et al., 2007) and, secondly, when children identify their own reasons for learning they learn more easily and more actively.

For adults, reading is a purposeful activity which has an outcome. Literacy helps them to fulfil their roles in many different areas of their lives. In the home they read a range of non-fiction and fiction texts for a variety of reasons. Textbooks, articles, advertisements and journals are read for employment and educational purposes. When they read bills, election leaflets, tax forms and newspapers people are helped to fulfil their roles as members of the community. As consumers, adults read advertisements, catalogues and credit-card statements. They can use reading for entertainment when they consult holiday brochures, knitting patterns, magazines, maps, TV listings and books. Adult readers read a range of writing, in a variety of situations and for many different reasons, but their reading is always purposeful.

When teachers and other adults are asked why children learn to read, their answers often fall into two categories: for the pleasure that reading can bring and for the information that reading can give them. These are valid and positive reasons but they may not be reflected in classroom practices or the day-to-day learning objectives that teachers plan. Practice at reading is often undertaken in order to help children to improve their reading ability and sometimes improvement and assessment, rather than pleasure or learning, become the main reasons for reading. When this happens children may develop a very limited picture of purposes for reading. They may be learning that reading is an important activity that gains adult approval but they may not be learning about how to use and enjoy reading. Materials and approaches influence children's perceptions of the uses of reading and reflect teachers' priorities about reading. The use of reading schemes, the teaching of skills and short periods of reading aloud are often associated with learning that reading is a competitive activity, relying on the use of technical skills and requiring only superficial understanding. They do not help to portray reading as a thoughtful, reflective activity nor do they reveal the wider purposes for reading.

The list of adult reasons for reading shows that being able to read gives individuals the opportunity to become more autonomous, to make choices, to evaluate different points of view, to analyse information, to make informed decisions and to gain access to new ideas and opinions. The ability to read places people in a powerful position. It enables individuals to decide what they read and what their purposes for reading will be. To be literate does not only include knowing how to read and write but also the place and value of these activities in one's life. The reason for teaching children to read is to empower them as individuals now and for the future. Resources and activities need to reflect this.

The changing conceptualisation of literacy

Literacy is changing as the ways in which we communicate develop. We now have a much broader understanding of texts and recognise that all texts in print, on screen and pictorial can be read. If we are to prepare children for life in the twenty-first century it is important to help them read a great variety of texts. As Adams and Hamm (2000: 3) state, 'Being literate now implies having the ability to decode information from all types of media.'

Visual literacy and media literacy are concerned with the sorts of texts children read and critical literacy is about adopting a questioning approach to reading all types of texts. Teaching children to read and respond to printed texts is likely to remain the central concern of teachers who work with young children but alongside this it is necessary to incorporate visual literacy, media literacy and critical literacy into the reading curriculum.

Visual literacy

Children live in homes and communities filled with visual stimuli and their experiences with visual images of all kinds mean that they have a sophisticated implicit knowledge of visual literacy from an early age (Buckingham, 1993). Visual literacy can be defined as the ability to understand and interpret the meaning of illustrations, symbols and images. In a good picture book both the illustrations and the text tell the story and reading the illustrations can dramatically alter the meaning and our interpretation of the book. If readers skip the illustrations they are likely to miss a great deal of the story. Illustrations in books by authors such as such as Anthony Browne or John Burningham do not just provide entertainment and enjoyment, they contribute significantly to the narrative by setting the scene, emphasising the plot and creating an atmosphere. They reveal aspects of the story that are not covered in the text. Young children know this when they pore over picture books for long periods and when they retell stories using the pictures as a support. Their retellings are often much more detailed than the words on the page. If we encourage children to continue to read the pictures even when they can read the words with ease they are likely to engage more deeply with the author's meaning and understand the power of the visual. During their research into how children read pictures Arizpe and Styles (2003) found that children as young as four were keen to discuss moral, social, spiritual and environmental issues as they responded to illustrations in books. It would be foolish to neglect 'the potential of picture books to develop visual literacy' which can help children to 'sort out, recognize and understand the many forms of visual information they encounter' (Kiefer, 1995: 10)

Visual literacy does not just apply to fiction, it is also used when reading information texts. Non-fiction contains photographs, line drawings, diagrams and charts all of which need to be read and interpreted. Reading information presented in a table or chart is a skill and not all children will be able to do this without assistance. The use of photographs can lead to questions from the reader. When was this photograph taken? In what circumstances was it taken? Why was this photograph included? Reading images may lead on to the exploration of issues such as stereotyping and bias.

Comics and magazines are a central part of many children's reading diet out of school. In 1996 a Children's Literature Research Centre survey discovered that up to the age of seven, 76 per cent of boys and 73 per cent of girls regularly read comics. Comics created for young children are often linked to toys, TV programmes or films. Magazines may be linked to leisure pursuits such as football or computers. There have been a number of projects which suggest that using comics in school can boost the literacy development of boys or poorer readers. These studies are usually concerned with children reading the words rather than the pictures. However, comics rely a great deal on the illustrations and are a good source for developing visual literacy. Children need to understand the conventions associated with comic illustrations including layout, the use of speech and thought bubbles, marks which indicate such things as speed or fear and the varied use of font size and type. Just as with picture books the illustrations have to be read carefully in order to understand the narrative. Indeed some children's authors such as Raymond Briggs and Colin McNaughton have drawn from the conventions of comics when creating their picture books.

A great deal of environmental print is visual. For example, road signs and logos associated with particular products are pictorial. Pictures play a significant part in the message communicated by other environmental print such as food wrappers, advertisements and greeting cards. Packaging and advertisements use colour, choice and style of illustration and overall design to appeal to different audiences. Children can discover which products are intended to appeal to them and how this is achieved by examining texts in the environment that are familiar to them.

Works of art such as paintings, drawings and photographs lend themselves to interpretation in the same way as pictures in books. Kenneth Clark (1960) suggested that viewers look at paintings in four stages. First, viewers look at the picture as a whole, getting an overall impression of the picture including the subject matter, the use of colour, the shape and size and the composition. The next stage is to look more carefully at the image noticing more details. Once the viewer is familiar with the picture he can start to make connections between the picture and his own experience and begin to ask questions about what he sees. The final stage is to re-examine the picture finding details that were perhaps overlooked and coming to some personal conclusions about the painting. This is a useful framework to use with children when looking at visual images. Most major art galleries now display their collections on line and many have produced notes to help children and adults read the pictures. The National Gallery of England's website is particularly helpful and a link to their teachers' resources is included on the website that accompanies this book.

Media literacy

There is some overlap between media literacy and visual literacy as most media is accompanied by pictures or symbols. This is true of television, film and websites. However, the term media is usually associated with texts which are not paper based and which include moving images and sound. There is an increasing interest in this aspect of literacy and many resources, particularly associated with film, have been produced for teachers by the British film institute (BFI, 2003) and in the planning exemplification for the literacy framework (PNS website: http://www.standards.dfes.gov.uk/primaryframework/). By the time children start school most of them will have an extensive experience of film and video and many will have experience of using websites and computer games. The role of the school in media literacy is to help children read the media at deeper levels by 'considering evidence and bias in an archive film in History, appreciating the affective power of short films, or comparing the different ways still images achieve an impact on our emotions' (BFI, 2003: 5). This involves using inference and deduction, looking at implied meanings and appreciating the craft of the creator which are all skills of comprehension.

Critical literacy

All texts are created in a context and for a particular purpose. They are socially, historically and culturally situated. Critical literacy involves examining and responding to texts by asking how, why and when was this created and by whom and for what purpose? Age-appropriate visual and media texts lend themselves to this kind of scrutiny by young children because they are a familiar part of their world and they may already have a great deal of knowledge about the origins of such texts. Their existing understanding can be drawn out and developed in the classroom. A telling example of critical literacy can be found in *Happy Birthday, Dilroy*, a poem by John Agard (1983). In the poem Dilroy is celebrating his birthday and as he looks at his birthday cards he asks,

> ... tell me why
> They don't put a little boy
> That looks a bit like me.
> Why the boy on the card so white?

Dilroy is questioning who this text is for and why it was created in this way. Questions about inclusion and exclusion, representation and misrepresentation, bias, power, what is considered normal, are all issues that can be explored through critical literacy. However, critical literacy is not necessarily negative; it is primarily about questioning and can be used to explore how texts bring pleasure and are of interest to children. Teachers can help children to develop critical literacy skills when looking at any kind of text by encouraging them to ask questions about what is before them. Below I have listed some questions that teachers and children can ask about what they read.

Looking at texts

Who produced this text?
Is the person or people who created this text named or anonymous?
What do I know about the producer of this text?

How was the text produced?
When was it produced?
Why was it produced?
Does the text reflect the how and why of its production?
How does the text reflect the time and place in which it was produced?

What kind of text is this?
Does it remind me of any other texts?
What conventions has the creator used?
What techniques has the creator used?
What kind of language, if any, has been used?

What effect did the creator want this text to have?
What were the creator's intentions?
Are these intentions openly stated or concealed in some way?

What thoughts has this text prompted?
What feelings has this text prompted?
How have I interpreted it?
Have I got evidence for my interpretation?

Translating theory into practice

The statutory requirements

Teachers can take account of how and what children have learned before and outside school when they plan a reading curriculum. There is now a far greater understanding of how children learn and how they learn to read and the official curriculum documents support approaches and activities that build on what children know and can do and that demand practical engagement. The Primary National Strategy (DfES, 2004) suggests that teachers should teach through modelling, demonstrating, sharing and guiding and providing opportunities for active learning. Its emphasis on personalised learning encourages teachers to accommodate children's individual needs and personal interests.

Official documents such as the Primary Literacy Framework (DfES, 2006a) do not prescribe exactly how teachers should work or the nature of the activities that they provide. Official requirements are a reference point for teaching. They require careful reading and thoughtful interpretation. Teachers need to draw upon their own knowledge when considering how to translate advice into practice and implement a reading curriculum that both teaches pupils how to read and gives them a love of reading.

Teachers and reading

All teachers of young children know a great deal about reading and readers. They have learned about reading during initial teacher education courses and continue to update their knowledge by participating in professional development. Any discussion of learning in school will almost always include some reference to reading. Teachers are aware of the debates and controversies surrounding practices and resources. They know that standards in reading are prominent in the minds of parents, governors, headteachers, Ofsted, employers and the media. As teachers of young children they will spend a great many teaching hours every week helping children to learn to read using a set of practices that seems to work for them and for the pupils they teach.

Despite the National Curriculum, official guidelines, policies and team planning the implementation of any curriculum in school will vary from class to class and teacher to teacher. Planning the curriculum begins with teachers' personal convictions about the purpose of education. Is it to prepare children for the world of work? To enable them to become good citizens? To enrich their lives? To place them in a better position to make choices about their lives? Whatever view one holds will influence the content of what is planned, the priorities that are established and the organisation of the curriculum. These will also be affected by teachers' assumptions about how children learn. Do children learn by being told? Do they learn through experience? Is learning only valid when it is directed by the teacher? How much do children learn outside school? From each other? By themselves?

Teachers also have beliefs about the value and use of reading. They are readers. They are aware of the value which society places on reading. They know how reading is applied outside school. They know that a major part of their role is to have a class filled with successful, developing readers and they know that their own aims for reading, even if they are achieved, will form only a part of the long-term development of each child's reading.

As the teacher plans her termly, weekly and daily reading programme she will be drawing on her beliefs about the purposes of education, about learners and learning and about the uses of reading, as well as her understanding of the reading process and her knowledge and awareness of practices and resources related to reading. Each individual will have his or her own model of reading which is related to his or her own definition of teaching and learning. One's own beliefs, knowledge and teaching style are a major influence on the content

and organisation of the reading curriculum which is planned and implemented. The list which follows contains the factors which influence how a
reading curriculum is planned and implemented and illustrates how a reading
curriculum is set within a wider framework of each individual's knowledge
about English, pedagogical knowledge and view of education.

Factors which influence practice include:

- beliefs about the purposes of education;
- beliefs about how learners learn;
- beliefs about what reading is for;
- awareness of the short- and long-term goals for teaching;
- teaching style;
- understanding of the reading process.

These factors influence plans and actual classroom practices including teacher
behaviour, the choice of resources, literacy priorities, the allocation of time
and organisation.

Creating a context for reading

The classroom environment

All classrooms should be rich and dynamic literacy environments, providing
children with opportunities to read, to write and to learn more about the nature
and purpose of literacy. They should have a writing area, a listening area and a
library area. Everyone in the class should contribute to displays of writing which
illustrate the nature, variety and uses of print. Children should be immersed in
the sounds of written language as stories, poems, rhymes, information books and
letters home are shared with them. There should be frequent story-reading and
story-telling sessions with opportunities for children to listen to and read known
stories and rhymes for themselves in the listening area. Children should have
access to books to read in class and to take home, as well as ready access to
resources for writing. From the first day children enter school or nursery there
should be an expectation that every child will read and write.

The atmosphere throughout the school and in the class should be conducive to risk-taking and independent learning. The teacher might make
explicit the expectation that children should make attempts to work things
out for themselves before asking for help. In an environment where the
process and effort of learning are valued it is easier to encourage children to
read in a way that allows them to take risks. Children who believe that reading is primarily about accuracy are likely to read deliberately and slowly and
to rely on adults for help rather than using their own capacity for problem-
solving and meaning-making. Children gain less practice at reading when
they read slowly and rely on others.

Models of literate behaviour

As Clark (1976) and Clay (1979) both found, children learn from and are motivated by seeing models and demonstrations of literacy and literate behaviour. So it is important that in school and in the classroom they see the teacher and other adults read stories, take the register, write captions for displays, refer to and use books for information, write letters or notes for children to take home, engage in literacy activities alongside the children and provide demonstrations of literacy through shared writing and reading. Displays, discussions and examinations of packaging and other print in the school and local environment also show children how reading is used.

The relationship between reading and writing

There is a mutually supportive relationship between learning to read and learning to write as both involve understanding and using written symbols. Writing supports reading by reinforcing the visual aspects of language. When writing children are encouraged to use their knowledge of the writing system, of what words look like and of how they are spelt. Developmental writing, in particular, encourages children to think about the sound and sight of words as they write. Children who learn to write in this way 'demonstrate greater phonological awareness than children who are used to copying under teachers' writing' and if time with groups and individuals is given to looking at words and spelling patterns, 'their growing knowledge of how words are constructed will support their reading' (Barrs and Thomas, 1991: 73).

Reading across the curriculum

Most children make progress in reading because they read a range of texts in a variety of circumstances. They read to others at home and in school. In class they read enlarged texts, personal reading books, computer screens, worksheets, instructions, their own writing, the teacher's writing and a range of environmental print. In addition they hear stories and engage in oral and written language games. Children receive practice at reading through all the activities involving literacy that occur during a normal school day. To make best use of the full range of literacy opportunities that exist teachers need to plan for reading beyond as well as within the literacy hour.

Classroom resources

Play areas

For many children imaginative play activities, drawing and games provide them with the opportunity to explore and experiment with literacy and it is in these situations that the beginnings of literacy frequently appear. Often it is in the context of play that children make up their first stories as they create and enact their own dramatic narratives either alone or with others. If play activities are equipped with resources for reading and writing, literacy will become more accessible to young children. During play they are able to explore the roles and activities of people who read and write and the uses of reading and writing. As they play at being readers and writers and play with the materials of reading and writing they will be gaining familiarity with the tools and activities of literacy, learning what reading and writing are and what they can do with them.

Children need easy physical access to play areas and need to be actively encouraged to make use of the literacy materials that they contain. Such materials might include notepads, memo boards, telephone pads, calendars, diaries, telephone directories, recipe books, TV guides, newspapers, books, magazines, cards, postcards, letters, bills, pens and pencils. If given the resources and opportunities, even children who cannot yet read or write in the formal sense will often behave as readers and writers.

The listening area

The listening area should be a permanent and recognisable area of the classroom. It will house the CD player, tape recorders or listening station and sets of headphones. Story tapes should be stored with their matching book. The area should contain blank tapes and children can be encouraged to make their own tapes perhaps to accompany their own books. A magnet board on which children can arrange story props as they listen is a useful way of encouraging children to think about their reading. Puppets and collections of other resources that support children's retellings of stories can also be stored in the listening area. The listening area provides children with opportunities to become familiar with books, to practise reading and to consolidate their understanding of the structure of texts.

The reading area

All classrooms should have a carefully arranged reading area. It should contain a wide variety of books that are attractively displayed. These should be in good condition and be appropriate to the age and interests of the children in the class. Books made by the class and by individual children as well as big books and one copy of the books that are used for group reading can be stored in the book area so that they are available for children to read and borrow. The book area may also contain comics, magazines, local newspapers, telephone directories, an A–Z of the area and a book in which children can write comments about the books they read. Time should be allotted for children to use the reading area to browse, to select books and to engage in extended personal reading.

The writing area

The writing area encourages children to experiment with letters, words and texts. If book making materials, empty diaries, notebooks and forms are provided in the area children have the opportunity to explore the style and organisation of different text types. Writing in the writing area provides children with additional practice with print and may help them to extend or consolidate what they are learning about reading. Further information about writing areas is given in Chapter 4.

ICT

Computers can be a helpful resource to develop children's reading. Software such as text disclosure programs, games, databases, word processing packages and CD-Rom format books all encourage reading as does the use of the internet.

Teaching methods

Shared reading

Introducing and developing reading using enlarged texts that could be read and listened to by large groups of children was first suggested by Holdaway (1979). Shared reading involves the use of commercially produced, teacher-made or children-produced books with enlarged texts and illustrations, popularly known as 'big books', which are shared with groups or classes of children. As the children become familiar with the text they are encouraged to join in reading the book with the teacher. This supportive, collaborative activity is helpful to all readers, giving them demonstrations of how to read and practice in reading.

   The book is positioned so that all the children can see the illustrations and the text clearly. Before reading the book the teacher discusses it with the children, asking questions such as: What is this book going to be about? How do we know? What is it called? Who wrote it? Who published it? Who illustrated it? Have we read any other books by this author or illustrator?

   Beginning with the title page the whole book is read straight through, with the adult pointing to each word as it is read. The book is read with the class a number of times so that it becomes well known to them and they can join in the reading. The children should have the opportunity to read the book without the teacher, either in its large form or in a smaller version which may have an accompanying tape. Smaller versions of familiar, enlarged texts are often among the first books that children share with adults during individual reading sessions. Once the children are familiar with the text they can take turns in reading it aloud to the class or individuals can take on the voices of the characters in the story. Sharing books in this way increases children's awareness of the layout of books, the narrative structure of stories, what is available to read as well as the pleasures and purposes of reading. The teacher may follow the reading by drawing the children's attention to words, letters, phonic blends, rhyming words, punctuation and other features of print. If the teacher wishes to focus on a particular letter or word in the text, she can write the letter or word on the flip chart, and ask the children to help compile collections of words to illustrate the teaching point.

Books that are used for shared reading need to:

- contain language suited to being read aloud;
- encourage prediction;
- encourage response;
- have a clear narrative structure;
- include illustrations that support the narrative;
- refer to situations with which readers can empathise;
- contain texts which have rhythm, rhyme or repetition.

The use of enlarged texts is very useful to early bilingual learners of English since shared reading provides a visual and oral demonstration of reading. Community language or dual language texts used in this way can be very helpful in supporting biliteracy, since when children see, hear and join in with reading, they are receiving the same experiences and insights about reading as English-speaking children.

Guided reading

In guided reading the teacher works with a small group, between four and six children, who have a similar level of reading ability. All the children in the group read the same book but each child has their own copy. The books that are used should match the children's present reading ability. They should be able to read them independently after the introduction but they should also present a small degree of challenge. When planning for guided reading the teacher will have decided on the learning objective for the group. She will have decided which reading behaviours need to be practised and developed by this particular group of children. It might be to encourage the use of contextual strategies when decoding an unfamiliar word, reading between the lines, justifying responses to what is read by using evidence from the text or reading an information book to find answers to specific questions.

At the start of the session the teacher introduces the text in a way that provides sufficient support for the children to read the book for themselves. The teacher might talk about the title, author, cover, illustrations and genre, and identify key words that the children might find difficult. It is also a good idea to remind the group of all the strategies they can use if they encounter an unknown word. Figure 2.2 is an example of a guided reading mat that one class of children made in order to help them remember to use a range of decoding strategies. To encourage thoughtful reading the teacher might pose a question that the children will be able to answer after they have read a number of pages. It is a good idea to set a task related to the text for children who finish reading early, such as:

- thinking of another title for the book;
- thinking of a who, when, where or why question to ask the group;
- thinking of a different ending;
- choosing part of the text to read aloud to the group;
- thinking of words to describe the main character.

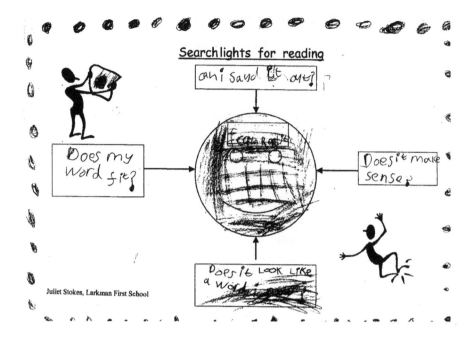

Figure 2.2   Guided reading mat

The next stage is for the children to read independently, quietly and at their own pace. The teacher's role is to observe and listen in to the children as they read in order to analyse how well the children are using the range of reading strategies. During this time she also works with individuals. If the teacher observes any difficulties she should help by asking the child to try different strategies rather than telling them the unknown word. After the children have read a few pages the teacher can stop the group and ask for answers to the question she asked at the beginning of the session. She can ask the children to substantiate their answer by reading from the text. She may ask the children to summarise what they have read so far. She may ask for comments about the type of language contained in the book or the structure of the text. After a short, focused discussion the children continue their reading.

At the end of the session the teacher can remind the group about the use of a particular strategy. Any words that caused particular difficulty can also be discussed. This last part of the session is an ideal time for the children to talk about the text and share their opinions and understanding. When reading fiction or poetry the children can discuss the effect of particular images, language or techniques used by the author. When reading non-fiction they might, for example, compare information found in two different reports. The discussion should help the children to develop a greater understanding of what they have read. As they talk their ideas can be clarified and extended, options explored and alternative views considered.

It is a good idea to set follow-up work related to the book. This could be an activity that the children can do immediately or at a later time. Examples of follow-up work include:

- drawing a story map;
- making a story board;
- looking up a new word in the dictionary;
- making a list of rhyming words;
- illustrating one part of the story;
- reading the text onto tape;
- making a character portrait with labels and speech bubbles;
- completing the sentence 'I like the part where ... because ...';
- writing a new blurb for the book.

Guided reading makes good use of the teacher's time. It is a powerful teaching and assessment opportunity. It enables pupils to practise their reading, think about what they are reading, extend their comprehension strategies, discuss texts and receive support that is related to their needs. During guided reading children can spend more time reading than they would if they were reading individually to the teacher. At Key Stage 1 and before children can often read a complete text in one session. Notes can be made about children's reading strategies and future targets at the end of the session. Figure 2.3 is an example of a guided reading record linked to the objectives in the primary framework. It reminds the teacher of the general objectives for the year and enables the teacher to make comments on how well the children are achieving these.

Group reading

Group reading is when four to six children grouped by ability take it in turn to read aloud from the same text. Those who are not reading aloud listen and read the words silently. If an adult is part of the group she should also take a turn at reading in order to provide children with a model of reading. It differs from guided reading as it is more concerned with giving children practice at reading rather than with teaching reading, although all practice helps children to develop their reading ability. HMI (2004) stressed that group reading is not the same as guided reading and that, as a means of teaching children to read, it is inferior to it. As it is less focused than guided reading it is an ideal activity for volunteers to lead. The books that are used during group reading may be taken from the class core collection and they may be taken home for the children to finish or reread. Sets of plays are a particularly useful resource for group reading.

Silent reading

The large-scale implementation of this practice grew in response to a suggestion from the Extending Beginning Reading Project (Southgate et al., 1981) which found that children's reading in school was often too limited in length for them to develop their experience and enjoyment of books. Periods

Guided Reading Year 1

Word recognition: decoding

Recognise and use alternative ways of pronouncing the graphemes already taught, e.g. the grapheme 'g' is pronounced differently in 'get' and 'gem'; the grapheme 'ow' is pronounced differently in 'how' and 'show'

Identify the constituent parts of two-syllable and three-syllable words to support the application of phonic knowledge and skills

Recognise automatically an increasing number of familiar high frequency words

Read more challenging texts which can be decoded using phonic knowledge and skills, along with automatic recognition of high frequency words

Read phonically decodable two-syllable and three-syllable words

Understanding and interpreting texts

Identify the main events and characters in stories, and find specific information in simple texts

Use syntax and context when reading for meaning

Make predictions showing an understanding of ideas, events and characters

Recognise the main elements that shape different texts

Explore the patterns of language and repeated words and phrases

Engaging with and responding to texts

Select books for personal reading and give reasons for choices

Visualise and comment on events, characters and ideas, making imaginative links to their own experiences

Distinguish fiction and non-fiction texts and the different purposes for reading them

Speaking

Retell stories, ordering events using story language

Interpret a text by reading aloud with some variety in pace and emphasis

Group discussion and interaction

Ask and answer questions, make relevant contributions, offer suggestions and take turns

	Book: *Willy the Champ*, A. Browne	Book	Book	Book
Lisa	Was able to discuss why Willy was an accidental champ			
Rosie	Identified the bullies as villains as well as Buster			
James	Split 'sometimes' into two words in order to read it			
Tom	Sounded out 'horrible' Identified Willy as old fashioned			

Figure 2.3 Guided reading record

of silent reading in class give children the opportunity for a sustained read from a book of their choice, enable them to see adults enjoying reading and enhance the status of reading for its own sake. The guidelines for organising silent reading were first described by McCracken (1971). He suggested that:

- a regular time should be allocated for silent reading each day;
- each child should have a personally selected book ready before the start of the session;
- the teacher should also read a book during this time;
- there should be no talking or movement around the class during the session;
- this is a time to enjoy reading and not a preparation for future work;
- after the session, some children might recommend to the class a book which they have particularly enjoyed reading.

Many teachers have found that periods of silent reading work best if they occur after a natural break in the school day such as playtime or lunchtime. Before the break the children select their books so that they are ready for the session when they return to class. Although ideally this should be a silent time, with very young children, who often read aloud to themselves, the time may be quiet rather than silent. As long as the rules of silent reading are explained to the children and it becomes a regular feature of the school day, children as young as four will happily read or look at a book for five minutes or more. By the time children are seven the silent reading period may be as long as 20 minutes. Normally the whole range of books in class will be available for children to choose from but, every so often, the pattern of silent reading sessions can be varied by having a theme for the session such as information books or books by named authors. Teachers may choose to include comics, magazines and the listening station in their provision for silent reading. Regular timetabled periods of silent reading take place in addition to the teaching of reading that occurs within the literacy hour in order to provide children with opportunities to practise their reading and time to explore and respond to texts.

Literature circles

For this activity children discuss texts that they have read independently. They may have read the book during silent reading, during library sessions or at home. The children will have been asked to remember the things that they found important or interesting when they were reading. The children and an adult meet in a small group to share and discuss their reading. They talk about what they noticed and question each other about the books. The discussion can follow a framework (Chambers, 1993). They can identify what they liked or disliked and then talk about what they found interesting or puzzling. This activity helps to develop children's understanding and response to what they read and can be used for both fiction and non-fiction. It can be incorporated into the groupwork section of the literacy hour.

Paired reading

With paired reading children choose or are allocated a regular reading partner. The two children take turns in reading aloud to each other from a book of their choice. During the reading the partner can give the reader help by supplying words or trying to work out unfamiliar words. The teacher and other adults can also be partners. If children have not yet reached the stage of reading alone they can 'tell' the story to their partner by reading the illustrations in the text. Paired reading can take place regularly as a whole-class activity or may appear on the daily plan for group activities with a different group engaging in paired reading each day throughout the week.

As part of the weekly literacy plan for the class, guided reading, group reading, sustained silent reading, literature circles and paired reading enable children to gain a great deal of reading practice at school. Providing children with the opportunities to spend time reading is important. Otherwise it might seem to children that they spend time learning to read but rarely have the opportunity to enjoy reading.

Individual reading

The practice of listening to young children read aloud for a few minutes a day, two or three times a week, used to be a common one in early years classrooms. Before the literacy hour it was often the main way in which children learned to read. It became standard practice because it gives the teacher the opportunity to:

- assess progress and keep track of development;
- provide help for individual needs;
- check the child's developing use of reading strategies;
- give every child individual contact time;
- demonstrate her interest in reading;
- give each child time to read.

Since the literacy hour was adopted by most schools in England there has been a decline in the use of individual reading. For some years prior to the literacy strategy arrangements this practice was questioned, for although the aims for individual reading sessions listed above are valid ones, critics doubted that listening to reading for short periods achieved these aims effectively. When teachers were trying to listen to the reading of whole classes of children every day individual reading sessions often only lasted between two and three minutes and were frequently interrupted as the teacher attended to other children's demands (Southgate et al., 1981). In this short period it was difficult for the teacher to provide quality individual time for each child, to provide the help needed and to make reading together a pleasurable activity. Moon (1988) described the practice as damaging to reading development because teachers who are conscious of time and are attending to other class members are probably most alert to the reader's mistakes and hesitations. This is likely to result in them providing unfamiliar words too quickly and so giving children the message that reading is about accuracy rather than comprehension. In such a short period it would be unlikely for sufficient text to have been read for the teacher to seek the child's response to the book and check understanding.

An interested adult who spends time on reading with individuals and who provides encouragement, enthusiasm and resources is crucial to children's reading development (Clark, 1976). So how might the teacher organise for individual reading efficiently and to good effect? Both Southgate et al. (1981) and Arnold (1982) suggested that reading sessions should be long enough for adults to teach and children to learn. HMI (1993) commented that the value of children reading to the teacher lies in the quality of preparation and follow-up work in which the individual reading session is embedded. There should be time for the child to read a whole story or episode and discuss this with the teacher, for diagnosis and help to be given, and for sharing enjoyment and interest in reading.

Individual reading sessions have an important place in nursery and reception classes where children may read with any of the adults who are available. These sessions are not the only way of teaching children to read as they will take place alongside other daily literacy activities. During individual reading sessions the adult works with a child as they read and discuss a book together (Browne, 2007). The process is undertaken in the spirit of genuine collaboration with the child. The adult's role is one of expert participant rather than expert instructor. She is there to provide the child with support and access to the text until the child is ready to take over. The focus of her interventions is to indicate how the child can enjoy the book more efficiently and independently rather than to judge progress or correct errors. Individual reading sessions take different forms depending on the experience and needs of the reader. The fluency of the reader will dictate which of the following elements are used when adults and children read together:

- a discussion of the title, author and possible content of the story before the book is shared if the text is unfamiliar to the child;
- the adult reading the text to the child so that he becomes familiar with it;
- the child retelling the story using the illustrations and text to guide him;
- the adult reading part of a book to the child and encouraging him to join in;
- the child joining in with the reading when he feels able to do so;
- the teacher and the child reading in unison;
- the child gradually taking over the reading until he is reading alone;
- the adult supporting the child by prompting or supplying words so that the meaning is not lost;
- a discussion about the child's response to the book;
- the child discussing the book with the teacher when he is able to read silently and without support.

Initially the majority of books that are read are familiar to the child from story times, shared reading sessions or previous readings with adults. At this point the child is using his memory of the story to join in with and retell the story. He is learning about print through behaving as a reader and, very importantly, he is establishing his belief in himself as a reader and gaining sufficient confidence to risk joining in with and taking over from the adult's reading. Gradually the child is able to approach more new texts with less preparation and to read with less support from the adult. But whatever stage the child has reached the teacher should tolerate hesitations and meaningful miscues and give the child opportunities to self-correct. During the reading the teacher responds to any difficulties that the child demonstrates in a way that causes least disruption to the reading. She limits her interventions to those miscues which detract from the child's understanding of the text. If the child substitutes an inappropriate word the teacher might read part of the sentence which led up to the miscued word. If the child makes no attempt at the word the teacher might provide the word, or draw the child's attention to the initial letter of the word. If the word is provided it can be returned to and discussed with the child after the reading has been completed. The teacher's interventions signal to the child the sort of cues that might be used when reading. Through rereading and reading on she is demonstrating how to use grammar and meaning to decode words and discussion of letters and sounds reinforces phonic and graphic strategies.

Spending time with children in this way gives the teacher the opportunity to monitor progress, note the range of strategies that the child uses, discuss the child's response to the book, his general reading interests and his difficulties, offer specific help and make suggestions about ways forward for the child. The teacher may set targets for the child and involve the child in this process. This approach places a great deal of emphasis on the quality of the texts that are shared in order to ensure that the child derives pleasure and meaning from the reading, to enable the child to use all the reading cues that are available and to sustain interest as the texts are returned to and read again.

The allocation of time and effective use of individual reading sessions depends on good classroom organisation (Campbell, 1990). The session needs to be long enough to allow the teacher time to listen to and observe the child. There needs to be time to talk in an unhurried manner. In order for this to happen the rest of the class needs to be engaged in activities which match their capabilities. They need to know what to do if they finish an activity and they need to know that they do not interrupt. It is helpful if the normal classroom routines support pupil autonomy and independence. Children may be allocated one reading session each week in class. This may be with the teacher but it can also take place with classroom assistants or volunteers.

Shared writing

During shared writing sessions the adult models writing for a large group or for the whole class. Because this activity involves a demonstration of writing it gives children insights into many aspects of texts and reading including words, letters, style and structure. As the children are concentrating on the content while the teacher transcribes, they have the opportunity to read and reread what is being written.

For shared writing the teacher can use the interactive whiteboard or have a number of large sheets of paper clipped to an easel and she should write with a large felt-tip so that all the children can see what and how she writes. As she writes, the teacher will demonstrate and may draw the children's attention to some of the following teaching points that she wishes to emphasise:

- where writing starts;
- spaces between words;
- punctuation;
- grammar;
- how phonic knowledge is applied to spelling;
- letter patterns in words;
- the sequencing of ideas;
- developing the plot;
- styles of writing;
- choice of words.

These will all add to children's knowledge about writing and consequently their understanding of how to read. Shared writing sessions are often used to write enlarged texts which can be used in shared reading sessions.

 Summary

When teaching reading we need to:

- be informed and reflective about reading in order to teach it successfully;
- teach children to use the full range of reading strategies;
- include visual, media and critical literacy in the reading curriculum;
- use a variety of teaching methods;
- foster in children an enduring love of and need for reading.

 Reflective activities

1. What are the central principles that guide your personal approach to teaching reading? How would you justify your principles and your approach?
2. Does this chapter have any implications for you as a teacher of reading? If so what are they?

(Continued)

(Continued)

3. Observe a guided reading session in school. What do you think the children were learning from the guided reading session? What were the rest of the class doing while one group was involved in guided reading? What organisational demands does guided reading make? What sort of worthwhile, independent activities could the class do if the teacher takes a guided reading session during an English hour?

Suggestions for further reading

Guppy, P. and Hughes, M. (1999) *The Development of Independent Reading*. Buckingham: Open University Press. This is a comprehensive account of the strategies readers use with suggestions about how to teach them.

Hall, K. (2003) *Listening to Stephen Read: Multiple Perspectives on Literacy*. Buckingham: Open University Press. In this book one child's reading is examined from different perspectives. A number of authors analyse the strategies he uses to decode and understand texts.

Harrison, C. and Coles, M. (eds) (2001) *The Reading for Real Handbook*, 2nd edn. Abingdon: Routledge Falmer (1st edn, 2001).The contributors explore theories of learning to read and look at how they can be applied in the classroom.

Lewis, M. and Ellis, S. (eds) (2006) *Phonics*. London: Paul Chapman. In this book a number of authors examine the place of phonics in reading and writing and offer practical suggestions about teaching phonics.

3

Resources and activities for reading

Introduction

> **This chapter covers:**
> - **why books are important;**
> - **selecting books for children;**
> - **activities which help children to read.**
>
>

What books offer

During the Foundation Stage and Key Stage 1 children read a great deal of fiction, non-fiction and poetry. Each of these genres has something distinct to offer but between them they introduce children to the pleasures and uses of reading.

Non-fiction

The majority of adult readers who do read usually do so for functional reasons rather than for sheer enjoyment (Wray et al., 1989). If we need to know how to … or we want to know about … we can consult the relevant text and discover the answer that we need. In order for children to be able to read and use non-fiction to further their learning at school and to access information out of school, learning to read and use information texts should be an important part of the reading curriculum at school. Non-fiction now has a significant place in the literacy curriculum in the early years perhaps as a result of the high profile it was given in the National Literacy Strategy (DfEE, 1998) and the Primary Literacy Framework (DfES, 2006a). Increasingly adults and children are using the internet as a source of information and this needs to be reflected in the resources we provide for children at school.

So while teachers will continue to provide non-fiction books they will also include other kinds of non-fiction texts in their provision for reading.

Fiction

Fiction has long been the core of the early years reading curriculum and much of the literacy curriculum is structured around stories. There are many good reasons for this. The ability to tell stories based on their own experiences and developed through their encounters with stories in books, on television, on film and on tape is a skill that all children bring to school (Barrs and Thomas, 1991). Introducing children to reading by providing them with story books to read is one way of building on what children can already do and know. Although this is important it is not the only justification for a literature-based reading curriculum. Stories have a value in their own right. Well written stories invite readers to recreate and examine familiar and unfamiliar worlds and experiences and offer readers the opportunity to know themselves, others and the world more fully. In the words of D. H. Lawrence, a story 'can teach us to live as nothing else can' (quoted in Wade, 1984).

To illustrate this, perhaps readers of this book would like to think about a story that they have read recently and consider what they gained from that reading experience. A memorable experience for me was reading *The Bone People* (1985) by Keri Hulme, a book that provoked a strong response in many people. For me reading *The Bone People* was a significant, rewarding and disturbing experience that enriched and challenged me in a number of ways.

At a personal level, reading *The Bone People* was an overwhelming emotional experience. As I began reading I admired the strength and sympathised with the dilemmas of the central character but, as the events of the book unfolded, I experienced a whole range of emotions including anger, fear and disgust at her actions and those of other characters in the book. Socially, the book gave me access to a society of which I have no direct experience. I was introduced to Maori traditions and values. I was confronted with the complexity of human actions and interactions and the recognition that these were linked to individual histories, relationships, communities and one's position in society. I was stimulated intellectually by examining the moral issues that confronted the characters. As I read, the unorthodox style of the book and the inclusion of Maori words and phrases encouraged me to pay close attention to the way in which the author used written language. And finally, because this was a book that had engaged my attention throughout, I wanted to read more by this author and to know more about her. I had experienced the power of story.

While this was an adult text, written for readers with abilities, understanding and experiences far greater than those possessed by young children, well-written children's books should offer their readers similar opportunities to those outlined above. Good stories should offer children the possibility of personal, social, intellectual and linguistic enrichment and leave children with the desire to read more. The list which follows identifies what stories have to offer young children as individuals and as learners.

To offer opportunities for personal development, books should:

- give enjoyment;
- extend imagination;
- develop empathy;
- widen experience;
- reflect experiences;
- present other perspectives.

To offer opportunities for social development, books should:

- reflect the nature of society;
- give access to secondary worlds;
- explore human relationships;
- express a variety of cultural traditions and values;
- demonstrate different ways of viewing the world.

To offer opportunities for intellectual development, books should:

- make abstract ideas accessible or intelligible;
- reveal deeper levels of meaning about familiar situations;
- invite consideration of moral issues;
- encourage reflection;
- modify or influence attitudes, values and understanding;
- give access to new ideas and knowledge.

To offer opportunities for language development, books should:

- allow readers to encounter different writing conventions and story structures;
- provide a range of writing styles;
- be a source of ideas about subject matter and writing techniques;
- demonstrate the beauty and power of language.

To offer opportunities for developing positive attitudes to reading, books should:

- leave the reader with the wish to read more.

Poetry

Poetry offers readers the opportunity to savour the sound and rhythm of language and to hear how ideas can be expressed in striking and unusual ways. It encourages children to explore and think about language and so has an important place in the reading curriculum. Young children, who might never have heard of poetry, often enjoy it and use it quite freely. Playground rhymes such as 'England, Ireland, Scotland, Wales, Inside, Outside, Inside, On' and 'Cowardy, cowardy custard, your legs are made of mustard' show us that children are attracted to memorable phrases and images. Readers might like to think of their own childhood rhymes and family sayings and think about their poetic qualities such as rhyme, repetition and pattern.

Books for young children

Books have the potential to enrich children's lives in so many ways. They are also a major force for exciting children into reading and persuading them that reading has a permanent place in their lives. Because books are such an important resource, teachers need to make careful selections of the books that they offer to children.

Every school needs a large collection of books to cater for the children's current and changing needs and interests. Some books should be kept centrally in the school library and the remainder distributed between each class. It has been suggested that every classroom should contain approximately one hundred books and that part of this selection should be changed once or twice each term (Somerfield et al., 1983). A collection that is changed will stimulate and maintain the children's interest in books and encourage them to discover the range of books and authors that are available.

There are so many different types and formats of good books available for children that it is worth making sure that any collection covers the full range. Each collection should contain books that will entice children, sustain their interest in reading and extend all the skills associated with textual and visual literacy. Outlined below are the main categories of books available for young readers. Each class and library collection should include books from each category in order to provide a balanced and varied selection catering for all the readers in the school from the youngest to the most sophisticated and experienced.

Books without words
These are usually considered to be most appropriate for very young readers as they do not require an ability to read text, yet they still teach children about books, directionality and story telling. However, their appeal is not limited to inexperienced readers, the quality of illustrations and the detail they contain can make them attractive to older readers as well. In order to enter into the story and construct the narrative the reader needs to read the pictures by closely observing the detail in the visual text. Each picture encapsulates a single stage of the action but a great deal might be happening at each stage. Sometimes the size of the pictures suggests the significance of the incident that is portrayed. Making sense of wordless books requires a number of reading skills including the ability to create a narrative with characters and plot.

Caption and concept books
These are very often alphabet, counting or naming books and contain limited text. Some books in this category consist of photographs each of which

describes an independent event. They are usually considered suitable for very young children.

Picture books

The majority of story books available for young children are picture books and they form the largest part of every collection. There are a number of subcategories in this section including traditional, dual-narrative, cartoon-style and novelty books.

Traditional picture books contain a combination of pictures and text. In the best books the pictures and the text combine to produce a satisfying and harmonious visual and textual experience. The illustrations support and clarify the text, helping the reader to understand and read the story. The illustrations may elaborate on the text by providing details of the setting or indicating the mood and the tone of the book. The pictures invite the reader to linger over the page and encourage children to reflect on and understand what is read. The length of the text on each page can vary from brief, repetitive sentences to long, complete paragraphs. Although they should be conceptually accessible to young children they need not be trite and can cover a range of themes from the familiar to those of universal and enduring significance. The artistic merit of artists who illustrate picture books is increasingly being recognised through awards as well as exhibitions and sales of their work.

Although in dual narratives the pictures and text are connected and may at first glance seem simple, the visual images often contain layers of meaning which show different perspectives and feelings. The illustrations extend the story far beyond the text and sometimes create a separate story. These books need to be read actively to fully appreciate the complex interweaving between the text and the several meanings expressed in the pictures. Reading books in this category can really develop children's understanding of the subtlety and meanings of books.

In cartoon-style books the narrative is usually found in the captions; dialogue, thoughts and dreams are contained in bubbles. The reader is asked to shift between at least two different styles of writing arranged within and around the pictures. Again these books encourage the reader to use all the clues on the page, in the text and in the pictures to make sense of the story.

Novelty books include books with pop-ups, flaps, cut-outs and hidden pictures. They can be used to entertain and maintain children's interest in books. They also make reading interactive by asking the reader to predict what is hidden beneath the flap or concealed on the next page. These qualities makes them ideal for very young children.

Longer narratives

These closely resemble paperbacks for adult readers. They vary in length, difficulty and in the number of illustrations they contain but generally provide a more sustained read than picture books. They may contain chapters or a number of short stories. Adults sometimes see these as the bridge between picture books and 'proper' books.

Picture books for experienced readers

Picture books are not just for beginning readers. Many of them can be read at different levels and evoke different responses depending on the age, experience and situation of the reader. Some picture books demand to be read by older children and adults because of the sophistication of the message, the length of the text and the intricacy of the illustrations. Even simple picture books should be read by older children since they can provide all readers with a visual treat and a satisfying read.

Books for sensitive situations

Feeling that it is 'their story' rather than 'my story' can give young readers and listeners a sense of safety when they encounter a subject that may be difficult. Death, loss, fear, bullying, abuse, illness, disability and inequality are all topics that have been written about by authors sensitive to young children's feelings. Including books on these subjects in the class collection acknowledges the existence of complex issues, presents them as normal and may prepare or bring comfort to children who are faced with situations that they find difficult.

Non-fiction books

Mallet (1992) identified three broad categories of non-fiction texts that have been written for young readers. These are narrative, non-narrative (reference) and non-narrative (exposition) texts.

Narrative texts can be written chronologically as information stories, biographies, autobiographies or diaries. Information stories have a narrower focus than true stories, since their function is to enable the reader to explore familiar and unfamiliar experiences, such as going to hospital, or to find out about topics linked to particular curriculum areas, for example facts about places and people. Some types of narrative non-fiction such as the story of a river from its source to the sea are considered easier for young children to read and understand than a more formal information book on the same topic. They can be seen as a bridge between fiction and traditional information books.

Non-narrative texts include dictionaries, thesauruses, encyclopaedias and atlases. This category also includes alphabet books, counting books and simple word books as well as those which provide facts through a combination of pictures and personal accounts. Expositionary texts which describe, explain and present arguments within their text are another, more complex, form of non-narrative information book. They may contain a considerable amount of text and make substantial demands on young readers. However, they are likely to be valuable in providing new information and extending children's understanding of a topic.

Poetry

There are many sorts of poetry books for the early years classroom including books of nursery rhymes, single author collections, collections of poems based on a theme and anthologies. They are often attractively illustrated. Many poems for young children are humorous but some children also enjoy poems that are more subtle or imaginative.

Plays

Short plays can be an excellent resource for group reading. Children have to concentrate carefully on the text and listen to others in order to know when to read their part. In order to bring their character to life they can vary their tone of voice. Play reading encourages children to think about the meaning of the text and about expression.

Big books

Big books are usually used when the teacher is sharing a book with a class of children. Their size means that children can see the text that is being read aloud. They can see how an adult reads and as they become more familiar with the text they can join in with the reading using the words that they can see. Poetry, songs, information texts, stories and plays are all available in big book format. Big books need to be selected with care. They are likely to be used with large numbers of children over many years and so need to be of sufficient quality to be read and reread with interest and enjoyment many times.

Reading schemes

Until the 1970s it was accepted that children in school learned to read using books specially written to provide practice in phonic and word recognition skills. This often resulted in texts containing unnatural language and lifeless stories. As a result of criticism that early reading schemes attracted and an increasing recognition of the importance of children's attitudes to reading, every scheme that has been published since the 1960s has claimed to contain 'real' stories and natural language and to be motivating to children. Many publishers and authors of reading schemes now make strenuous efforts to ensure that the texts in their books are written in natural language, contain stories that have some relevance to children's interests and lives and include colourful and lively illustrations. However, schemes still attract criticism for a number of reasons. They are criticised for their uniform appearance, the way in which they encourage competition, the distinction that their use creates between learning to read and reading, the way that they delay children's access into the world of books and their bland content.

Meek (1988) wrote about the disconnection, emptiness and arbitrariness of reading-scheme books in contrast to the coherence, fulfilment and pattern of individual books written for children. Her remarks are not dissimilar to those made by Stebbing and Raban (1982: 159) who described one reading scheme as containing 'narrative without structure. There is no plot requiring resolution … There is no introductory "Once upon a time …" or anything suggestive of development … The characters are insubstantial and little occurs in the train of events to make the reader wonder what will happen next.' While some individual books within reading schemes are enjoyable, even the best stories can be emotionally barren. By concentrating on the instant appeal of 'fun', they seldom, if ever, contain new material or stories or illustrations which evoke an emotional response from the reader. Scheme books are rarely 'an instrument for entering possible worlds of human experience' (Bruner, 1984). In their survey of reading for 'purpose and pleasure' HMI (2004: 13) noted that following the structure of a reading scheme 'did little to encourage positive attitudes or help [pupils] to see reading as a way of developing their personal interests'. Overall reading schemes do not compare well with books written by authors who have a commitment to a story and a sensitivity to language.

It is very difficult for all the books in a reading scheme to match the quality of well-loved picture books, particularly when they have been written to meet a number of constraining requirements, such as the need to have:

- introductory books containing very few words;
- a simple, limited vocabulary;
- some phonic regularity;
- word repetition;
- appeal to a mass audience;
- attention to the prevailing 'isms' of the day;
- a uniform appearance;
- a grading system for ease of administration.

Reading schemes only work as well as the teachers who manage them. Teachers with a thorough understanding of the reading process, who are organised, who know how children learn, who are aware of the abilities and needs of pupils in their classes and who are familiar with children's books will experience little difficulty in selecting suitable books and using these rather than scheme books for reading.

Selecting books

Good books for young children are written by authors and illustrators who care about what children read, have something worthwhile to say, are committed to writing well and are concerned about the quality of young children's encounters with print. In good books, the illustrations and the language unite to capture the reader's attention and support the child in his attempts to read. They can be read and reread by adults and children, revealing something new at each reading (Meek, 1982). Because books play such an important role in learning to read they must be selected with care and thought. They are used and reused and they should embody all that the teacher thinks is important for children who are learning to read. They play an important part in influencing children's short- and long-term attitudes towards reading, since 'What the beginning reader reads makes all the difference to his view of reading' (Meek, 1982).

Criteria for selecting fiction

Teachers can ask themselves a number of questions when they are selecting books for children. In this section I have included a few. Is the external appearance of the book attractive? Will it encourage the potential reader to look beyond the cover? Is the book well written? Does it contain a story that is worth reading? Is it inspiring, entertaining or thought provoking? Is the story coherent and convincing? Is the language vivid yet accessible to young readers? Can today's readers identify and sympathise with the characters? Are the moral and social assumptions in the text positive and constructive? Does it offer a fair representation of the world in the twenty-first century? Does it represent the experiences of the children in this school? Are the illustrations of good quality? Do the illustrations enhance and support the text? Is it a book that children will like? Do I like it? Will the book contribute to the breadth, balance, range and variety of the present book collection?

Criteria for selecting non-fiction

Many of the questions referred to in the previous section also apply here but there are some additional considerations about the choice of non-fiction books for very young children. They should:

- look inviting;
- be clearly laid out;
- contain a factually reliable summary of information about the subject appropriate to the age and knowledge of the pupils;
- introduce key words and technical language in context;
- contain the characteristic features of information texts such as a list of contents, index, glossary and headings;
- have illustrations, diagrams, photographs or drawings which complement, extend and explain the written text;
- be free of bias, stereotyping and misrepresentation;
- make reference to disturbing as well as comfortable aspects of subjects, for example controversial practices related to farming;
- help young learners to organise their existing knowledge and provide unfamiliar information which is likely to extend what is already known.

All teachers need to be aware of the sorts of books that can be offered to children, as an important part of their role is to help children to make choices about reading material. At times the teacher will need to extend the range of books that the child is reading, suggest more books that appear to match the child's current interests and increase or reduce the difficulty level of the books for the child. In order to be able to recommend a wide and rich reading journey for all children, teachers need to be familiar with all the books in the classroom. They need to be aware of the demands they make on readers and their subject matter. Keeping up to date with books that are available is an important, time-consuming but often delightful part of every teacher's role. As well as reading children's books, teachers can keep up to date through reading book reviews, sharing information with colleagues, attending book exhibitions and visiting bookshops and children's libraries. Some sources of information about children's books are given on the website accompanying this book.

Promoting books

Having a range of carefully selected books is important but teachers have actively to promote the books if they are to be used to their full potential in the classroom. As Klein (1986: 148) wrote, 'resources ... cannot in themselves teach the pupils'. The teacher's own enthusiasm and knowledge about books plays a great part in influencing children's attitudes and interests but there are also a great many practical ways of encouraging children to read and use the book stock in the class and in the school library.

Keeping children interested in books

- Have a variety of books in the classroom. Don't forget joke books, recipe books and poetry.
- Make sure that the books are interestingly, attractively and accessibly displayed, and that they are in good condition and clearly organised.
- Regularly change the books that are displayed.
- Have a comfortable, welcoming, inviting reading area in the classroom.
- Read regularly to the class.
- Have commercial and home-made audio stories available with the appropriate books.
- Keep a stock of blank tapes available for children who wish to record favourite stories.
- Have books available that span a range of difficulty levels.
- Include books written and 'published' by the children in the book displays and library area.
- Use adults, parents, helpers, visitors and other children to share books.
- Have specific times such as silent or quiet reading periods set aside for reading.
- Make time for children to share opinions with others about books they have read at home and at school.
- Make links with books in all curriculum areas.
- Plan work that culminates in the production of a class book which can be placed in the library.
- Discover individual children's reading interests and recommend titles that will appeal.
- Make sure children take books home and check they have read them.
- Organise a book week every year.
- Organise a book club.
- Have a book sale or exchange of second-hand books once a year.

- Use books from the school library for story times and for class projects.
- Organise visits to the public library.
- Introduce new books in assembly or class-sharing times.
- Make a display of new books.
- Read aloud the first half of a book, ask the children to predict the ending then offer the book to the children for reading in their own time.
- Offer inspection copies of books to children to evaluate.
- Make displays of each chapter of the class book as it is read.
- Organise story-telling or story-reading sessions for groups of children. The teller or reader can be an adult or an older or more confident reader.
- Be alert to children's book programmes on TV or radio and sometimes match the book that is read to the class with these.
- Have a 'Book of the Week' display. After reading the book the children could write or draw a response to add to the display.
- Play games based on books. For example, 'I'm thinking of a book in which the young girl is ill and has to stay at home with her dad ... I wonder who can guess which book I'm thinking of ...?'
- Use extracts from books on computer programs such as TRAY.
- Use computer programs that are based on books.
- Begin and add to a large chart listing good books as and when children mention them.
- Have a puppet box to provide opportunities for children to act out stories and repeat the language of books.
- Before buying books for the class ask the children, 'What is the best book you have read?' to give you an indication of what to buy.
- Put some of the children's book reviews inside the back covers of books for others to read.
- Have a class discussion, such as 'If you could only take one book to a desert island, which would it be?'
- Have a permanent display board for children to pin up their spontaneous book reviews and for others to display their responses.
- Use DVDs of stories and authors talking about their books.
- Invite more confident readers to read to the class.

Story times

These are often the most valuable times for promoting children's interest in books. Traditionally story time occurs at the end of the day or at the end of each session in the nursery, but books can be shared at any point in the day. In the course of a week a teacher will probably select a range of stories that offer children opportunities for personal, social, intellectual and language development, that are varied in content, style and length and that appeal to the children she teaches. It is at story time that the teacher's enthusiasm for books is transmitted regularly to children. Her choices of books and the way in which she reads or tells the story will do much to affect children's attitudes to books, authors and reading.

Telling and reading stories to children is a real art. One only has to listen to and watch professional story tellers to realise how limited one's own performance is and what a spellbinding experience it can be. Listening to and watching actors telling or reading stories on TV, radio, story tapes and CDs can provide teachers with ideas about how to share stories well. Sharing stories with children is a communicative activity, bringing together the teller and the listener and enabling the teller to respond to the feedback he receives from the audience. It depends not only on the use of the voice, including clarity, projection, level, varieties, intonation, pace and the use of pauses, but also on the use of a whole range of facial expressions and gestures. This means that story times can be particularly valuable for children with special needs and those whose first language is not English. There are a few guidelines that may help to convince children that stories are extraordinary and that make story time a truly magical time for children and adults.

Selecting the story:

- Choose a story that you like or enjoy.
- Make sure that you are familiar with the story.
- Make sure that what you have prepared is appropriate for the audience.
- Consider where you will be able to use sound effects, emphasis and repetition.
- Prepare and use props such as puppets or examples of items that are mentioned in the story.

Before the reading or telling:

- Ask the children to look at the cover, title and author of the book.
- Ask for the children's ideas about the content and the characters.
- Make links with stories they have previously encountered.
- Explain any words that may not be understood.
- Ensure that you have the children's full attention before beginning the story.

During the reading or telling:

- Do not be afraid to take a risk: children enjoy something different.
- Allow the children time to respond and, if possible, incorporate their contributions into the story.
- Encourage the children to examine the illustrations to enrich their understanding of the story.
- Leave plenty of time for story sessions.
- Do not rush to finish the story – pauses and silences can be very effective for creating tension and drama.
- Involve the children by keeping them guessing, by asking them what they think might happen next and by encouraging them to help with props and sound effects.

- If you are sharing a story in episodes, summarise with the children what has happened so far before beginning the next session.
- Enjoy yourself and so will the children.

After the story has been shared:

- Give the children the opportunity to express their opinions and reactions.
- Take the children through the illustrations again.
- Provide opportunities for the children to recreate or retell the story orally.
- Place the book in a prominent place in the classroom so that the children can read or browse through it at their leisure.
- If a tape of the story is available place this and the book in the listening area.
- Ask a group of children to create story visuals for the book so that the story can be retold and enjoyed in a different way.

Reading stories is important and enjoyable but *telling* stories allows even more contact between the adult and the audience, so you might consider using some of the above suggestions to sometimes tell rather than read stories to children.

Book-related activities

Book-related activities are at the heart of the curriculum for teaching children to read. They can have a significant impact on children's attitudes to reading and so they should be pleasurable and motivating. They are usually related to the three main types of texts that exist, fiction, non-fiction and poetry, but other types of texts including plays, visual texts and media texts should also be included in the reading curriculum. Activities should help children to learn and practise word recognition as well as encouraging children to delve more deeply into books by exploring the meaning, the structure, the language and the function of texts. They should also provide opportunities for children to express and develop their own responses to text and encourage them to read thoughtfully. The activities in the following sections can be used with a range of books and are suitable for use across the 3–8 age range. They are arranged in a way that matches the reading strategies described in Chapter 2.

Word recognition activities

Snap
Each child needs to make two identical playing cards. On one side they should draw a character from a book they know well and on the other side write the title of the book in which the character appears or the name of the character. The cards are used to play a conventional game of 'Snap', using a match between the words, the pictures or either. A set of similar cards but without the pictures can be used to play matching games such as 'Pelmanism' or 'Memory'.

Lotto

In order to make this game the children need to divide a piece of A4 card into four sections. In each section they should draw a character or an object from a book. On smaller pieces of card that will each cover one section of the playing board the children should write the name of a character or object they have drawn. Four boards are needed to play the game. One player reads the word from the small cards and the other players look for the match on their lotto boards. A variant that is particularly useful for very young children is to ask the children to draw four items or characters from a book that they know well. The A4 boards are photocopied. The photocopies are cut into four pieces and used to cover the cards when the lotto game is played.

Names

Making a collection of children's names can be a rich starting point for examining words and letters. Names can be sorted and matched according to initial letters, number of syllables and length. They can be arranged in alphabetical order and may be used to make an alphabet frieze or poster for the class. Children can experiment with writing their names in various colours and sizes using a variety of tools and materials. The sounds, names, shapes and formation of all the letters contained in the names can be discussed and compared during the activities and later when the poster or the frieze is referred to.

Signing in

Instead of calling the register the teacher can introduce a large signing-in sheet on which the children can write their name each day. This can be read by the whole class at the start of the morning and illustrates the uses of reading and writing for keeping records and providing information.

Making collections of words

Collections of words that begin with the same letter or that contain the same letter strings can be started and added to over the course of a week. Each time something is added the sounds and names of letters can be discussed and the words read by the class.

Rhymes and games

Nursery and other rhymes as well as advertising slogans and jingles can be sung and recited together. Other oral language games such as 'I Spy' and 'Odd One Out' can be played with and by the children. These activities provide relevant introductions to phonic awareness as well as helping children to see the fun and use of literacy.

Collections of objects

It can be useful to use a collection of objects related to the story when sharing a story with children. This is especially helpful if the story contains unfamiliar vocabulary or experiences that are distant from the children's lives. Real objects may help to increase children's understanding of the story and extend their vocabulary. The collection might also contain items related to the subject or the issue that is being raised. After using the items during the story session, the collection could be used to make a display and the objects labelled in English and other languages known to the children in the class.

ICT

Computers, audio equipment and videos are useful resources for language and literacy. They allow children opportunities to learn and reinforce their learning in different ways. Computer software can provide children with a means of learning and writing letters, developing a sight vocabulary and reading a complete text from a CD-Rom. Tape recorders can be used to record reading or to listen to tapes of books. There are DVDs of children's books, of authors talking about their books and their writing and of TV programmes intended to develop language and literacy.

I read a book ...

In turn the children think of a book, author or character beginning with each letter of the alphabet. For example, 'I read a book called *Anancy and Mr Dry-Bone* (French, 1991), 'I read a book written by Anthony Browne.' This activity could arise from or lead on to making an alphabet frieze incorporating books and authors that are known to the class.

Reading with understanding

Understanding stories involves appreciating their structure and recognising features such as setting, character, plot, openings, endings and conflict. Activities which allow children to explore aspects of structure help them to comprehend what they read at a literal level. They encourage recognition and recall of main ideas, sequence, character traits, comparison and cause and effect. There are a number of activities and resources which can be used to develop children's understanding and their awareness of narrative features.

Retelling the story

Children can retell a story in a number of different ways. It can be done orally as children take turns to recall an episode from the story. It can be done using role play, masks, puppets or story props. Objects from a story collection can also be used. Sometimes children can be asked to retell the story by identifying four significant elements. These can be recorded in the same order in which they occurred in the book, using pictures or words and pictures. All these activities can be done individually or in pairs. They help children to consider story structure, language, characterisation and content. Retelling a dual-narrative story where the words and the illustrations tell different stories can be an exacting and revealing activity. Retelling a wordless story can be a stimulating talk activity for a group of children. The teacher might want the children to use books without words as a stimulus for writing. One way of organising this is to ask groups of children to rehearse orally the dialogue that could accompany the pictures in the book. They could then draw some of the pictures, adding speech bubbles containing the dialogue that they had composed. Written retellings can be incorporated into a large book of class stories or made into individual books. When asking children to retell the story they need time to discuss the events and issues contained in the story and rehearse their retelling so that they will be able to remember the events and their sequence.

Role play

The role-play area can be transformed into the setting for a favourite or important story. This can provide children with the opportunity to explore the characters and repeat and adapt the action. Asking the children to make a large window for the home corner could transform it into the setting for *Through My Window* (Bradman, 1986). During their play the children could experiment with the roles of Jo and the people she sees during her day at home. With the addition of a wicker basket or a cardboard box painted to resemble a large toy box, the home corner could become the setting for *Bet You Can't!* (Dale, 1987). Involving the children in the production of props for imaginative play can give them further opportunities to reflect on the story and imagine how they would behave in similar circumstances.

Story sacks

A story sack is a large cloth bag containing a story book and a range of objects which can be used to explore the story. They are used by teachers and parents to read, enjoy and talk about books with children. A typical story sack includes:

- a picture book;
- an information book related to the story;
- soft toys of the characters;
- games related to the story;
- objects from the story;
- a taped version of the book;
- an ideas card for activities.

Story props

Story props are pictures of the characters and important objects from a story that are made by the teacher or by the children. They can be attached to a board with a magnet or with reusable adhesive pads. When the story is told or read to the class the props are placed on to the board as they appear in the narrative. The figures are then moved around as the story develops. Words and key phrases from the text may be placed alongside the pictures. Once the children have seen the story props in use they can be kept in the listening area with the book and an accompanying tape for the children to use when they read the book again.

In the following lists I have made some suggestions about other activities which could be used for whole-class teaching or for group or individual work.

Exploring setting:

- Read the opening and discuss where and when the story is taking place, who has been introduced, what sort of atmosphere is being established and how you know.
- Make a chart to record the information in the book using the headings where, when, who and atmosphere.
- Complete a similar chart using a different but similar story.
- With a journey story locate the journey in a different setting and draw a story map to show the new story.
- If the story has a specific or interesting geographical or historical location identify some research that could be done to add to the children's understanding of the setting.

Exploring character:

- Write a list of what the main character likes and dislikes.
- Design a birthday card for the main character.
- Discuss how the characters are made to seem frightening or familiar.
- Retell the story reading the words spoken by the characters.
- Make a collection of characters from books and compare and contrast them.
- Retell the story from the point of view of one of the minor characters or an onlooker.
- Make a character card for each character in the book listing their name, their part in the story, words in the text that describe them and what you think of them.
- Write a postcard or letter to one of the characters in the book.
- Plan a birthday celebration for one of the characters thinking about presents, games and guests to invite.
- Consider what would happen if the main character came to your home.

Exploring plot:

- Make story props to retell the story.
- In pairs play a game of consequences using the headings 'one day', 'then', 'in the end'.

- Draw a sequence of pictures to retell the story.
- Act out the story.
- Reread the book in a group or retell it taking it in turn to tell a section of the story.
- Draw a story map to represent the plot.
- Change one element in the plot and consider the implications for the story and what else needs to be changed.
- Identify when the action gets complicated and identify the problem and the solution.
- Make a zig-zag book with one event from the story on each page.
- Create an alternative opening for the story.
- Write a sequel to the story.
- Make a set of sequence cards to be used to retell the story.
- With a journey story write the story of the return journey.
- Write a diary entry related to the events in the book.
- Look at a number of books and the nature of the conflict in each one.

These activities encourage children to reread and reflect on texts. This gives them extra practice at reading and improves their reading abilities. Many of the activities also contribute to children's speaking, listening and writing development as well as their reading.

Reading between the lines

Reading between the lines calls for a more active response from the reader than reading at a literal level. The reader has to infer what might only be implied in the text. It involves thinking about cause and effect, making deductions and making comparisons. Many of the activities that are used to help children to read between the lines arose from a project conducted by Lunzer and Gardner (1979). They called these activities DARTs or Directed Activities Related to Text. Prediction, cloze procedure, summarising, sequencing, questioning, comparing texts and using alternative representations were all suggested by Lunzer and Gardner and I have included them and some other suggestions in this section.

Activating prior knowledge
This helps children to make links between what they already know and what they might encounter in a book. Consequently it puts them in a stronger position to make inferences about what is read. This can be achieved through:

- brainstorming around the title, the front cover or the opening pages;
- making a word association chain around a key word in the title;
- generating ideas around a key word or an item from the text. *This reminds me of ... This makes me think of ...*

Title: *Something Else* **Author:** Kathryn Cave **Ilustrator:** Chris Riddell	**On a windy hill** **alone** **with nothing to be friends with** **lived Something Else.** From *Something Else*. (Cave,1994)	**What do these words make you think of?** sad spooky cold lonely afraid
Who or what is Something Else? Something strange An alien		**What do you notice about the illustrations?** blue tall mountain cold
Do the opening or the illustrations make you think of any other books or anything else? Dracula's castle	**What do you want to find out as you read this story?** Why does Something Else live in a spooky house? What will happen to him	**What do you think is going to happen in this story?** Might make friends

Figure 3.1   Activating prior knowledge

This can be done as a whole-class activity using talk partners during a shared reading or as an independent activity. In Figure 3.1 the children were reading the opening page of *Something Else* (Cave, 1994) and working in pairs to complete the chart.

Prediction

Here the text is read in sections. As the teacher or the children pause during their reading the children are asked to recap what has happened so far and predict what might happen next. The children can work with talk partners to do this. As they read or hear more of the text they might revise their original predictions. All the predictions should be supported with reasons and where possible evidence from the book.

Sequencing

Sequencing activities develop children's familiarity with stories, story structure and narrative language. Pictures and words taken from a book are given to pairs of children. Working together the children are asked to arrange the pictures and or sentences in order. When engaged in this activity the children are practising the oral and written language of the story. By doing this activity collaboratively they are negotiating meaning, recalling past experiences and sharing ideas as well as listening to one another. After the children have sequenced the cards they can use them as the framework for narrating a story to other children or to an adult. They often embellish their story including details that were only inferred in the original. The children can also make their own cards for this activity based on their favourite books.

Alternative representations

The children can draw a part of the story that is not represented in the illustrations, for example what Red Riding Hood's mother is doing while Red Riding Hood is visiting her grandmother. An image can also be constructed through a freeze frame of a moment in the story to bring it to life in the children's minds. Another way of representing something from a story is to make a model based on the text, for example making houses for the three little pigs.

Discussion

All stories can be followed by a discussion and questions. This may take the form of comparing the events in the story with the children's own experience, for example how does the action described in *I Am Not Sleepy and I Will Not Go to Bed* (Child, 2001) compare with events in their own homes? Or, after reading *Phoebe and the Hot Water Bottles* (Furchgott and Dawson, 1977), the teacher might ask whether the children have ever received a present they did not want and what has been their favourite present. Children can also be asked to think about what they might have done at different points in a story. When asking questions adults need to be careful that discussion times do not become quizzes about how well children have been listening but that they are genuine starting points for exploring the story. To vary the format the children can sometimes be asked to discuss their answers to questions that the teacher has asked about the story in pairs or groups. The questions can be written on a flip chart and the children given ten minutes' discussion time before they report back to the class.

Questioning

The children can imagine that they going to interview the author. In preparation they write questions related to the text. They can do this around a photocopied image or section of the text. The questions could be used during an author's chair activity where one child or the teacher takes on the role of the author and answers questions about the book.

Children can question the characters through a hot-seating activity. They might want to ask *Why did you do that?* or *What if you had … ?* As an alternative to hot-seating, pairs of children can conduct a telephone interview with one child acting as the interviewer and the other in role as a character from the book.

Playing a questioning game such as 'Who Am I?' allows children to think of traits appropriate to characters in books they are familiar with. To play the game one child thinks of a character from a book and gives the class a brief description. The children then have to try to guess who it is and what book the character comes from. For example, a child might say, 'I am a girl who wants to be a star in the school concert. Who am I?' In this case it is Grace in *Amazing Grace* (Hoffman, 1991). Alternatively, after the first child has secretly selected the character the rest of the class take turns to ask him questions, such as 'Are you a girl?' 'Are you naughty?' 'Do you go to school?', in order to identify the character. Only yes or no answers to their questions are allowed.

Children can also devise their own comprehension exercises by setting questions related to the book for other children to answer. The questions should require answers that are both literal and inferential.

Creating speech or thought bubbles

Writing speech or thought bubbles for characters at different stages in the story can help children to get under the skin of the character and to understand what the character is feeling or thinking. Doing this at key moments in the text such as during a dilemma or a moment of fear can be most productive. This activity can stand alone or be a follow-up to 'conscience alley' described in Chapter 1.

Rewriting a story

Children can rewrite or retell a story using a different starting point from that used by the author. For example *Rosie's Walk* (Hutchins, 1970) could be rewritten from the fox's perspective, beginning, 'One day I saw a hen in the farmyard …' Using *On The Way Home* (Murphy, 1982) each child could write an account of the grazed knee in the role of one of the characters in the book. They might begin and continue their account with phrases such as 'My friend told me that …, but I think …, because …' These activities can help to develop empathy by looking at the story from a different viewpoint.

Cloze procedure

A cloze text has words deleted from the original text. The reader has to complete the text using their understanding of the meaning and their understanding of grammar. The aim is to find words that make sense in the context of the passage. These do not need to be the same as the original words. In order to do this readers have to think carefully about the content, the style and the type of text they are reading. To illustrate this think about the sort of knowledge you are drawing on to complete the following passage taken from the opening of *Thank You, Mr Falker* (Polacco, 1998):

Trisha, the littlest girl in the family, grew up loving _____. Her schoolteacher mother read to her every _____. Her redheaded brother brought his books home from _____ and shared them. And whenever she visited the family _____, her grandfather or grandmother read to her by the _____ fireplace.

In order to fill in the missing words you have to read on and back. The first missing word is a noun and it could be anything that a young child might like such as dolls, cats or sweets. Reading further it becomes clear that her enjoyment is related to reading and so the missing word in the first sentence could be stories, books or words. The second deletion could be filled with another noun, possibly day, night or morning.

Cloze passages for young children should have no more than one deletion in every ten words. The deleted words should not be provided for the children as this limits their interrogation of the text and their possible solutions. The children's suggestions and their reasons for choosing them should be discussed. Discussion helps children to identify clues in the text and adopt a more questioning approach to reading. Teachers can make their own cloze passages using text completion software packages such as *Developing Tray* (2Simple Software, 2004) which can be used on the interactive whiteboard or individual computers.

Reading the illustrations

Children can be asked to create a story using a set of pictures, without any text, from a book. The stories the children make can be compared with the original. During the discussion the children can identify the differences.

Reading beyond the lines

Reading beyond the lines involves evaluating and appreciating the author's work. To do this readers need to make judgements about style, characterisation and the effectiveness of the writing, to express reasoned opinions and preferences about books, illustrations and authors. The ability to evaluate and respond to what is read are aspects of critical literacy which was described in Chapter 2.

Story comparison

Comparing stories helps readers to understand how different authors use similar features in different ways. It helps readers to explore style, characterisation and plot in ways that allow them to make judgements about the effectiveness of the writing. A simple way of doing this with young children is to compare versions of stories which contain slightly different elements. For example, in *The Three Little Pigs*, the wolf sometimes meets his end in the pigs' cooking pot. In other versions he repents and changes his ways and in others the pigs build him a house of his own. What effect does the changed ending have on the story and which is the most satisfying? Figure 3.2 shows a story comparison chart that the children were completing in a shared writing session. The children were comparing *Puss in Boots* with *Jamil's Clever Cat* (French, 1999). Both are traditional stories about cunning cats who help their impoverished masters become wealthy through some form of trickery.

Although both stories are very similar there are differences in the characters, motives and the outcomes of the stories. These differences provide a way into

	Setting	Hero	Cat	Opening	Problem	Ending
Puss in Boots	French countryside	Jacques, a miller's son, poor, not very clever	Puss, scheming frightened for his own life	Jacques has no money Puss is afraid that he might be eaten by poor, hungry Jacques	Puss needs to help his master become rich in order to avoid being eaten	Jacques marries the princess He lives in a large castle He is called the Marquis of Carabas Puss lives well and happily
Jamil's Clever Cat	A village in Bengal	Jamil, a weaver, poor, ambitious	Sardul, cunning, helpful, loves his master	Jamil has no money He wants to marry a princess and become rich Sardul wants to help his master	Jamil needs to appear rich in order to marry the princess	Jamil marries the princess Together they become rich They live in a beautiful house The villagers also become richer Sardul is happy

Figure 3.2   Comparison of *Puss in Boots* and *Jamil's Clever Cat*

discussing how the children feel about the characters and analysing why they feel differently about Jacques and Jamil.

Author study

Reading a number of books written by the same author can be the starting point for exploring style, characterisation and themes. Once the children are familiar with a few of the author's books they can begin to compare them by using a story comparison chart. They might be able to identify common themes in the books. For example, many of Anthony Browne's books feature characters who are powerless or marginalised and provide insights into how this feels. They could compare how the author begins and ends his or her books. Are there any similarities? During the project the children can find out about the author and this might involve searching through reference books, book catalogues and using the Internet as well as writing letters to publishers and to the author. If the author can visit the class as part of the project this is ideal. The project might be drawn to a close by asking groups of children to compile a list of questions about the author and the author's books for their peers to answer; it could then end with a class quiz.

Exploring language

Many authors have their own distinct style of writing and most use language to create particular effects. Jez Alborough's (1992) use of rhyme in *Where's My Teddy?* creates a comic and rhythmic effect which makes it very hard not to sing the text as one reads. In *Owl Babies* (Waddell, 1992) we know that Bill is the youngest owl and Sarah is the most sensible by the things they say. In *Don't Forget the Bacon!* (Hutchins, 1976) the child's determination to remember the shopping and her anxiety about forgetting are mirrored by the increasingly odd items she thinks about on her journey to the shops. Children may notice these effects themselves but teachers might want to draw children's attention to them by asking children to join in with repeated sequences of words or asking children to think up their own lines that fit into the story. When writing new lines they need to understand the effect the author wanted to create and the sort of language they used.

Exploring messages in books

Some books contain messages about important issues within their stories. Gender stereotyping is explored in books such as *William's Doll* (Zolotow, 1972), *Princess Smartypants* (Cole, 1986), *Henry's Baby* (Hoffman, 1993) and *Piggybook* (Browne, 1986). Reading one of these books to the class and following this with a discussion can be a valuable way of exploring ideas and issues with young children. After reading *Piggybook* the children could be asked questions such as: What is a piggyback? Look at the front cover of the book. Who is giving a piggyback to whom? What does this make us think the book is about? What does 'pigs might fly' mean on the inside cover? These initial questions might be followed by going through the book and making a list of the images of pigs that occur in the book. Finally the children could be asked, 'What do you think *Piggybook* is about?' 'What do you think about this?' As part of the process of understanding the message contained in the book the children might be asked to write to a character in the book expressing empathy, giving advice or stating an opinion about his or her actions. Other representations in books of girls, boys, women and men could be examined and the children could be asked to retell or rewrite a familiar story changing the sex or actions of some of the characters.

Establishing preferences

Identifying favourite books and giving reasons for preferences gives children the opportunity to articulate their emotional response to a book. This type of thinking can be encouraged from the earliest stages of learning to read by discussing with children whether they liked or disliked a story and the characters in it, and asking them to give reasons for their point of view. They can share their thoughts about the books they read in silent reading sessions. From time to time the children can undertake a class survey of favourite books and the results could be used to create a class top ten or compile a database which would reveal the most and least popular books and authors in the class. Designing posters or advertisements for a favourite book or writing to a friend inviting them to read a favourite book encourages children to think carefully about the book they want to promote and why. Short book reviews ranging from a short caption such as 'THIS IS A GREAT READ! READ IT TODAY' to a list of three reasons why other children should read this book or three reasons why they should not also encourage children to think about what makes a good book for them.

Writing a sequel

Some stories are part of a published series; for example, *Through My Window* (Bradman, 1986) was followed by *Wait and See* (1988) and *In a Minute* (1990). Reading all three could give rise to a discussion about further events that could form part of Jo's life and the children could produce their own book about her further adventures. The children could write replies to the letters that are delivered in *The Jolly Postman* (Ahlberg and Ahlberg, 1986) or they could write about what happened after the original letters were received. When writing a credible sequel children need to understand the setting, the characters and the sort of story the author wrote in the original so that their story can be seen as one of a series.

Reading poetry

Poetry is a key part of the National Curriculum for English and children are expected to spend a number of weeks each term reading and writing poetry. They should encounter poems from a range of cultures, good quality modern poetry and classic poetry. A survey by Ofsted (2007) found that there was room for improvement in the teaching of poetry in primary schools. Although many of the pupils said that they enjoyed reading poetry, inspectors found that work on poetry was often planned around the need to improve skills in writing. They suggested that, 'Used in this way, poetry becomes primarily a teaching tool for language development rather than a medium for exploring experience' and that 'this approach limited the variety and quality of poems studied' (Ofsted, 2007: 3). In particular they noted that few poems or poets from other cultures were included in the English curriculum and that most poems which teachers introduced to young children were rather 'lightweight', a finding that corresponded with that of a survey which found that teachers' awareness of children's poetry was often limited to the light hearted or humorous (Cremin et al., 2007). Poetry for young children does not always need to be comic. It can entertain and be enjoyable when it prompts readers to look at what is usual and everyday in a fresh way and when it includes language used with sensitivity and versatility.

By the time children start in nursery or reception classes they will already have had some experience of poetry through hearing television jingles, pop songs and nursery rhymes. Teachers can extend these early experiences by continuing to provide children with opportunities to hear and join in with familiar rhymes, simple poems and rhyming stories. To deepen their enjoyment of poetry children need to become aware of patterns of rhythm, rhyme and sounds and to think about the way in which these features are used to enhance the meaning. Young children need to be immersed in poetry if they are to appreciate its qualities. In the early years teachers can help children to become aware of the patterns of rhythm, rhyme and sounds by:

- saying and singing nursery, playground and action rhymes with the class;
- regularly reading and rereading poems to children;
- encouraging children to listen intently to rhymes and poems;
- asking children to participate through actions and by joining in with the words;
- discussing the content and significant features of poems with children;
- discussing memorable or striking words and phrases;
- asking children to provide illustrations or select images for poems they hear;
- making collections of favourite poems;
- using poetry in shared, guided and quiet reading;
- having a poem of the week on display in the classroom;
- relating poetry to children's own experiences;
- teaching children the terminology of poetry such as rhythm, rhyme and sounds;
- providing audio tapes and CDs of poems for children to listen to at school or at home;
- using cloze and sequencing activities to encourage rereading and attention to meaning;
- concealing the title of a poem and asking children to think of a title after they have heard the poem;
- creating opportunities for children to read and perform poems in assemblies;
- participating in poetry celebrations such as National Poetry Day.

Reading non-fiction

Key features of information texts

The appearance and presentation of text in most information books differs substantially from that of story books, as do the readers' purposes for reading them. Information books have their own particular set of features to guide readers and help them understand the content. The number and use of organising features of information texts vary, often according to the length and nature of the book, but all information books contain some of them. Among the typical features of information books for young readers are:

- an introductory summary of what the book contains;
- a final summary;
- an afterword containing extra information;
- the use of retrieval devices such as a list of contents, index, glossary and headings;
- illustrations in the form of charts, diagrams, drawings and photographs;
- headings, subheadings, captions and lists;
- technical vocabulary;
- an impersonal style of writing.

Activities for teaching non-fiction reading

Before teaching children how to read non-fiction or expecting children to be able to use information books teachers need to provide opportunities for children to become familiar with their function and layout. This can be done in many ways. Teachers often place non-fiction books close to classroom displays and encourage children to look at books associated with those topics. They may read from non-fiction books during the course of a topic or share books with children when planning imaginative play activities. Classrooms contain many examples of information texts such as lists, instructions, explanations, posters and captions which are written and read by teachers and children. Children often take home information in the form of letters or booklets. Teachers can make good use of these varied texts by discussing them with children and by encouraging them to read and use them. This helps to familiarise children with information writing and helps them to appreciate the usefulness of non-fiction.

Non-fiction is a resource for learning and if children wish to pursue an interest, explore an idea or discover the answer to a question an information book may be able to help them. The best way of illustrating this is for the teacher to model ways of reading and using information books. Teachers can show children how to find the book that they need for a particular purpose, to appraise books quickly by using the cover, title, list of contents, index, headings and subheadings, to scan the book to locate the section that they want, to skim through the pages that they think will be useful and to carefully read the parts which contain relevant information.

Children need regular opportunities to practise using the strategies for reading non-fiction. These can occur during shared, guided reading and independent reading. Teaching children how to use and read non-fiction texts can often take place in the context of subjects other than English. This can give children a real purpose for using books and other texts and provide opportunities for using the information they discover.

Some of the activities which help children to read and understand fiction and poetry are also helpful when learning to read non-fiction. The directed activities related to texts (Lunzer and Gardner, 1979), which include prediction, cloze procedure, summarising, sequencing, questioning, comparing texts and using alternative representations, can all be used with non-fiction. Suggestions about these and other activities are given below.

Key words

Different curriculum areas and topics introduce children to subject-specific vocabulary. This vocabulary is important to understand both the topic and any related books that the children read. For example in Year 2 when children are studying plants and animals in the local environment (QCA, 1998) they are expected to understand and use words which have a different meaning in other contexts such as shoot, fruit, earth, table as well as less common words like reproduce and produce. They also need to be able to name and distinguish between any animals and plants that they might find in the local environment. As the children encounter these new words they can be added to a class word bank or a subject-specific dictionary or glossary. The definitions and illustrations can be made by the children.

Another way of creating glossaries is for the children to write individual key words onto small rectangles of paper and write their definitions on other pieces of paper. After a number of these have been made the definitions and the key words can be jumbled up and given to other children who have to correctly match the definition and the key word.

Sequencing

Many non-fiction texts contain words such as *first, next, then* and *because*. Cutting up a text into chunks of individual sentences or groups of sentences and asking the children to remake the text encourages them to see that non-fiction texts are carefully organised and that joining words are an organising device. During sequencing activities children need to read and reread the chunks of text which can help them to become familiar with the style of writing that is used for non-fiction.

An easier sequencing activity can involve giving pairs of children pictures and words taken from a book or photographs and sentences recounting an activity the children have undertaken. The activities might include an experiment, a school event or an outing. Working together the children arrange the pictures and/or sentences in order and then provide an oral recount or report for their sequence.

Questions

Many people read non-fiction to find out the answers to particular questions. It gives reading a purpose and a focus. Children can approach reading in this way too. When working on a project about animals, Hannah devised the questions in Figure 3. 3. After reading some non-fiction books she was able to answer her questions and the answers are seen in Figure 3.4.

Alternative representations

After the children have listened to or read an information text they can produce a diagrammatic summary of what they have understood. This is particularly helpful if children are learning about life cycles or learning to interpret

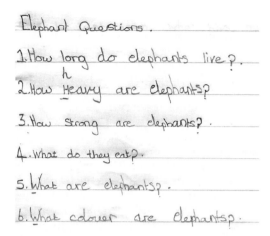

Figure 3.3   Hannah's questions

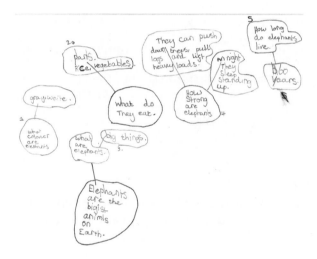

Figure 3.4   Hannah's answers

instructions. A visual representation can help a child to remember what they have read or heard and encourages them to think about organisation and order.

Summaries

Making a summary involves deciding what are the most important or interesting elements of the text. To do this the text has to be read thoroughly and thoughtfully. It involves reading a text once to become familiar with it and then reading it again to make a selection. The children can select key ideas by highlighting important sentences or words. When the highlighted parts of the text are put together these should produce a summary. Children can also summarise a text by producing a diagram, a labelled picture or a set of pictures. Summarising techniques need to be modelled by the teacher before children can use them independently.

Classroom example: reading non-fiction

The following examples of introductory work with non-fiction books are taken from work in a class of Year 1 and Year 2 pupils. They are examples of summaries and alternative representations. The first example, Figure 3.5, shows the initial activity which followed on from a reading to the class of an information book about life in China (Flint, 1993). The teacher began by summarising what the children had learned about China.

The children then went on to consider which aspects of life in China are similar to life in Britain and which are different. They began by constructing a chart about food, like the one that appears in Figure 3.6. Later they used their own experience and other information books to extend and complete the chart. The questions at the end of the chart were the starting point for reading other books about China. By starting the project with a whole-class session, reading an information book with the children and constructing two simple diagrams, the teacher had introduced children to one way of using non-fiction texts, had demonstrated how to organise the information this text contained and had provided a structure and a starting point for the further use of information texts.

The next example in Figure 3.7 is a table constructed after the teacher had read an information text about games with the children (Deshpande, 1988). It was important to summarise what the class had found out as the intention was to play the games so those that were not fully explained in the book needed to be investigated further. Later the instructions for playing the unfamiliar games were written up by the children.

Visits and visitors

These can bring work on non-fiction to life for young children. They can extend their knowledge and give them a real purpose for finding out. For example, a parent who has recently had a baby might be asked to come in to talk and answer questions about the preparations for the birth and the items she uses for the care of the baby. To prepare for her visit the children might have consulted information books and used these as a prompt for the questions they decided to ask.

Linking non-fiction and fiction

Work on non-fiction can also arise from work on stories. For example, as part of the follow-up work to *Mrs Lather's Laundry* (Ahlberg, 1981b) groups of children could visit a local launderette to observe it in use. In order to make best use of their time there they might have read some books about laundries and laundrettes in order to prepare some questions which they can put to the manager of the launderette. Afterwards they might compare what they had found out during their visit with the events in the book. They could continue to research the topic of launderettes and laundry practices using books and the internet.

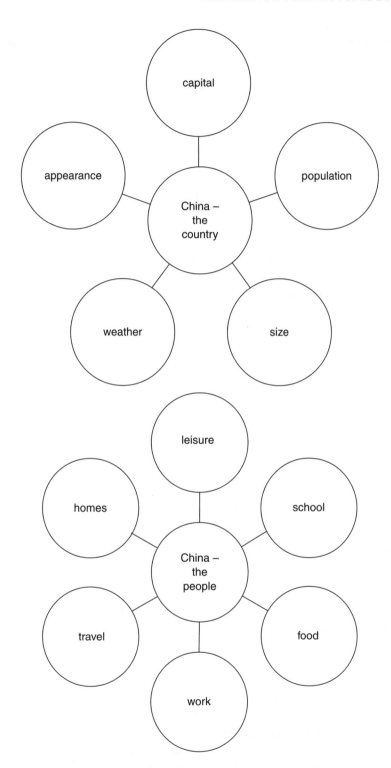

Figure 3.5 A summary of what the children found out about China

Food and drink	China	Britain
noodles	yes	yes
rice	yes	yes
chicken	yes	yes
fish	yes	yes
pork	yes	yes
tea	yes	yes
rice wine	yes	no
beer	yes	yes
What else do Chinese people eat and drink?		
What do they eat on special occasions?		

Figure 3.6   Food and drink in China and Britain

Game	What you need	Number of players	Where to play
marbles	marbles	2+	in/outside
bombardiers	marbles	2+	outside
brown girl in the ring	people/song	lots	outside
hopscotch	chalk, stone	2+	outside
slide	slide	1	outside
higher and higher	skipping rope	3+	outside
jacks	jacks	2+	
people puzzle	people	4+	
grandmother's footsteps	people	3+	
giant's footsteps		1+	outside
follow my leader	people	3+	

Figure 3.7   Summary of games

ICT

The National Curriculum for Information and Communication Technology at Key Stage 1 (DfEE/QCA, 1999b) states that pupils should be taught to use ICT to find things out and exchange and share information. Both of these aspects have implications for literacy learning. CD-Roms, videos and the internet as well as books can be sources of information. Many of the activities suggested for reading non-fiction books can be applied to reading on-screen texts.

Children need to have one or more questions in mind before they begin to search for suitable material and before they begin to read. When they are reading they can use the highlighter tool to mark sections of the text that will be useful to them. These sections can then be copied and pasted to the child's own document where they can be edited and organised. It might be helpful for children to have a grid or a list of their questions on their document before they begin to copy and paste as this will help them to structure their material more easily. When working with young children it is probably best for teachers to have identified useful websites before the children begin their research and to model how to read and use electronic texts.

Organising a book week

A special week, devoted to books, can help children to become more informed about books and stimulate them into reading more widely. A school book week can help to reinforce the idea that reading can be exciting, stimulating and informative. A national book week is timetabled for the first full week of October each year but schools can hold a book week at any time. Organising a successful book week needs a great deal of prior planning as authors, illustrators, story-tellers, book sales, sponsored events and displays provided by local bookshops need to be organised well in advance. Any of the activities outlined in this chapter could be usefully incorporated into a week devoted to books. The *Children's Book Week Resource Guide* available from the Book Trust (http://www.booktrust.org.uk) provides detailed guidance on all aspects of organising a book week.

 Summary

When teaching reading we need to:

- make careful and informed choices about the books we provide for children to read;
- provide varied and interesting activities which cover the full range of reading strategies;
- promote reading as an enjoyable and rewarding activity.

 Reflective activities

1. Think of six of your favourite picture books. Why do you like these books? What makes them stand out from the other books that have been written for young children? What would you want children to enjoy or learn from them?

(Continued)

(Continued)

2. Select a story that you know well. Could you use a collection of objects to introduce the story or bring it to life? How would you make use of the objects as you shared the story with children?
3. What do you think makes a good quality book for children? Are there any books in the classes you work with that are not good quality? What happens to these books? What should happen to them?

Suggestions for further reading

Ellis, S. and Barrs, M. (1996) *The Core Book*. London: Centre for Language in Primary Education. This booklet explains how teachers can put children's books at the heart of a structured approach to teaching reading. It provides a rationale for selecting and organising core collections of books and suggests ways of planning activities around them. It is complemented by Lazim, A. (2008) *The Core Book List*. London: CLPE, which is a comprehensive booklist of fiction, non-fiction and poetry for primary schools.

Gamble, N. and Yates, S. (2008) *Exploring Children's Literature: Teaching the Language and reading of Fiction*, 2nd edn. London: Sage (1st edn, 2002). This is an authoritative and enthusiastic exploration of books written for children.

Meek, M. (1988) *How Texts Teach What Children Learn*. Stroud: The Thimble Press. In this classic pamphlet Margaret Meek demonstrates the power of books and how they affect young children's reading.

Merchant, G. and Thomas, H. (1999) *Picture Books for the Literacy Hour*. London: David Fulton. Merchant, G. and Thomas, H. (2001) *Non-fiction for the Literacy Hour*. London: David Fulton. These two books provide practical suggestions for reading and writing activities.

4

Writing

Introduction

> **This chapter covers:**
>
> - composition, that is conveying ideas and meaning through writing;
> - why we write and why children learn to write;
> - what is involved in the writing process;
> - the teacher's role;
> - classroom organisation;
> - teaching methods;
> - writing fiction;
> - writing poetry;
> - writing non-fiction.

Reasons for writing

Writing in the world outside school

Writing is a significant feature of life in the twenty-first century. It is all around us, on our clothes, in our homes and on our streets. We all use writing at some point every day. Think for a minute about all the writing you have done in the past 24 hours. You might have written:

- a birthday card;
- a shopping list;
- a letter;
- a diary entry;
- an e-mail.

Why did you write these things? You probably wrote to keep in touch with someone, to remember something or to record something. Adult writers know that writing is about the communication or expression of ideas. They write because they have something to communicate and someone to communicate with or because they have something to remember or clarify. We usually write to people who are some distance away. It is unusual to write an e-mail or a letter to someone who is in the same room as you or if the message could have been conveyed orally. Writing is time-consuming. It can take ten times longer to write something than to say the same thing (Smith, 1983). Writing is a useful skill but one that adults use selectively.

Children's understanding of the functions of writing

Children are active and avid learners almost from the moment of their birth. This is clearly demonstrated through their achievements as oral language users. However, two conditions need to be present for their learning to take place. They need to see a purpose for their learning and that purpose has to be relevant to their present needs. In Whitehead's words, children seem to ask themselves two questions when engaging in a task, 'What is it for?' and 'What's in it for me?' (Whitehead, 2004: 178). Most young children are aware of writing in their homes and their communities. They have seen adults responding to written messages and using writing. Children may have been encouraged to join in with the writing that adults do when writing greetings cards or sending letters and e-mails to relations and friends. They may have begun to formulate some ideas about the use of writing in the world. What seems to be more difficult is for children to understand the relevance of writing in school to their own lives. During the course of the National Writing Project (1990) children were asked why they wrote. They gave replies such as because 'teacher says so' and 'so we don't get told off'. These children saw writing as a school activity whose primary purpose is to show adults what has been learned. They were unclear about the reasons for doing the writing they were asked to do in school and could not relate writing to their own lives or their present needs.

If children learn most effectively when they can see reasons for what they are learning, then it is important for adults to explain and demonstrate the communicative and exploratory functions of writing. We need to offer children reasons for becoming interested and adept users of written language. To this end, as far as possible, the writing curriculum in school should contain activities that are relevant to children's lives and needs.

What writing involves

Writing is an activity that is undertaken for a reason and with a specific audience in mind, and the form that writing takes is determined by its purpose and its audience. Read the following extracts and consider:

- Who was the author?
- Who was the intended reader?
- Why was it written?
- How do you know?

Gone to Tom's. Back at 5ish

Am I the only reader who finds the new bus service hopelessly inadequate?

Thank you so much for the book.
I have already started it and am
enjoying it very much. It was an
excellent choice.

The first extract is a note written to someone who is familiar to the writer. You have probably left similar notes for family members or friends. There is an assumption that the reader will know who Tom is and who has written the note. It is brief and informal. The sentences are incomplete and contain abbreviations.

The second extract is from a letter written to a local newspaper. The writer has selected his words carefully. Words such as 'hopelessly' and 'inadequate' are rather formal and may have been chosen to impress the unknown audience. The writer is also looking for allies who will perhaps join in his campaign of complaint about the bus service. He does this by assuming other readers will also have found the bus service wanting. The choice of language and the sentence construction give this extract a rather indignant and pompous tone.

The last extract is formal but it is clear that the writer knows the person she is writing to as she is thanking them for a present. It is typical of a letter written by a child to a relative that they do not know very well or see very often. The words have been selected with care and the tone is polite. Figure 4.1 shows how we could categorise the three extracts.

Writing can be a hastily written note jotted down on a scrap of paper or it can be a carefully crafted piece of text that has been drafted and redrafted before being sent to the recipient. A letter to a friend may be quite lengthy, may describe events and feelings in some detail, may contain advice or comment and may vary in tone from humorous to serious. It may be loosely structured, may refer to shared knowledge and experiences and convey the personality of the writer. A letter to the bank manager might be quite formal. The writer may take a great deal of care in organising the content, presenting the information clearly, ensuring that the writing is legible and checking spelling and grammar. It might be written out a number of times and the writer may use a word processor. A shopping list written for oneself may contain abbreviations, words which are crossed out and it may be added to over a few days. In all these pieces of writing the interplay among the purpose for writing, the audience and the content will affect the form and style of the writing, the care with which it is undertaken and the length of time spent on it.

Text type	Purpose	Audience	Tone	How it was written	Outcome
Note	To convey information	Close family member	Informal, casual	Quickly	Thrown away after having been read
Letter	To complain, persuade	Unknown, not specific but living in the same area	Formal, pompous	Drafted and possibly word processed	Published in a newspaper, possibly responded to
Letter	To say thank you, keep in touch	Known audience but different to the writer in status or age	Formal, polite	Carefully, possibly drafted and spellings checked	Possibly kept for some time after being received, possibly shown to others

Figure 4.1   Table of text types

Text types

There are four main text types that children learn about in school. These are fiction, non-fiction, poetry and plays. Each of these can be subdivided further. For example, there are many types of fiction including fantasy, traditional stories, animal stories and realistic stories. The major non-fiction text types include recounts, reports, procedural texts, persuasive texts and discussion. Poetry may rhyme but sometimes it does not. It can be humorous or serious. Children also learn to compose more everyday texts such as lists, notes and letters. Each of these text types has a different function, a different structure, uses a particular type of vocabulary and may have its own layout. If children are to learn how to write these different types of texts there is a great deal for them to learn. Learning to compose or to make informed decisions about what is written and how it is expressed is a complex undertaking and one that requires a great deal of help from a knowledgeable adult. When children first begin to write they usually write for themselves. They write using formats that are simple such as lists or notes and use words that are familiar to them. During their time in school they will learn to extend this repertoire and write in formats that are unfamiliar. Being aware of the characteristics of different types of texts helps teachers to appreciate precisely what needs to be taught and what children need to learn.

Audience

Writing is an act of communication and as such has both an author and an audience. Before beginning any writing, writers identify not only why they are writing but also for whom they are writing. During the course of a week an adult might write to a friend, to the bank manager, to a colleague, to readers of a newspaper, for themselves. The extracts discussed in Figure 4.1 were all forms of letters but, depending on their audience, each was different in content, style and the care that was taken to write them.

In the world outside school most writing is written in order to communicate with people who are separated from the author by distance and time. Much of the writing undertaken in school is only read by the teacher who is present in the classroom. Children do not need to communicate with the teacher through writing – they could just as easily speak to her. Children soon learn that the purpose of most of the writing done in school is for practice or for assessment by the teacher. This can obscure the functions of writing. Wherever possible we need to create opportunities for children to write to real audiences outside school. For example, children can write invitations to school functions to parents and governors. They can write their own end of term reports. They can write thank you letters to visitors and owners of facilities that they visit. When it is not possible to give children an outside audience we can provide them with audiences that they can visualise or imagine such as characters in picture books.

Outcome

Outcome describes what happens to writing once it has been written and read. Writing can be kept, published or thrown away. In school much of what children write remains in their books. However, there are opportunities to use children's writing and as far as possible we should try to provide children with outcomes for their writing that reflect its communicative function and show children that their writing is valued.

Children's writing can be used in the following ways:

- for labels, captions and commentaries for paintings, models and displays (see Figure 4.2);
- for cards, letters and e-mails that require a response from others or written to thank visitors to the school;
- for invitations to parents and carers to attend events at school;
- for records of books read or projects that have been undertaken;
- for instructions to users of games or equipment;
- for reviews of books and posters to display in the book corner;
- for charts or graphs recording surveys and discoveries;
- for newspapers for the class or school;
- for information leaflets about the school for new entrants to the class or school.

Another way of providing children with an audience for their writing is through publishing it in books. It enables children to feel that their writing is valued and it provides a purpose and an incentive for writing. When published, children's

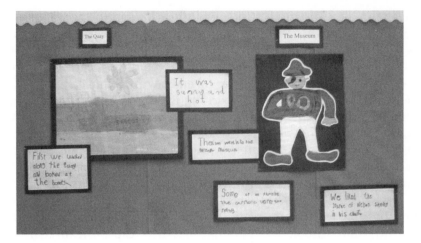

Figure 4.2 Display

writing reaches a wider audience than the class teacher as the books can be read to others and by others, in class, in assemblies or in the school library.

Children can incorporate the features of commercially published books into the books they make. They can include an index, a list of contents, notes about the author, summaries, dedications and reviews by others. Before beginning to write children will have to think about the sort of book they are writing and who will read it. This will have implications for the length, style, content and organisation. When writing their books children need to plan, draft, revise and produce a best copy. Publishing writing provides a motivating context in which children can practise all the stages of writing.

Drafting

Few writers have the skill of producing perfect writing at the first attempt. Most writers need to draft important pieces of writing before producing a final copy. Often this includes

- rehearsal – thinking, preparing to write, jotting down initial ideas;
- planning – ordering ideas;
- writing a first draft – developing ideas from the plan into structured written text;
- revising – reviewing, altering and improving the draft;
- proofreading – checking the writing for spelling and punctuation errors, omissions or repetitions;
- making a final draft – preparing a neat, correct and clear final copy.

The first stage is to think about what one wants to write and to gather ideas. Recollecting and remembering information, events and feelings is an essential part of writing. At this stage the writer might make a note of what he has thought about. As well as ideas, key words or phrases might also be recorded. The next stage is to make a plan which outlines what will be included and in what order. This may be revised but it provides the writer with a starting point. The first draft of the writing is about getting it down fast, without worrying about the transcription elements such as spelling, punctuation or handwriting. It often appears messy and may contain misspellings and crossings out. When the first draft is complete it is time to read through the writing looking for clarity of meaning and changing words, phrases and sentences to make a more satisfactory piece of writing. This is followed by proofreading for spelling and punctuation errors. The final stage for a piece of writing that is going to be made public is to produce a final draft.

Not all the writing that children do needs to be drafted – it depends on its purpose and audience. However, all writing can benefit from using elements of the drafting process, particularly rehearsal and revision. Children can be taught to spend some time thinking before they write. Children who think before they write are less likely to feel they have nothing to write about. Thinking can be done alone or with a partner. Children can also be shown how to plan, perhaps by drawing a picture or a story board or creating a spider diagram or list. This helps them to organise what they want to say and when writing fiction helps them to write good endings to stories rather than stopping when they run out of ideas. After producing a piece of writing children can be taught to read through their work to see if there is anything that they would like to change about the content. The writing can be shown to a partner who may be able to check it for clarity. After reading to check the content children can read their writing again to check for spelling errors. More experienced writers may be able to use a dictionary to correct some words. Any problems that the child cannot reconcile on his own can be highlighted and discussed with the teacher. The only time children need to make a final draft is when the writing is going to be published or if it is to be read by other children or adults. Using the drafting process in this way does not mean that children have to write and rewrite complete pieces of work. Instead it encourages them to think about their writing before, during and after they write and to take an active part in improving their own writing.

Drafting takes pupils through the stages of writing. It enables pupils to take risks since it does not matter if they make mistakes in a draft – these can be rectified later. It helps pupils to focus on composition and transcription at separate times and encourages them to see that writing is about the expression of ideas, not just the production of neat handwriting or correct spellings. In order for drafting to work, the class may need to be organised so that a piece of writing can be worked on over a period of days.

The teacher's role

Learning to write is more likely to flourish in an atmosphere which encourages risk-taking and where mistakes are regarded as opportunities for learning. Children can learn a great deal about writing in an environment that encourages pupils to share what they know with others and where learning is seen as a collaborative enterprise between the teacher and her pupils and among the pupils themselves.

As a facilitator the teacher provides the resources that children need when they write. She makes sure that there is a varied and plentiful stock of writing materials and other resources such as alphabet friezes, collections of words and dictionaries to support the children's independent writing. The teacher designs a reading–writing classroom with a writing corner, displays of writing, a well-stocked library and literate role-play areas. As a facilitator the teacher is responsible for planning writing tasks that are necessary, purposeful, varied and interesting and for ensuring that the writing that is produced is valued and displayed. As well as organising resources and activities the teacher may organise other adults in the classroom to work alongside children as scribes, to operate the computer keyboard or in other ways that help children to learn about writing.

The teacher demonstrates what writers do through her attitude to writing, her own writing in the classroom and in shared and guided writing sessions with the children. She may want to demonstrate her own use of a dictionary to the children and she may draw their attention to features of writing when reading stories and sharing big books with the class. When the opportunity arises the teacher will explain the function of the writing that she does in the classroom to the children. Situations such as taking the register, writing for displays and writing letters and notes provide these opportunities. She can also engage in written dialogues with the children. Through the examples of writing she provides she demonstrates the many uses of writing as well as how to write.

When working as an adviser the teacher works with the pupils on their writing. At all times she will be responding positively to what the children do while looking for ways to help them improve. In the early stages of writing she may be encouraging children to have a go at writing, to focus on what words look like or what letter words begin with. She may write the correctly transcribed version of what the child has written beneath the child's writing and discuss this with him. As the child progresses in confidence and competence she may teach specific skills such as letter formation or strategies for spelling correctly, such as 'look, cover, write, check' or how to use word banks and dictionaries. Later she may demonstrate strategies such as drafting and revising. The teacher may advise on various ways of representing written responses such as using lists and diagrams as alternatives to prose. She will also make suggestions about how to improve the content, organisation and vocabulary of writing. Some of this teaching may take place in guided writing sessions but it will also take place at other times including when children write in other curriculum areas and when they are writing during their play.

Finally the teacher acts as an observer of children as they write. As she monitors the children and their work she considers how successful she has been as a facilitator. Would the children benefit more from different tasks? Do they need more or different resources? She considers her role as a model. Is this sufficient for the children's development, or do they perhaps need more demonstrations in shared-writing sessions? She also thinks about when she should intervene and how to intervene to support each child's writing development. In the light of her observations she can then change aspects of her teaching and the writing opportunities she plans for the class.

Classroom organisation

It is easier to help children with their writing if only one group of children is writing at a time. It is difficult for the teacher to provide effective teaching if she is dealing with 30 writers at once. Daily organisation needs to take account of this. A classroom where groups of children are engaged in a mix of activities and where some need little adult support will put less pressure on the teacher and allow her to spend more time with children who are writing.

Children who are writing do not always need to write alone. The teacher may ask children to work in pairs to compose and write using each other as sources of ideas and help. This again helps the teacher to use her time more effectively as she can work with two children at once when she checks on their progress or, if the children are providing effective help for one another, she can let them get on alone and spend time with other children in the class.

If the writing that is done in school mirrors the way writers write in the world outside school, the children will plan, draft, revise and publish many of the pieces of writing that they produce. All this takes time and not all children will finish each stage at the same time. Within a group of writers there may be children who are planning and some who are making a final copy of their writing. Again this helps to take pressure off the teacher since at the final draft stage she will not be needed by the children and will be able to concentrate on working with those pupils who are planning or revising their work. When children are used to working independently there is less demand on the teacher for fragmented help with spellings and more time for the teacher to give help on other aspects of writing including content, structure and style.

The classroom as a writing environment

A well-resourced classroom offers children many models of writing, provides the opportunity to practise writing in a variety of ways and gives children a positive image of writing. Children are more likely to respond positively to writing if it is given a high profile in the classroom and if it is clear that the teacher values writing.

The writing area
Most classrooms contain resources that support children's writing development such as books, alphabet friezes, wooden, plastic, velvet and magnetic letters, paper and writing implements. It is helpful if these are readily available and stored in or near the writing area. An attractive and well-resourced writing area

transmits the message that writing is important and worthwhile and signifies its status to the class. Practicalities such as the size of the classroom influence the amount of space that can be given to the area and how many children can work there at one time. Children can choose either to work in this area or they can collect the resources and materials they need for writing from it.

Resources in the writing area might include:

- a variety of different sizes, shapes, colours and quality of paper and card;
- coupons and forms;
- envelopes;
- postcards and greeting cards representing a variety of festivals and featuring a range of languages;
- note and message pads;
- ready-made booklets of different types and sizes;
- in- and out-trays;
- a variety of writing implements;
- a stapler, a hole punch, rubber stamps, glue, labels, pencil sharpener, Sellotape, string, paper clips, ring binders, scissors, rulers;
- diaries and calendars;
- line guides and borders;
- a paper trimmer;
- stencils;
- reference materials such as alphabet books, dictionaries, thesauruses and word banks and lists;
- a post box;
- a computer.

It helps to keep the children's interest if the resources are changed regularly. Knowing how to use resources such as the paper trimmer and the stapler and how to mount their work and make their own books helps the children to work independently and use the area purposefully. The children can also be involved in organising the writing area. They can make labels for the equipment and write notices for the area. The use of the writing area should be discussed with the class and some of the writing that is produced there can be shared, displayed and responded to by others.

The writing area should invite children to use it. It should be a quiet place where writing is seen as an enjoyable and purposeful activity. Children should be encouraged to use it both at set writing times, including during the literacy hour, and when they can make choices about their activities. Written suggestions about what children might write when they choose to use the area, such as an invitation to rewrite a story that has recently been shared with the class or to write to a child who is away from school, can maintain the children's involvement in using the writing area. There might be notices such as 'Come and Make a Book' or 'Make a List of Your Favourite Books'. If it is available for use at any time by the children it can give them the chance to experiment with writing for their own purposes and at their own pace, without pressure for particular results and usually without needing much adult intervention. Used in this way the writing area can be a place where children are in control of the writing process, giving them the opportunity to initiate and carry out ideas of their own. Using the resources provided, Patrick, aged five, wrote the letter in Figure 4.3 to his granny as he experimented alone in the writing area. It reads, 'Thank you for the Smarties'.

The writing area can also be used to display writing including writing in a variety of scripts and languages, writing from home, a range of handwriting styles, writing that has been received by the class and writing that has been done at school. Writing that is displayed may reflect current events in the classroom or in the locality. The writing area can demonstrate writing used for a variety of purposes and in a variety of styles.

Writing and reading

There is a significant relationship between learning about reading and learning about writing. An important part of the classroom writing environment is provided by books. This includes books that are in the library or book corner, books that are taken home by the children, books that are read to children, books that are made by children, books that are made by the teacher and big books that are shared with the class. Familiarity with books provides children with important lessons about how writing works, what it can do and how they can use it.

From books children learn that print carries a message and as they begin to write they will want their own writing to convey meaning. When reading they learn that symbols used in writing are not arbitrary and that writers use

Figure 4.3 Patrick: 'Thank you for the smarties'

a set of symbols with a particular form. They can see that writing is arranged in a particular way. In the English language it moves from left to right and top to bottom on a page. Spaces separate words and punctuation is used to separate ideas. As children read they are engaging in a visual examination of words and as they read aloud they are using the grapho-phonic aspects of written language. Both of these are important in helping to increase children's awareness of letter shapes and in developing their knowledge about spelling.

Written language is used in particular ways that have to be experienced and understood before they can be produced. Experience with reading introduces children to the pattern, style and the explicit nature of written language. Children may also learn about structuring their own writing by thinking about how different sorts of texts are organised. When texts are shared with children teachers are familiarising children with the notion of authorship. As children realise that books are written by people they can be introduced to the idea that they too can be authors and produce texts for others to read. Books and other forms of text provide ideas for writing. In order to learn about writing it is essential that children have access to a wide range of good-quality books which present a range of ideas, styles and organisational structures.

Role play

The classroom environment cannot always provide opportunities for the full range of writing that children encounter in the world outside school. Role play is one way of extending the range of purposes, audiences and variety of writing available to children in the classroom. It is also a means of demonstrating the variety and purpose of writing. Role-play areas often arise from the theme that is being undertaken by the class. For example, a clinic, a hospital or a garden centre might be set up if the children are working on the theme of 'Growth'.

Whatever type of role-play area is established, it is important that children have some knowledge and experience of the context to support them as they engage in the writing activities that may arise. When setting up a new role-play area the children can write the signs, notices, menus and price lists that will become part of it. The children also benefit from the teacher joining in and modelling the types of writing that are appropriate, for example writing a receipt or taking a phone message. By doing this the children will understand the purpose, style and audience of the writing that accompanies their play.

The sort of writing that might emerge from setting up a post office in the classroom could include:

- letters, postcards, cards, notes, invitations;
- form-filling;
- record-keeping;
- notices, signs, posters, advertisements;
- writing incorporated into design with stamps and posters;
- passports;
- addresses.

If the imaginative play area is used as a home corner this too can be a valuable source of literacy activities. Children can write books to read to the dolls, invitations for a dolls' party, greetings cards, telephone messages, shopping lists, items in a diary and messages on a memo board. It is useful to use the home corner to illustrate the different sorts of writing that may be found in the home. To this end it might contain magazines, newspapers, letters, postcards, recipe books, a calendar, a telephone directory, as well as packets and containers with writing on them. It should also have resources for writing such as pens, paper and notepads.

Drama can provide a context for writing. There might be opportunities to write notes, lists or diary entries in role. Sometimes characters can receive letters or postcards or consult maps and notes. Questions can be written before hot-seating, words and captions can be written during role on the wall and speech bubbles or captions added to a freeze frame which has been captured as a photograph.

By using writing in role play children come to recognise the uses of writing and the many types of writing that exist. They are given the opportunity to experiment with writing in a relaxed environment. The writing they produce need not be assessed, improved or redrafted, but by observing children writing in play or drama the teacher can gain insights into their understanding of the writing process and may seek to extend this in the more formal writing sessions that take place in the classroom.

Writing across the curriculum

Writing is both part of a distinct curriculum area, English, and a part of every other area of the curriculum. Most of the learning about writing may take place during literacy sessions but there are opportunities for developing and reinforcing learning during science, technology, geography or history. Other subjects can provide a context for learning about different formats and styles of writing. Recipes may be written as part of a science investigation into change. Children can describe and evaluate how they made a musical instrument as part of a technology session. They can use writing to plan a route from the school to a local park in geography or compile a set of questions to ask a visitor in a history session.

There should also be opportunities for personal writing at school and children can be given their own private journals where they are free to write anything they like without it being read by others. When children write in journals they may be organising their thoughts, recording feelings or experimenting with different forms of writing. The opportunities for writing and the possible types of writing that can emerge in school are plentiful and varied. Writing does not need to be a distinct part of the curriculum only taking place with status during literacy sessions.

Teaching young children to write

Independent writing

Independent writing gives children the opportunity to experiment with and practise writing. Most of the teaching occurs through the help and support the teacher gives to the child as he writes and the feedback and discussion that occurs after the writing is completed. Although during the past twenty years there have been substantial changes in the way in which independent writing is organised, the picture is not uniform. Currently two main teaching approaches are used when children are writing independently: a developmental approach and a traditional approach.

A developmental approach

Studies of young children's early writing reveal that before starting school many children know a great deal about the writing system and its uses (Bissex, 1984). They often know that, in English, print goes from left to right across the page and from top to bottom down the page. They may know about letter shapes and symbols and how these represent meaning, and have discovered that not all symbols are writing and not all letter combinations are words. Children have gained this understanding through seeing writing around them, imitating what they see, exploring its features for themselves and discovering what is and what is not acceptable as part of the system (Ferreiro and Teberosky, 1983). Even without formal teaching the majority of children are able to produce marks on a page that are the beginnings of writing.

Teachers who work developmentally work with the knowledge and ability that children bring to school. From the start children are expected to try to write for themselves. They are given the opportunity to 'have a go' at writing without copying or waiting for the teacher to help them. Children do not learn to write quickly. It takes time for them to move from marks on a page to fluent writing. Expressing what is meant through the written word is both time-consuming and hard work. Children need to be given time to experiment with writing and to feel that their written efforts are valuable if they are to continue to learn and to develop positive attitudes to writing. To this end the teacher does not correct every error that they make; instead she talks to them about their writing and provides correct models for them to see. As their writing develops she works with them on one or two mistakes or difficulties at a time. The examples which follow show how children's writing can develop when teachers respond positively and sensitively to children's writing.

Figure 4.4 was produced by three-year-old Dhanyal. When asked about his writing he said: 'It says, "I'm sad because my brother took my toys".' In the writing it is possible to see how Dhanyal has used some letters from his name in his writing. The teacher took the opportunity to talk to him about what he had written and then to talk about the letter shapes he had used.

Sally, aged four, wrote the words in Figure 4.5 about herself. The teacher responded positively to what Sally had written and then modelled the correct version. Next she wrote out a question for Sally to answer in her writing. Sally copied what the teacher had written and then she responded to the question she had been asked. Her response shows how attentive she has been to the adult's intervention. She has thought carefully about the spelling of *Funnybones* and included several letters from this word in her writing. When the teacher read Sally's answer she was able to draw her attention to the letters which Sally wrote and those present in the title of the book.

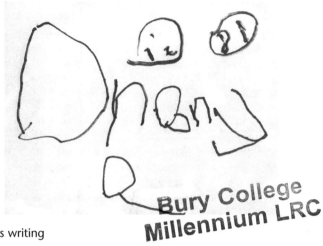

Figure 4.4 Dhanyal's writing

Figure 4.5 Sally: 'I am reading a book'

Michelle, aged six, a speaker of Ibo as well as English, was writing in her duck diary shortly after some eggs, which had been kept in an incubator in the class, had hatched (Figure 4.6). Michelle wrote very quickly and could be quite careless. As Michelle read her entry aloud, the teacher wrote some of the correct spellings above Michelle's words. She did not particularly draw Michelle's attention to the correct versions as she had written these to remind herself what had been written rather than for the child's benefit. She did

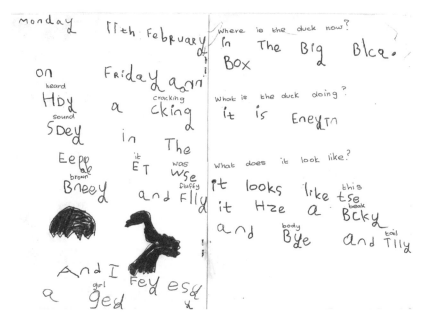

Figure 4.6   Michelle's duck diary

think that Michelle could write more about the ducklings, so she wrote out a series of questions which were intended to show Michelle how to include detail in her writing. Michelle's responses show how she has incorporated some of the teacher's models into her own writing, for example 'it' rather than 'ET' and 'is' rather than 'esy'. She may also have used the teacher's spelling of 'look like' in order to write 'looks like'. After writing her answers to the questions, the teacher commented positively on the correct spellings that Michelle had produced. She then discussed with Michelle how the answers could have been made into complete sentences in order to produce an extended and structured text of her own.

The final example in Figure 4.7 shows a recount of a science activity written by six-year-old Joe. Joe has taken a great deal of care over this writing. He has used some features of a recount such as 'first' and 'then'. He has told what happened clearly and in a logical order. Although there are some incorrect spellings all the words are readable and closely resemble the correct versions. This is a good piece of writing but discussion and demonstration could improve it. The teacher could show Joe how to structure his writing using full stops and perhaps ask him to write about his findings from the experiment.

In a developmental approach children are initially encouraged to write without worrying too much about spelling and handwriting. They are given purposeful tasks and, wherever possible, an audience other than the teacher. Before they begin to write independently the teacher may use shared writing to demonstrate the sort of writing she wants the children to produce and to teach children about writing. After the children's independent writing is completed the teacher works with individuals to develop their writing further. The discussion and feedback encourages children to think about the content of

Fist we were blid foldid
and then we were taken into
a cuJerd and we had to taste
abcand d and I got them
all rite and a was oring and
B was lemom and c was
apale and d was black –
curunt .

Figure 4.7 Joe's recount

their writing and to think about how things should be written. The feedback may involve showing the child how to do something and will include the teacher demonstrating writing either through a question or a statement that refers to the content of what the child has written.

A developmental approach to teaching writing is based on an understanding of the different elements of writing, an understanding of how writing develops and an understanding of how children learn. This understanding enables teachers to make decisions about when and how to intervene in order to develop each child's writing ability.

A developmental approach to writing allows children to:

- believe in themselves as writers from the outset, since the knowledge and understanding that they have is valued;
- participate actively in their own writing development;
- solve problems, form hypotheses and apply learning;
- take a chance and risk being wrong;
- be independent by using their own resources and knowledge;
- develop positive attitudes towards writing by not being overly concerned with correct letter formation, correct spelling and neatness;

- understand that writing is primarily about communication of content;
- discover the ways in which writing is used; and
- receive individual teaching tailored to their needs.

The teacher's role as a model and a guide is crucial to the success of a developmental approach.

Traditional approaches

A traditional approach to teaching writing is based on the premise that because young children have very little knowledge about writing they cannot write independently. This means that when children are first learning to write they need to copy an adult model. When this happens correct spelling and recognisable letter shapes are prioritised. Because children are copying their writing looks right from the start and children learn that how writing looks is at least as important as what it says. This belief is often reinforced by the practice of using word books in which adults write the words that children cannot spell.

The writing in Figure 4.8 was produced by a six-year-old working in a class with a traditional approach to writing. The activity was intended to encourage

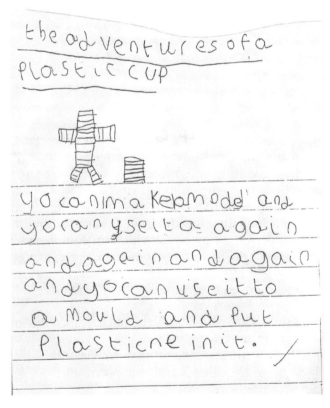

Figure 4.8   The adventures of a plastic cup

the children to consider the subject of recycling everyday objects. The writing was done straight into the children's writing books and the only person to read the writing was the teacher. The spelling is good, since it was supplied by the teacher, and the handwriting is clear, although the letters are not formed correctly. However, what is worrying about this writing is the tired content and lack of enthusiasm for writing that this child seems to have. In order to finish the task the child has merely repeated the same phrase until, presumably, he judged that he had written enough to satisfy the teacher.

Traditional approaches to teaching writing have a number of disadvantages. Copying and asking for words encourage children to become reliant on the teacher. A great deal of time can be wasted by children as they wait for help, as they follow the teacher around the classroom with their word books open, or as they sit at their tables with their hands up waiting for the teacher to write their sentence for them to copy. Writing out sentences for children to copy and writing spellings for children takes up a lot of the teacher's time and leaves little time for teachers to talk about content and to show children how to compose. While urging children to produce exciting, interesting, detailed and well constructed pieces of writing, it is possible for teachers to spend most of their time not helping with any of these aspects of writing.

The main difference between developmental and traditional approaches is the aspect of writing that they prioritise. Traditional approaches tend to emphasise transcription and a developmental approach emphasises composition. In both approaches, teachers work with children in order to help them learn to write. In a traditional approach most of the teaching occurs before the child writes and in a developmental approach the teaching occurs after the child has written. Teachers make a choice about how they organise independent writing but as Wyse and Jones (2001) remind us classroom choices are influenced by our understanding of how children learn and by our knowledge of writing development.

Shared writing

Shared writing refers to the times when a whole class or group of children compose a text together, with the teacher acting as the scribe for the group. When children are familiar with the format they may take over some of the scribing but initially it is more helpful if the teacher does this. It is generally best organised by having the children sitting as a group on the carpet and the teacher writing on large sheets of paper on a flip chart or on the interactive whiteboard.

The activity usually begins with the teacher and children discussing the topic for the writing. It is important to make the purpose and audience for the writing clear as this will affect the format and the style. After the initial discussion the teacher takes the pupils through all the processes of writing as she writes. The first stage is to generate ideas which could be included in the writing. As the children contribute their ideas the teacher records these as a list or diagram. After collecting the ideas the group considers which ideas should come at the beginning, middle and end of the writing. The teacher then numbers the ideas in the order that they will occur in the text to form a plan.

Working from the plan, the children and the teacher begin to compose the writing. The initial ideas are reworked, words are changed and sentences are composed as the group focuses on the writing. At the end of this stage the first draft of the writing, probably containing false starts and crossing out, is complete. The first draft is read through and may be revised or edited before the final draft is produced by the teacher or the pupils.

A piece of shared writing may take a number of sessions to complete. This provides a useful message about the permanence of text and how it helps people to remember ideas. It also signals that writing that is worth doing need not be completed in one session. Reading and reviewing what has been written at the beginning of each session may lead to further revisions and improvements. This illustrates the benefits of rereading a piece of writing showing children that when writers take time to think about what has been written they often bring new ideas to the writing.

The completed writing may be copied out by the children to form individual letters or books that they can illustrate. With a long piece individual children may copy out one section of the text to form the writing for one page of a class book. They can then illustrate their page. Alternatively the teacher may make the final draft of the writing and the children may provide the illustrations. The text and the pictures can be placed in a large book that can be used for shared reading. Sometimes the teacher may stop scribing before the final draft of the writing and the children can use the plan and the draft to compose their own individual ending to the story, poem, letter or account. Alternatively the writing and the teaching that has occurred in a shared writing session may act as a model for the children as they compose their own text.

Shared writing encourages children to reflect on all aspects of the writing process. The children see all the stages of rehearsing, planning, drafting, revising, proofreading and redrafting taking place, and from this model they can learn valuable lessons about how they might work on their own writing when they are working independently. As the children see the teacher writing, their attention may be drawn to spelling patterns, punctuation, word boundaries, the layout of text as well as the patterns and conventions associated with different genres of written language. The children benefit from seeing how the transcription of writing takes place and this will help them in their own writing.

Writing in this way enables children to work collaboratively and to draw on each other's strengths and knowledge. As the transcriptional aspects of writing are taken over by the teacher the children can focus on the composition and as a result can often create longer, more complex texts than they could do alone. In particular, less confident or less able writers benefit from shared writing since they can see that writing does not have to be perfect at the first attempt and that writing is as much about composition as transcription. Such children may also experience a great sense of satisfaction from seeing their ideas in print.

Guided writing

During guided writing sessions the teacher works with a group of five or six children. The session will have been carefully planned and there will be a clear objective for the children's learning. For this reason it is usual for the children to be grouped according to learning need. The session may begin with a brief teaching input about what the children are going to do. This may refer the children back to their earlier experiences of writing in a particular genre or using planning techniques. They may have participated in these in a shared writing session. Once the children have started to write, the teacher's role is to provide support when it is needed and to encourage the children to think about their writing. While it may be necessary to help children with transcription during guided writing the main teaching focus is on helping children with the content and organisation of their writing.

Scribing

More experienced writers, such as older children, parents or other adult volunteers, can be invited into the classroom to write with and for the children. They can scribe for individuals or small groups of children leaving the children free to concentrate on the composition of the text. While they write they can discuss the choice of words, spelling, the use of punctuation and layout with the children. They can also act as prompts if the composition dries up and they can encourage the children to get ideas by reading and reflecting on what has been written so far. The scribes may do all the writing, including a plan and the first draft. They can write by hand or on the computer. They may tape record a child's story and then work with the child as he writes his story using the tape recording as a first draft.

Before volunteers start to work with the pupils it is essential that they know exactly what is required of them. The teacher needs to spend some time explaining the way that she would like them to work with the children and the purpose of the activity. Experienced writers, writing alongside children, can encourage children to compose at greater length than they could manage alone and enable children to see how writing should be tackled. The satisfaction children gain from seeing their words in print is enormous and often motivates children into wanting to write alone (Smith, 1994). Scribing is particularly beneficial for children who find writing difficult. It can also be used to help younger children compose an extended text. Scribing makes very good use of additional helpers in the class.

Writing conferences

During writing conferences individual children discuss their writing with the teacher. It can last from five minutes to as long as the child needs and classroom organisation permits. The main aim is for the teacher to provide the child with feedback about his writing and to provide help for the difficulties that the child identifies. The conference may begin with the child reading or summarising his writing so far. The teacher then asks the child questions about the writing. These questions might include:

- How is your writing going?
- What do you think that you will do next?
- Could you add anything else to interest the reader?
- Do you need to give the reader more information?
- What do you do when you aren't sure about how to spell a word?
- How do you work out where to put full stops in your writing?
- Is there anything you are finding difficult?
- Are you pleased with your writing?

Through questioning and discussion the teacher can find out about the writing strategies the child uses as well as where he would like help. The conference should occur as the child is writing so that he can revise and improve his writing as a result of the discussion and advice. Conferencing can lead to 'dramatic changes in children's writing' (Graves, 1983), since it is an opportunity for the teacher to provide the help that the child identifies as important and that meets his current needs.

Response partners

The idea of pairing children to act as consultants for each other's writing developed during the course of the National Writing Project (1989) where it was found that children as young as five were able to work successfully in this way. In their pairs children listen to or read their partner's writing and comment on how the writing might be improved or extended. They can comment on the clarity of the meaning, the structure and the style as well as helping with spelling and punctuation. Children need to be shown how they can help to improve the work of others and they will probably benefit from their own experiences of working in this way during conferences and shared writing sessions with the teacher. They can be given simple instructions about how to act as a supportive partner, such as:

- Ask questions if anything is not clear.
- Say two good things about the writing.
- Suggest one way of making the writing better.

Teaching writing using a range of methods

During a block of teaching designed to introduce children to writing a new type of text the children's learning has to be carefully structured to ensure that they learn how to write it well. The structure recommended in the Primary Framework for Literacy (DfES, 2006a) is one of familiarisation, teach, practise, apply and review. These five elements both follow on from one another and can also be used side by side.

To become familiar with a new text type, children first need to read and explore examples. More than one text might be read or viewed and then analysed to identify the key elements. This might occur through shared reading, guided reading and talk activities. Teaching children how to write the new text type might take place through teacher demonstration in shared writing and guided writing sessions. These direct teaching sessions provide children with the information they need to try out this new type of writing independently. Paired writing, scribing and guided writing might also be used to give children opportunities to practise. Applying their ability to write will take place when the children are ready to produce their final piece of writing for this block of work. It will have been preceded by evaluating the writing which has been done so far and more teacher input in shared and guided writing sessions where children can be shown how to improve their writing. The block of work should end with a final review of what has been learned. Figure 4.9 shows how each stage of the writing process can be taught using the variety of teaching methods described in this chapter.

	Teaching methods
Familiarisation	Shared reading, guided reading, analysis of text, talk partners, drama
Teach	Shared writing, guided writing, feedback on children's independent efforts
Practise	Independent writing, guided writing, scribing, paired writing of drafts and plans
Apply	Independent writing, guided writing, scribing, paired writing of final versions
Review	Writing conferences, response partners, teacher feedback, shared reading and discussion of children's writing, pupil revision and proofreading

Figure 4.9 Using a variety of methods to teach writing

Writing fiction

Despite their familiarity with fiction through listening to and reading stories children do not find it easy to write literary texts (Bereiter and Scardamalia, 1985). To write a successful story, children need to recognise that stories are carefully organised forms that have their own characteristics and structure which include:

- an opening;
- a setting;
- characters;
- a structure incorporating a sequence of events;
- a problem;
- an ending.

In order to identify these characteristics children need to be guided through some of the books that they know and enjoy. Many of the activities in Chapter 3 in the section about reading with understanding help children to become familiar with the characteristics of stories. They then need to be shown how to write each of these elements and how to use them in their own stories.

Openings

As they listen to and read stories, the teacher and the children can start to compile lists of sentences that begin and end stories. This helps children to understand that stories can begin and end in many different ways. They can begin by introducing or describing a character as in:

Ginger was a lucky cat. (Voake, 1998)

or by setting the scene as in:

It was night, and some fireflies danced around the moon. (Carle, 1977)

Once a number of openings have been collected the children can examine them to see whether there are any similarities between them and the range of ways there are to begin a story. They may also be able to model their own opening sentences on one used in a published story.

Endings

Endings also differ. They may contain a statement that summarises the story, that reassures the reader that order has been restored or that leaves the reader wondering as in:

And now Ginger and the naughty kitten get along very well ... most of the time! (Voake, 1998)

They may refer to the beginning of the story and show the passage of time as with:

The fireflies, who had been sleeping all day, came out to dance around the moon. (Carle, 1977)

Writing good endings can be particularly difficult for young children. It is often helpful for them to plan the ending to their story before they begin writing. We often give children story starters to help them begin writing but sometimes it can be helpful to give them a story ending and ask them to write the beginning and middle of the story. Trying to write the story that precedes, 'He woke up' is difficult as anything could have happened to anyone before this ending. An ending such as 'When the new baby came to Tom's house they all took it in turns to look after the bears ... and the baby' (Waddell, 1994) suggests the characters, the setting and the main events of the story. To write a good story for this ending the children need to link the story and the ending closely together. This can help them to appreciate that the ending is integral to the whole story and needs to connect to what goes before.

By analysing how stories begin and end children can be helped to understand that first and final sentences are important. They need to be planned carefully in order to avoid plunging the reader into the middle of the plot or leaving the reader wondering what happened.

Plot and structure

As it is common practice to ask children to base their fiction writing on stories that are familiar to them it is helpful to be aware of some of the most common plot structures in children's picture books. Lewis (2001) identified seven main story structures in books that are read by young children. These are:

- Cumulative stories – events, objects or characters are added until a climax is reached as in *Mr Gumpy's Outing* (Burningham, 1978) or *Mrs Armitage on Wheels* (Blake, 1987).
- Reverse cumulative stories – characters or objects are lost until a climax is reached as in *Handa's Surprise* (Browne, 1994) or *Five Little Ducks* (Beck, 1993).
- Journey stories – these can take different forms including:

  - linear journeys such as *On the Way Home* (Murphy, 1984);
  - return journeys such as *We're Going on a Bear Hunt!* (Rosen, 1993);
  - circular journeys such as *Patrick* (Blake, 1968).

- Three wishes stories – the wishes may be wasted or used positively. Many traditional stories follow this pattern.
- Turning point stories – character, circumstances or physical characteristics are changed by a significant event.
- Simple problem and resolution stories – contain a problem that is quickly solved such as *Where's Spot?* (Hill, 1980) or *Ginger* (Voake, 1998).
- Days of the week stories – stories with a simple structure such as *Jasper's Beanstalk* (Butterworth, 1992).

Careful plotting is one of the most important elements of a successful story. Children need to spend time examining plots and story structure and on planning their own plots to ensure that their stories have shape. After identifying the key events in a story they know well children can draw story maps, story boards or a picture to represent the sequence of events. The format that is chosen will depend on the structure of the original. The diagram should include the opening, the ending and the main events. They can then recreate the story that the author wrote. For example, the main events in *Ginger* (Voake, 1998), a problem and resolution story, are:

A kitten comes to live at Ginger's house.
He teases Ginger and tries to sleep in Ginger's basket.
Ginger leaves home.
The little girl finds Ginger and brings him home.
She gives the kitten a box to sleep in.
Ginger and the kitten play and sleep together.

Each of these events can be represented by a picture on a story board. Isolating the key events and completing the story board helps to identify the opening, the problem and the resolution, and the ending. A story board can also act as a plan for the children's own writing and so next the children could be asked to write sentences to accompany their pictures as in Figure 4.10.

| One day a kitten came to live with Ginger and his family. | The kitten wanted to sleep in Ginger's basket. | Ginger was unhappy so he ran away. |
| The little girl found Ginger. | To make Ginger happy she gave the kitten his own bed to sleep in. | Ginger was happy again. |

Figure 4.10 Rewriting *Ginger*

A more demanding activity is to ask children to use the plot elements of a known text to write their own version. To do this they will need to change some aspects of the existing plot. For example, in *Ginger* there could be a different solution to the problem of the kitten. Instead of leaving home the cat could find a place for the kitten to sleep or Ginger could find a new place to sleep, perhaps in the little girl's room. A further activity is to ask children to use a familiar plot to write a completely new story. For example, Ginger could be replaced by a young child. The problem could be similar and involve the arrival of a new baby who gets lots of attention. The writer then has to decide how to solve this problem. Figure 4.11 shows how this new story might read.

| One day a new baby came to live at Sandra's house. | Everybody played with the baby and gave him presents. | Sandra felt left out. |
| Sandra's dad found her crying behind the couch. | He gave her a big cuddle and a new teddy. | Sandra showed her new teddy to the baby. |

Figure 4.11 Writing a story based on *Ginger*

Setting

Stories are usually set in a particular location and at a particular time. The location can be domestic, urban, rural, local, far away or fantastic. The time can be the past, the present or the future. The setting has to fit in with the plot and the characters that the writer chooses. Traditional stories are often given settings such as dark woods or enchanted castles that allow for the introduction of magical or mysterious figures. Stories where animals are the main characters are often given domestic or natural settings. If children are asked to consider how published authors use settings in their book they can then be asked to include a setting in their stories both through their writing and in their illustrations.

Characterisation

In discussions about books children often comment about the characters. They may say that they like or dislike certain characters or that characters are good or bad. Exploring character goes beyond this. Children need to be encouraged to think about what qualities make a character likeable, unlikeable, good or bad. They can be asked to say what they know about a character and what they can imagine about the character. This kind of discussion helps them to investigate character and to think about the ways in which authors portray their characters.

Painting and drawing posters depicting characters from books gives children the opportunity to reflect on the characters' feelings and activities as well as their appearance. In pairs children can sort pictures of characters from familiar books into different types. This exercise can generate a lot of useful vocabulary to describe characters. Making a collection of words that match a character gives children a bank of words to draw on when they are writing.

Style

One of the features of good writing is the author's use of language. To encourage children to be adventurous in their choice of vocabulary in their writing the teacher might start a word chart on which the class can note interesting words that they encounter in their reading. It may also contain a list of the many words that are used to introduce or conclude dialogue. When they are writing children can consult the chart to see if they can enliven their own work by using more unusual vocabulary.

Style can also be developed through adding detail or more description to what is written. For example the child who wrote the introductory sentence about Ginger in Figure 4.10 could be asked to add detail by including more information in response to some questions as in Figure 4.12.

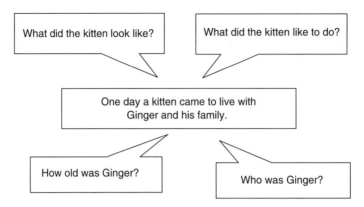

Figure 4.12   Adding detail to writing

Classroom example: children learning to write a complete story

During Key Stage 1 children are expected to write complete stories. The easiest way for children to write a complete story is to base their writing on a story they know well. This also prepares them to write original stories because the activities which lead up to the rewriting of a story help them to become aware of how to produce a satisfying and well crafted piece of writing. The following activities outline a block of work linked to *Jamil's Clever Cat* (French, 1999) culminating in the children producing their own version of this traditional tale.

This is a summary of the story for readers who are not familiar with it:

Jamil, a poor weaver, and his cat Sardul live in a village in Bengal. Jamil longs to marry the princess, become richer and work less hard. Sardul decides to help his master achieve his dreams. He takes a beautiful sari woven by Jamil to the princess. He tells her that the sari is a present from his master who is the richest man in the world. She and her father the Rajah are very impressed and the Rajah tells Sardul that he would like the princess to marry Jamil. Jamil and Sardul weave themselves beautiful clothes for the wedding. To give the impression that Jamil is truly a rich man Sardul gathers tigers, monkeys and elephants and takes them to the palace garden where, hiding in the trees, they create a terrific din. The Rajah assumes that the noise is made by Jamil's courtiers and because there is so much noise he assumes the retinue is too large to enter the palace so he asks Sardul to send them away. Jamil marries the princess but when he takes her home she is surprised to find that he is only a poor weaver not a wealthy man. However she loves Jamil and so helps him to weave and sell beautiful cloth. Together they become very rich and are able to build a fine house. When the Rajah visits his daughter and Jamil, Sardul is able to say to him, 'Did I not tell you the truth? … My master is the richest man in the world.'

The project began with a shared reading of the text followed by an analysis and discussion of the elements that made this a story: characters, plot, opening, ending and setting. After this the children began to look at plot and structure in more depth. Examining the plot began with a shared writing session in which eight key events were written on the interactive whiteboard. The children worked with talk partners to decide on the most significant events. The children then used the text on the interactive whiteboard to create a story board which recorded the eight key events. Depending on their ability as writers the children wrote out the events in their own words, copied the text from the interactive whiteboard or drew pictures to represent the events. Other activities to familiarise the children with the plot included making and using story props to retell the story, making and using sequencing cards to retell the story and sequencing the printed out sentences from the shared writing activity.

The children then moved on to thinking about the setting. The activities which helped them to do this included drawing a map of the area in which the story takes place showing the location of Jamil's house, the village in which he lived, the palace, the palace garden and the forest. They added descriptive words such as fine, dark, poor and magnificent to the images they had drawn. Next they drew and labelled pictures of Jamil's first house and the house he built after he became rich. Some children were asked to imagine that they were walking through the area and then wrote words in response to the questions:

- What can I see?
- What can I hear?
- What can I feel?
- What can I smell?

Some of the children used information books and the internet to research the setting further. They found out about the garment industry in Bengal and found pictures of weddings and the architecture of the region. This helped them to think of more words to describe the places and the events in the story.

Next the class began to think about the characters in the story. They took part in a drama activity where, led by the teacher, they re-enacted the story. They used freeze frame and thought tracking during the drama to explore the characters of Jamil, Sardul and the princess. This was followed by role on the wall and hot-seating. In pairs they made collages depicting one of the key characters and added thought or speech bubbles to their pictures. Some children wrote character portraits of one of the main characters by filling in a writing frame like the one in Figure 4.13.

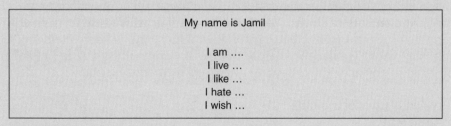

My name is Jamil

I am ….
I live …
I like …
I hate …
I wish …

Figure 4.13   Writing frame for a character portrait

(Continued)

(*Continued*)

The teacher organised a shared writing session to compose a list of story openings that were suitable for retelling the story. These included 'One morning', 'Once upon a time' and 'A long time ago'. In pairs the children then composed their own more extended opening for their writing. They were asked to include when, where and who in their opening and to refer back to their notes on setting and character for words and ideas. This helped them to create openings such as, 'A long time ago in Bengal there was a poor weaver called Jamil. He lived in a small house with his clever and crafty cat who was called Sardul'. The teacher used a guided writing session to help the less experienced writers compose an opening.

The final stage, before the children began to write their complete stories, was to compose an ending. In preparation the children drew the ending and added words and phrases to their pictures. Some children were given photocopies of the last two pages of the book with the words erased, and were asked to write the ending in their own words.

The children were now ready to write their own story. They were each given a small book containing 16 pages. They were asked to use about ten pages for their story and the others for a front and back cover and additional illustrations. The ten pages of story were to include their own opening and their own ending. In between the children were to use the eight pictures or sentences from their story board as a plan for their story. Some children wrote sentences very similar to those that were composed during the first shared writing session or that they had written on their story board. Other children were encouraged to add a reason to their description of each event and so write sentences like: 'Jamil wanted to get married to the princess because he thought this would help him to become rich'. Some children used dialogue in their stories or added speech bubbles to their illustrations. All the activities that the children had undertaken before they began to write their complete story provided them with a stock of ideas and words to use. During the project the children had rehearsed and planned each element of the story but had not had to do too much writing. Although the children had been thoroughly prepared to write independently and to produce a piece of writing that was polished, satisfying and fit to be read by others, they were able to come to their writing feeling fresh and motivated. Spending time on thinking and preparation gave them the opportunity to care about telling the story well.

When writing original stories children need to use their understanding of the different elements of stories. They will be familiar with these from rewriting known stories and from creating stories in which one or more elements of a published story is changed. Before writing an original story it is helpful for children to consider the following questions to produce a plan.

- What is my story about?
- Who will be in it?
- Where and when will it be set?
- What is the first event?
- What is the problem?

- What happens to solve the problem?
- How will my story begin?
- How will my story end?

Once children have a plan that is manageable and that they are satisfied with they can begin to write their story. At this stage it is often helpful if the teacher holds conferences with the children to discuss their work. Some children can expend a great deal of energy on their opening and initial events, so much so that they run out of steam and fail to complete a promising piece of work in a satisfactory way. Planning guided writing sessions, making use of response partners and providing feedback helps to move children's writing on and helps children to write a complete story in the best possible way.

Writing poetry

Poetry is '... the best words in the best order, language used with the greatest possible inclusiveness and power' (DES, 1975), so it offers children the opportunity to experiment with language and express their ideas imaginatively and creatively.

Many teachers introduce children to writing poetry by giving them simple writing frames based on a poem that the children have read. The writing frame allows children to use the original poem as a prompt but allows them to alter some words and so create their own poem. When children alter the original version they have to pay attention to the patterns of language in the published version but the framework enables them to concentrate on their own choice of words and meaning. Figure 4.14 is an example of a young child's

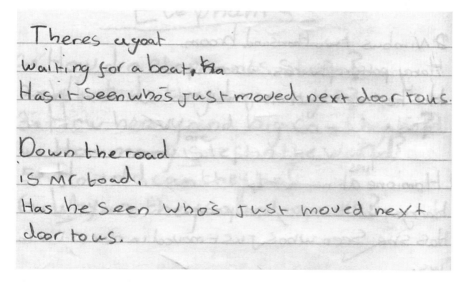

Figure 4.14 Lily's poem

poem based on *Have You Seen Who's Just Moved in Next Door to Us?* (McNaughton, 1991).

Frameworks do not have to be followed without thought. Published poems can provide a starting point and the children's own poems can differ significantly from the original. Anthony Wilson (1998) describes how he read *Isn't My Name Magical?* by James Berry to a Year 3 class. One child said that the poem was about liking yourself. Wilson used this as a starting point for the children to write poems that described what they liked about themselves. A teacher who used this idea asked some children to list what they could do as a series of 'I can …' and then asked the children to change this into a list of 'I like it when I can … '. The following is an extract from a poem that two children wrote together:

I like walking through the trees when I can kick the spinning leaves.

I like it when I can run into the whirling, biting wind.

A very popular starting point for children's own writing is *The Magic Box* (Wright, 1989). As a follow-up to listening to the poem children can create their own real box, imagining that the box and its contents will be a present for someone who is important to them. The colours and decoration on the box should be chosen to appeal to the person they are making it for. In the box the children will place a poem that has been specially written for the recipient of the present. The teacher asks the children to think carefully about the person who will receive the box and imagine what they might like in response to the following prompts:

- Something you can see
- Something you can hear
- Something you can touch
- A special colour
- A feeling
- A dream or hope
- Something from the natural world.

Then, making a selection from their ideas, they can fill in the following frame:

A Gift

In my box I will put

For you

The advantage of this activity is that it encourages children to think carefully about their choice of words and images. They can then change and polish their ideas as they make a selection. Giving the children a real person to concentrate on and a real audience for their poem also helps them to become more deeply involved in their writing. More ideas for writing in response to *The Magic Box* are given on the website that accompanies this book.

It is important that children are given opportunities to enjoy their own creativity and explore the power of language when they write poetry. Overuse of writing frames may limit opportunities to do this. As well as using published poems to stimulate writing, children can also write about:

• pictures, photographs, sculptures;
• places, people, objects;
• dreams, memories.

Understanding what is distinctive about poetry as a genre should guide the activities and feedback that teachers give to children. This should focus on choice of language, rhythm, striking phrases and images. In poetry less is often more, quality rather than quantity is important, and so poetry benefits from reviewing and redrafting where the aim is to take out anything extraneous and make every word count.

Writing non-fiction

Young children are expected to gain experience in writing instructions, non-chronological reports, recounts, explanations and non-fiction texts such as captions, dictionaries and notes. Non-fiction writing is highly structured, explicit, impersonal, and often includes the use of specialist terminology and formal language structures. In order to be able to write the variety of non-fiction described in the Framework for Literacy (DfES, 2006a) children need to learn about the distinctive features of each text type. The main non-fiction text types that are read and written in Key Stage 1 are illustrated in Figure 4.15.

Writing non-fiction is best done with a real purpose in mind and so it may be practised in subjects other than English. For example, children can write instructions in design and technology sessions, explanations in science or reports in geography or history. Alternatively topics that are selected should be relevant and of interest to children such as toys, TV programmes or their locality.

Recounts

In their classroom talk children are often asked to convey information to others. For example, children share news with each other. Telling others about an event or an experience is a recount. Children can be asked to organise their oral news before sharing it with the class. They might be asked to think about when the event took place, with whom, where and what happened. Following the 'when, who, where, what' framework could result in a piece of news such as 'Last night my brother and I went to visit my aunty in her new house'. Children can rehearse their news and practise using the framework with a

Text type	Purpose	Text structure	Sentence and word features	Example
Recount	To retell events	Opening sets the scene Recount of events as they occurred A closing statement	Written in the past tense In chronological order Connectives that signal time, e.g. then, next, after Focus on individual or group participants, e.g. I, we	Diary entry, newspaper account, biography account of a visit or event
Non-chronological report	To describe the way things are	An opening, general classification or topic sentence Description of the phenomenon, including some or all of its: • qualities • parts and functions • habits, behaviours or uses May include diagrams Information ordered logically	Written in the present tense Non-chronological Initial focus on generic participants Moves from the general to the specific	Report on hamsters or volcanoes, a guidebook or a book review
Procedural	To describe, or instruct, how something is done through a series of sequenced steps	A statement of what is to be achieved Materials or equipment needed listed in order Sequenced steps to achieve the goal Often includes diagrams or illustrations	Written in the imperative In chronological order May use numbers, alphabet or bullet points to signal order Focus on generalised human agents rather than named individuals	Recipes, instructions, rules
Explanation	To explain the processes involved in natural and social phenomena, or to explain how something works	General statement to introduce the topic A series of logical steps explaining how or why something occurs Steps continue until the final state is produced or the explanation is complete	Written in the simple present tense Uses connectives that signal time, e.g. then, next Uses causal connectives, e.g. because, so	Why we need to eat vegetables or how the eye works Flow charts, diagrams

Figure 4.15   Description of non-fiction text types

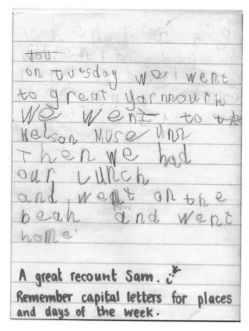

on Tuesday we went
to great yarmouth
We went to the
Nelson Muse Ums
Then we had
our Lunch
and went on the
beach and went
home.

A great recount Sam.
Remember capital letters for places
and days of the week.

Figure 4.16 Sam's recount

response partner. This activity helps children to convey information clearly and explicitly and to take account of the needs of an audience who do not know the participants and who were not present at the event. This is an important feature of information writing. The plenary session during the literacy hour often involves children talking about what they have done or produced. This can also be structured using the recount format. Recounts are often written after a class visit or an event that all the children participated in. Figure 4.16 is a written recount of a class visit in which Sam has included who, where, when and what happened.

Classroom example: children learning about report writing

When teaching children to write a particular type of non-fiction text the teaching sequence moves through the same stages as those for teaching fiction, that is: familiarise, teach, practise, apply and review. In the following example the Year 1 class were learning to write reports. The subject for their report was an animal of their choice. During the teaching sequence the children were researching facts about their chosen animal.

The sequence of work began with the shared reading and analysis of some sample reports that the teacher had written. These were analysed to identify the particular characteristics of a report. An example of one of these annotated shared texts is given in Figure 4.17.

The next stage was to write a report in a shared writing session using the language and structural features that had been identified during the shared reading sessions.

(Continued)

(Continued)

The children chose to write about sheep in this session. The report was organised into sections and each section was given a heading. Later this was printed out, cut up and given to the children as a sequencing exercise as in Figure 4.18.

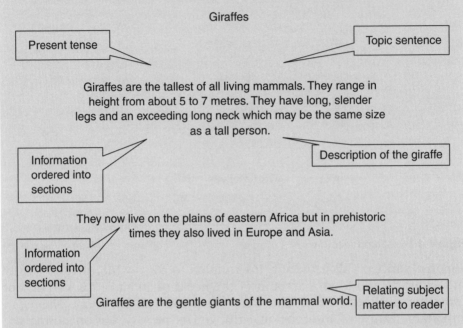

Giraffes

Present tense

Topic sentence

Giraffes are the tallest of all living mammals. They range in height from about 5 to 7 metres. They have long, slender legs and an exceeding long neck which may be the same size as a tall person.

Information ordered into sections

Description of the giraffe

They now live on the plains of eastern Africa but in prehistoric times they also lived in Europe and Asia.

Information ordered into sections

Giraffes are the gentle giants of the mammal world.

Relating subject matter to reader

Figure 4.17   'Giraffes' text

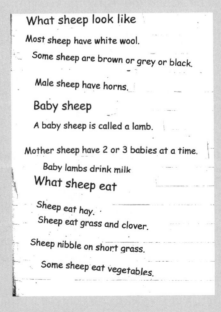

What sheep look like

Most sheep have white wool.

Some sheep are brown or grey or black.

Male sheep have horns.

Baby sheep

A baby sheep is called a lamb.

Mother sheep have 2 or 3 babies at a time.

Baby lambs drink milk

What sheep eat

Sheep eat hay.

Sheep eat grass and clover.

Sheep nibble on short grass.

Some sheep eat vegetables.

Figure 4.18   Sequencing activity

In the next session the children were given a writing frame to complete to help them plan and organise their own report. The prompts corresponded to the headings they had used in shared writing and the sequencing activity. They then used this as the basis for writing their own formal report. An example of one child's plan and final draft including a diagram are shown in Figures 4.19 and 4.20.

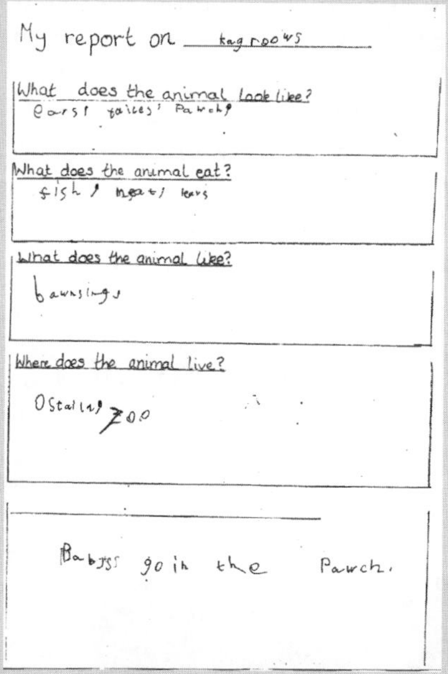

My report on kagroows

What does the animal look like?
ears, tailes, pawchs

What does the animal eat?
fish, meat, leavs

What does the animal like?
bawnsings

Where does the animal live?
Ostalia, zoo

Babyss go in the pawch.

Figure 4.19 Plan for a report about kangaroos

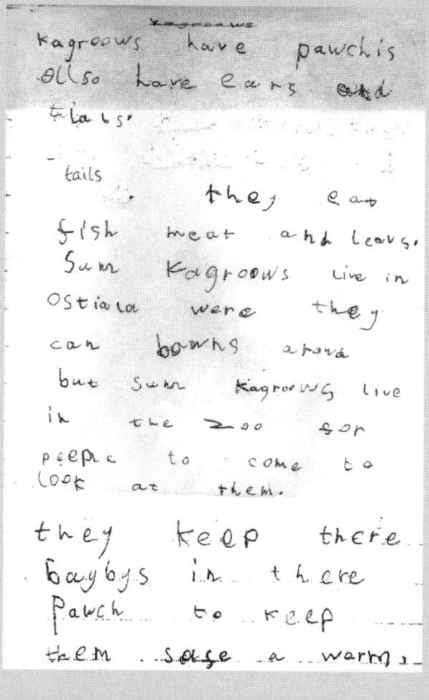

kagroows have pawchis allso have ears and tials.

tails

they eat fish meat and leavs. Sum kagroows live in Ostiala were they can bowns arond but sum kagroows live in the zoo for peepl to come to look at them.

they keep there baybys in there pawch to keep them safe a warm.

Figure 4.20 Report about kangaroos

Note-making

Note-making is a vital skill when preparing to write many information texts. Children need to be shown how to make notes from their reading or to use in a plan. To help children learn about note-making they can be given photocopied pages from an information book and asked to highlight key facts. This can be demonstrated using the interactive whiteboard. Sticky notes can be used to jot down facts and then grouped together to provide prompts for one section of an information text or a plan for the whole text. Showing children how to use spider diagrams where key words or phrases are recorded also helps them to understand more about note-making. The children in the earlier example of report writing were given a chart similar to the one in Figure 4.21 and asked to record some facts about their animal. The space available for writing was limited and this reminded the children that notes can be words or phrases, not long pieces of writing.

Planning a Report

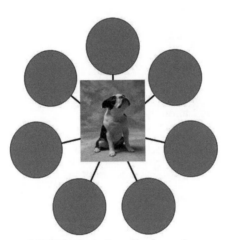

Use the report bubbles to make notes to use in your report about dogs

Figure 4.21   Planning a report

Alphabet books

Making alphabetically ordered texts is a simple way to introduce children to writing non-fiction. All sorts of topics can be used. For example, the animal reports referred to earlier could have been included in a class book. A simple and relevant topic is a guidebook to places that the children know and visit. Parks, playgrounds, streets, shops, restaurants and places of interest can all be listed alphabetically and then written about. For example, the Airport, Bowthorpe and Castle Mall would all be familiar to children living in Norwich. An alphabet book can also incorporate some of the features of an information book such as diagrams, captions and a glossary.

Summary

When teaching writing we need to:

- take account of how children learn to write;
- allow children to behave like writers and use all aspects of the writing process;
- devise activities that show children that writing is a communicative and purposeful activity;
- teach children how to compose a variety of text types;
- give children feedback to develop their ability to compose.

∿ Reflective activities

1. Explore any inconsistencies between your own understanding of writing and what you do in the classroom. If there are inconsistencies between what you know and what you do, why is this the case? Could you make more use of your own understanding and personal approach to writing when teaching children?
2. Think of a school that you know well. How do the teachers promote the enjoyment of writing? How do they ensure that all children engage in a wide range of stimulating writing experiences? Do all the children enjoy writing most of the time? Can you think of ways to increase children's enjoyment of writing?

📖 Suggestions for further reading

Browne, A. (1999) Writing at Key Stage 1 and Before. Cheltenham: Stanley Thornes. This book provides guidance on teaching writing in the early years.

Evans, J. (ed.) (2001) *The Writing Classroom: Aspects of Writing and the Primary Child 3–11.* London: David Fulton. In this book a number of authors look at writing development from many different angles and consider how to help children develop into competent writers.

Wilson, A. (1998) *The Poetry Book for Primary Schools.* London: Poetry Society. Anthony Wilson is a poet and a lecturer in primary education. In this book he discusses the value and delight of poetry and suggests practical ways of helping children to write poetry.

5

Spelling, handwriting and punctuation

Introduction

This chapter covers:

- maintaining a balance between teaching transcription and composition;
- teaching spelling;
- teaching handwriting;
- teaching punctuation;
- teaching layout;
- investigating language conventions.

Maintaining a balance between transcription and composition

Transcription – the skills of spelling, handwriting and punctuation – has a place in writing development. Mastering transcription enables writers to communicate clearly and once they have a good grasp of transcription they can concentrate more easily on content. In spite of its value, transcription should not become the prime concern of the teacher or the child; it should not take on a significance that is out of proportion for the beginning writer who needs to explore the purposes of writing and to learn about content, structure, coherence, clarity, choice of language, style and audience, not just how to transcribe.

Transcription can preoccupy adults when they examine and discuss children's writing and this can be detrimental to the teaching of composition. When children have been asked about writing their answers reveal that they too have learned to place too much importance on transcription. During the

National Writing Project (1985–88) teachers found that 'Children often judge the success of their writing by its neatness, spelling and punctuation rather than the message it conveys' (National Writing Project, 1990: 19). Two further surveys, one conducted by Shook et al. (1989) and another by Wray (1994), found that the majority of young children thought that good writing was synonymous with correct spelling, good punctuation neat handwriting and length. Wray suggested that these results reveal as much about the priorities of the children's teachers as they do about the pupils.

Teachers who are trying to develop children's abilities in all aspects of writing will know that writing is, first and most importantly, about the creation and transmission of meaning rather than the accuracy of presentation. They realise that transcription forms only one part of the writing curriculum and that giving too much attention to transcription can undermine children's confidence and limit their experiments with writing. Adults should not have unrealistic expectations that conventional spelling, neat handwriting and accurate punctuation will develop quickly. They develop as children gain greater familiarity with written language both as readers and as writers, as they appreciate the need to make their writing accessible to others and as a result of sensitive, well-timed intervention by the teacher.

Spelling

When we look at children's writing it is easy to focus on spelling errors first and the content of what was written second. This may be because spelling is more visible than style, structure or choice of vocabulary. We can quickly see spelling errors but to identify errors in composition we need to read the writing carefully and understand what the writer is attempting to say. Because spelling is either right or wrong, it is easy to correct. Problems with composition are more subtle and take longer to explain and correct. Too much emphasis on correct spelling can produce writers who are frightened to 'have a go' alone and who play safe with the words they include in their writing, limiting their choice of words to those which they think they can spell correctly rather than using words which add colour and atmosphere to writing. If the role of spelling in writing is overemphasised, teachers may be teaching children that learning to write is just about learning to spell correctly and that children who cannot spell cannot write. It is possible to transmit this message in many ways, not just by overly correcting children's spelling errors but also by only displaying perfectly spelt work, by training children in the indiscriminate use of word books and by encouraging children to use erasers to correct every mistake they make as they write. It is important to maintain a realistic awareness of what children may be expected to achieve in unaided spelling as they begin to discover how the spelling system of the English language works and to let this sense of proportion guide the response, assessment, correction and teaching of spelling to young children.

English spelling

One of the problems for writers is that the English writing system is not completely alphabetic. In alphabetic systems each speech sound or phoneme is consistently represented by a single grapheme, that is a letter or a combination of letters. Some English words are written alphabetically such as, *cat* or *log* but many are not. The 44 phonemes that are used in English are represented by 26 individual letters and 435 combinations of letters, giving us 461 graphemes in total (Dombey, 2006). If writers try to spell by matching letters to sounds they have to make a great many choices. For example, trying to spell the word *through* by sounding it out could be very difficult. The phoneme represented by the letters *ough* may also be represented by *ou* as in *you*, *u* as in *prudent*, *oo* as in *boo*, *oe* as in *shoe*, *ue* as in *clue* or *ew* as in *chew*. Just to add to the confusion the sequence of letters in *ough* can also stand for the *off* sound in *cough* or the *ow* sound in *bough* and the *up* sound in *hiccough*! Some words that children use frequently in their writing are similarly difficult. The word *there* could be written as *their*, *thare* (*fare*) or *thair* (*fair*). Moseley (1990) suggested that only one-third of the words used by beginning readers contain a one-to-one correspondence between letter and sound.

Asking children to sound out a word is often the first strategy that adults use to teach children about spelling. When children ask for help with spelling a word an adult's first response is often to ask the child to say the word and to listen for the sounds that it contains. Not only is it difficult for a young child to take in auditory information and translate it into a visual image but also the problem of how to spell words such as *some*, *the* and *have* cannot be solved in this way. Neither are spelling problems solved by giving children rules such as 'i before e except after c'. This rule does not apply to words such as, *their*, *eight*, *weigh* and *height*, which are frequently used in the early years classroom. If writers could rely on the regularity of sounds and rules then spelling correctly would be a lot easier than it is.

Although adults often give a great deal of attention to spelling by writing in children's word books and correcting spelling in children's writing, they spend less time teaching children how to spell (Barnes, 1994). However, in spite of the difficulties that English presents to the inexperienced writer, children can be taught to spell.

The development of children's spelling

Research suggests that accuracy in spelling develops as children explore the writing system for themselves and as they gain more familiarity with written language (Gentry, 1982; Read, 1986). Each of the stages they pass through shows children developing new insights into writing and attempting to understand and use a system for conventional spelling.

During the first stage, known as the pre-communicative stage of spelling development, children imitate the writing that they see in the world around them and as they do they make their first discoveries about writing. The writing that is produced at this stage may incorporate letter-like shapes, numerals or the letters that are found in the child's name. There is no correspondence between the words the child writes and the correct spelling of the words, as in the example in Figure 5.1.

Figure 5.1   Pre-phonemic stage

The next stage, known as the semi-phonetic stage, shows children developing an awareness of the alphabetic and phonic principles of the English language and exploiting their understanding of this complex relationship. Letter names are used to represent words, for example *R* for *are* and *NIT* for *night*. Sometimes only the most dominant sounds are represented as in *wac* for *walked*. Elements of this stage may persist for some time and are helpful to the speller and the reader in communicating and understanding the message.

In the third stage, known as the phonetic stage, the child recognises that all the sounds in words can be represented by letters. More letters are included in the words and the words become more complete. Examples of spellings at this stage include *baf* for *bath*, *cist* for *kissed* and *cercul* for *circle*, and in the example in Figure 5.2 the words *cwyuet* for *quiet* and *care* for *carry*. Simple phonically regular words such as *can* are usually spelt correctly. This is the stage that many

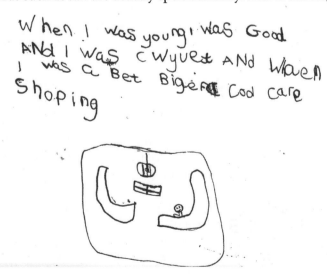

Figure 5.2   Phonetic stage

children reach by the end of the Foundation Stage and spelling in this way may continue during Key Stage 1.

As children move closer to conventional spelling they enter the transitional stage. They are no longer almost wholly dependent on phonic strategies. They begin to combine their understanding of how words sound with their knowledge of how words look. They are becoming aware of the visual features of words through their experience of seeing adults modelling correct spellings and through their reading. Increasingly they begin to write words that look right, showing an understanding of letter combinations that are frequently found in the English language. In the example in Figure 5.3, *too* and *moterway* and the experiments with letter strings in *rian* and *siad* show Nicola's growing awareness of how words look. In this stage commonly used words such as *the* or *there* are often spelt correctly.

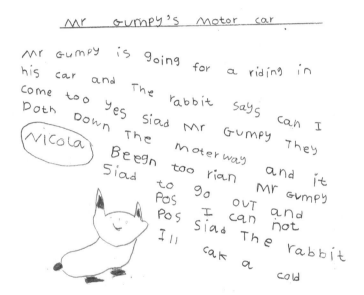

Figure 5.3 Transitional stage

The final or conventional spelling stage is when correct spellings are produced almost all the time. At this stage writers use a combination of strategies including letter sounds, letter names, letter strings, visual strategies and memory to produce close approximations or correct spellings of short and multisyllabic words. As children gain more experience of reading and writing and as they are taught how to spell their spellings become increasingly conventional but, realistically, most children will reach this stage after the age of eight.

Tracing how children's spelling develops shows that the mistakes that children make are usually transitory and often logical. They are an important part of their learning about spelling, providing them with the opportunity to experiment with and internalise the system and enabling them to make intelligent and informed attempts at spelling words correctly.

Adults frequently use a variety of strategies to help them spell correctly. They may use aids such as dictionaries and spell checks, exaggeratedly pronounce each syllable of a word or write down several versions of an unknown word. Sometimes they use a known spelling to provide clues about the spelling of a more difficult word, for example using *finite* to spell *definite* or *lie* to spell *believe*. On occasion adults draw on their awareness of how the English language is constructed, using their understanding of roots, prefixes and suffixes or their knowledge about the sequence of letters in words. When spelling difficult or unfamiliar words adults often use a combination of these strategies. Children need to be given access to the strategies that adults use, including the visual appearance of words, knowledge about language, memory, external resources as well as awareness of sounds and syllables. By being aware of how children learn about spelling and by examining the strategies that competent spellers use, it is possible to respond positively to what children can do, appreciate progress, identify good errors and discover some effective ways of helping children to learn how to spell.

Practical ways of supporting children's development in spelling

Most children find it easy to use phonic strategies to help them spell and the phonic work they do as they are learning to read supports this. Children who apply phonic strategies to spelling are making good progress but in order to become accurate spellers they need to use other strategies as well. It has been suggested that direct teaching about spelling should begin when children reach the transitional stage (Whitehead, 2004). By this time children will have had opportunities to experiment with writing and make some valuable discoveries about English spelling.

There is considerable evidence to suggest that accurate spellers draw on visual rather than phonic strategies when spelling (Peters, 1985). Good spellers can often 'see' correct spellings inside their heads, they 'know' by 'looking' at words whether they are spelt correctly. To help children 'see' and 'know' they need opportunities to look at, visualise and memorise words that are relevant to their needs and that they use frequently. Asking children to copy out corrections, to learn lists of words, to copy from word books or to sound out words does not help children to become good spellers and does not provide them with reliable strategies for spelling unfamiliar words independently (Peters, 1985; Moseley, 1990; Redfern, 1993). Earlier, I explained why a wholly phonic approach is unreliable. Copying is cognitively unchallenging and can be done without thinking. The words on lists that are learned by heart are usually not immediately connected to the writing children do in school. Once learned they are not used and reinforced and so are quickly forgotten. The strategies that follow develop and activate children's visual awareness and memory for words and should be used regularly as part of a systematic approach to developing spelling.

Developing word awareness

Developing children's awareness of words and letters benefits all children regardless of the spelling stage that they have reached. Simple, everyday activities which encourage children to examine and talk about words can be used with even the youngest children. When teachers draw children's attention to classroom displays, labels and notices they are providing them with opportunities to visualise and remember words. Children can make letter shapes and letter strings in a variety of media. Seeing adults writing either as scribes or during shared writing sessions provides children with visual models of words and letter combinations. The teacher can use story and reading periods to draw attention to print. For example after reading the big book *Mrs Wishy Washy* (Melser and Cowley, 1980), the teacher could ask the children to think of words that they know that contain the *sh* sound. These could be recorded by the teacher on a flip chart or interactive whiteboard. After a list has been compiled the teacher could ask individual pupils to find particular words on the chart.

Collections

The teacher and children can make collections of words. The teacher can issue a challenge to the class by writing 'How many words do we know that begin with B or b?' on a flip chart. The children can be encouraged to find words and add them to the collection. This activity can continue for several days. The collection can be examined daily and the words discussed by the class. Collections of words that have been written onto small cards can be sorted by the children into categories such as words that begin with *c* or words that end with *ay*.

Language games

Games such as Snap and Lotto using the names of children in the class and later using common words that are familiar to and used by the children encourage the visual examination of words. To make this even more relevant and useful, the children can make the games. Making the cards and writing the words carefully will help to concentrate and develop their memory for conventional spellings.

Reciting and singing rhymes and sharing poems and jokes provides a rich opportunity to interest children in language and to discuss words with them. Even very young children understand the humour of a 'Knock, Knock' joke, such as:

'Knock, knock.'
'Who's there?'
'Mary.'
'Mary who?'
'Merry Christmas.'

Recognising letter patterns

Teachers can talk about letter patterns in words to children in order to help them 'see' words more clearly. For example, looking at the word *heart* would reveal the following words

---

Heart leads to

- hear
- ear
- he
- art

After talking about all the words and the letters they contain, the children would be more likely to remember how to spell the original word and may have added more words to their spelling vocabulary. The activity also gives children the chance to remember some of the spelling patterns found in the English language such as *ear*. This may help them when spelling *tear*, *wear* or *dear*. Games such as 'Hangman' can help increase children's awareness of letter combinations in words. For example, the initial letter *b* can only be followed by one of the five vowels or by *l*, *r* or *y* and this and other letter sequences become clearer as children play. An associated activity is to find a long word that is of interest to children or drawn from the current theme in the classroom, for example a word such as 'gardening', and ask the children to make as many words as possible using the letters that are contained in the word. Other words to discuss include families of words, for example *play*, *playing* and *played,* and words that have prefixes and suffixes.

Look, cover, write, check

The most helpful way of giving spellings is to write the word down for the child using the 'look, cover, write, check' routine originally devised by Peters and Cripps (1980). First the teacher writes the word for the child and then asks the child to look at the word and to memorise it. This can be done by tracing or copying it. The correct version is then removed or covered and the child is asked to write the word from memory without help. The child's spelling is then checked against the correct version. If the spelling is correct the child can incorporate the word into his writing. If the word is incorrect the teacher and the child compare the two versions, identify where the problem lies and repeat the whole procedure.

This strategy helps children to:

- memorise the correct spelling;
- look at the whole word;
- get the overall visual pattern of the word.

Positive correction

When correcting children's spelling it is best to work with the errors that arise in what the child is writing. These words are of use and interest to the child and for that reason the correct spelling is more likely to be remembered. Some teachers ask children to identify the words that cause them problems or those that they think are incorrect. One way of doing this is to ask children to put a mark such as a dot next to words that they think are incorrectly spelt and which they would like help with. If the child has made a good attempt at the word the teacher might write the correct version of the word beneath the child's version and draw attention to the letters in the child's word that are correct. This can be illustrated by putting a tick above each of the letters in the child's word that correspond with the letters in the standard spelling. The teacher might then ask the child to look at the letters that are incorrect and compare these with the correct letters. After doing this with one or two identified errors the teacher can then ask the child to follow the 'look, cover, write, check' routine. One or two words from a piece of writing might be corrected like this. The extract in Figure 5.4 shows a teacher working in this way.

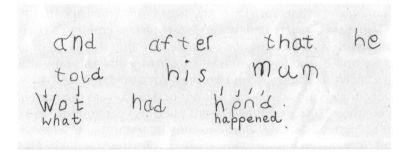

Figure 5.4   Positive correction

If children are totally stuck on a word and unwilling to have a go, the teacher can suggest that they write down any letters that they think are in the word and indicate by spaces or dashes where the missing letters are. A word attempted in this way might look like be——s for *because*. When the teacher reads through the child's writing she can talk about the word with him and fill in the spaces. This strategy encourages less confident children to 'have a go' without risking an error and it helps the teacher to identify the words to tackle first when she is helping the child with his spelling.

Some children feel more confident about 'having a go' in a 'try book' or 'try pad' before writing their chosen version in their writing. This practice encourages children to have several attempts at a word and to compare the versions visually. It develops the habit of visualising and recalling the appearance of words.

Drafting and redrafting

If children are producing first and second drafts of their writing, help with spelling can be given when the first draft has been completed. Before the teacher reads the writing the children can be encouraged to proofread the writing, identifying words that they think are incorrectly spelt and either try to correct these by having another go at the word or searching for the word in a dictionary, or they can indicate the words that they are unsure of by means of a mark. Children can ask another child in the class to read their writing and identify mistakes in the text before it is shown to the teacher.

Computers and spelling

Word processing can help to improve children's spelling. Incorrect spellings are automatically highlighted when they appear on the screen and children can then try to correct these themselves or use the spell check. In order to prevent children from becoming too engrossed with correct spelling at the cost of composition it is suggested that spell checks are not used until after the first draft of a piece of writing has been completed. The computer can certainly reduce emphasis on the transcription elements of writing since it automatically produces clearly written text that is easily readable, can make the correction of spellings simple and takes the effort out of redrafting. All this means that children can be freed to concentrate on the composition of writing and yet still produce a perfectly presented piece of writing.

Dictionaries

Children can be introduced to the use of commercially produced dictionaries by making large class dictionaries for topics that are studied by the class. The new vocabulary can be entered by the children, giving them a purpose for spelling carefully and correctly. Making a dictionary gives children a sense of alphabetical order and introduces the idea of looking for spellings in other dictionaries and books. For younger children or as an alternative way of introducing alphabetical order, the children can produce an alphabet frieze or poster. A good starting point for the words on class-made alphabet friezes are the names of the children in the class and the school or topics such as food and animals. To reinforce alphabetical order older children can be asked to write an ABC book for younger children in the school.

When introducing the more difficult alphabetical ordering skills using letters beyond the initial letter, children's names are a good starting point. The children can begin by producing an alphabetical list of class names using initial letters and then asked how they could order Shirley and Sophie or Rosie and Rachel. The principle of using the second and subsequent letters of the alphabet when looking for words in a dictionary can then be explained. Class names can be extended to include the names of family members and friends if there is not sufficient variety within the class.

Practice at using alphabetical order may also be gained in play situations in the classroom. For example, children can make patient record cards that are kept in name order in the hospital, or enter names in an address or telephone book in the home corner.

Spelling and handwriting

There have been suggestions that introducing young children to cursive script can help with correct spelling. When a writer prints, each letter is isolated from the one before it and the one after it and the hand does not build up a memory for how it feels to produce certain patterns of letters. When letters in words are joined there is an increased possibility that the correct version of a word will be remembered since both the visual and the motor memory are being used. Peters (1985) suggested that this is particularly helpful for memorising letter patterns such as *ough* or *ight*. Fernald (1943) suggested a multisensory approach to spelling helps children to learn how to spell difficult words. This involves children tracing or writing words and at the same time saying the letters out loud. This is similar to Peters's suggestion but adds an auditory and oral element.

Some children adapt their handwriting to help their spelling on their own initiative. It is quite common to see children use a capital D in the middle of a word or sentence. They may write *Dog* instead of *dog*. This is often a device for avoiding reversals and distinguishing between letters that are commonly confused. Handwriting corrections involving words that are incorrectly spelt because of letter reversals may improve some children's spelling.

Spelling conferences

Writing conferences between the teacher and the pupil might sometimes focus particularly on spelling. Conferences give teachers time to discuss spelling errors in a piece of writing that has just been completed and to find out what the child finds difficult in spelling, what strategies he uses when spelling unfamiliar words and which words he would like to be able to spell correctly. As a result of a spelling conference the teacher might have a better understanding of the child's needs and be able to plan to meet them.

Advice to children

Children can become preoccupied with correct spelling and be reluctant to write if they are unsure of how to spell a word. Children need to think about how to spell. Trying to solve a spelling problem encourages them to think about how words look. If they ask adults to spell words for them they are likely to copy the word unthinkingly. This does not help them to learn about spelling or to remember how to spell. To avoid this it can be useful to make some classroom rules about spelling like the ones in Figure 5.5.

If you can't spell a word

Sound it out
Find it in the room
Write down the parts you know
Leave a gap and come back to it later
Ask a friend
Finally ... ask an adult.

Figure 5.5   Spelling advice

Handwriting

One of the aims of every school's English policy is to teach children to write legibly, fluently and with reasonable speed. Since the purpose of all writing is to communicate, the writer needs to do this easily and the recipient of the writing needs to understand the message easily. Clear handwriting helps this act of communication. There is a correct way to form letters and this is shown in Figure 5.6 which is taken from *Developing Early Writing* (DfEE, 2001). The reason for teaching children to use the correct formation is that it is economical and legible and for the most part leaves the pen in the appropriate place for a joining stroke when cursive script is introduced. Fluency in writing means

Alphabet showing starting point and direction of each letter

Figure 5.6 Letter formation chart

that the writer is at ease with the writing system and with writing implements, pencil or pen grip is firm but not tense and the letters are correctly formed. When children can form letters correctly and feel comfortable with writing implements they can usually write quickly.

Handwriting style

Schools make their own choice about the handwriting style that they teach. Most styles have a manual that provides information about letter formation and the development of good handwriting. The important point is that one style is taught and modelled consistently throughout the school to ensure continuity and progression as children develop as writers. All staff should use the style of handwriting chosen by the school when writing for displays and providing models for children.

The debate about whether joined writing should be introduced to children as soon as they begin to write at school has been with us for many years. Joined-up writing has been viewed as a progression from preliterate patterns (Jarman, 1993), as an aid to spelling (Peters, 1985) and as a means of maintaining the flow when writing creatively (Graves, 1983). When the statement, 'Handwriting is joined', was included in the description of a level 3 writer in the National Curriculum (DfE, 1995; DfEE/QCA, 1999a) a number of schools decided to introduce joined-up handwriting in Reception and Year 1.

One of the disadvantages of introducing joined writing early is that this style conflicts with the stages children go through when they are beginning to write. When children first begin to write they often produce capital letters, then a mixture of capital and lower-case letters and finally lower case with the correct use of capitals. The use of capitals plays a part in spelling development when children use letter names to help them write words. Joined writing would seem to be at variance with the models children see and the materials teachers use to teach children lessons about literacy as the type face in children's books is usually print script.

Sassoon (2003) suggested a compromise for those concerned about the merits and demerits of the early introduction of cursive script. She proposed that from the start, children should be introduced to letters with exit strokes. Letters that are made in this way retain the print form similar to that found in books, give children the opportunity to absorb and use correct letter formation and provide a model for the flowing movement needed for cursive script. With this style children only need to extend the exit strokes to form joins as their handwriting matures. The example in Figure 5.7 illustrates how this works. The teacher has written the correct spelling of 'home' using print with exit strokes.

For schools which prefer to teach a traditional form of infant script to younger children and joined writing to older children, the order of introduction might be as follows:

- beginning writers – print script;
- children using lower-case print well and forming letters correctly – begin to introduce them to joining letters when it is comfortable and quicker for them.

Figure 5.7   Exit strokes

When children get to the stage of joining letters they need to be taught the four basic handwriting joins:

- diagonal joins to letters without ascenders, e.g. *ai, ar, un;*
- horizontal joins to letters without ascenders, e.g. *ou, or;*
- diagonal joins to letters with ascenders, e.g. *ab, ul, it;*
- horizontal joins to letters with ascenders, e.g. *ol, ot.*

The degree of care that children take with their writing should be related to the purpose and audience for their writing. A first draft may be written quickly and contain a number of crossings out and corrections. Normal everyday writing will need to be both legible and fast. Writing for special occasions such as public writing on invitations, letters home and displays will require care and attention. In time each writer will develop his own personal style of writing and this is not a problem as long as it is legible, fluent and fast.

Resources

Writing implements

Sassoon (2003) wrote that thick pencils are not necessarily helpful for small fingers and suggested that young children should use a variety of writing implements. Different sizes of pencils, fibre-tipped pens, felt-tips, wax crayons, pencil crayons and chalk can make writing more interesting. Most children will have had experience of using pens at home so pens can be introduced to children as soon as they start school. If children do not use erasers when writing first drafts they can write in any medium, but it might be most appropriate for children to use pencils for first drafts of writing. Roller-ball pens, fibre-tips or felt-tips can make writing look attractive and are suitable for work that is going to be published.

Paper

Traditionally beginning writers have used unlined paper to write on. Young children may have problems keeping to lines. They are not always sure which part of a letter rests on the line and may place the tails of letters such as *p* and *g* on the lines if given lined paper too quickly. Unlined paper gives young children the freedom to experiment with letter formation and size as well as giving them the flexibility to incorporate drawings into or near to their writing. As children begin to use smaller writing and to form letters correctly they can be introduced to line guides to help them keep their writing straight. Line guides are made from strong white card on which bold black lines are drawn at the desired width. The guides are placed beneath the child's writing paper and can be kept in place with paper clips. The lines show through and provide a guide for writing. They have the advantage over lined paper of allowing children the freedom to choose where to place their illustrations.

Alphabets

Most classes contain commercial or pupil-made alphabet friezes that children can refer to when writing. Sassoon (2003) suggested that each child could also have an alphabet strip which could be placed on the table when writing. This might help children to remember the order of the alphabet and help them to sort out which way letters face. They also remind children of the writing style that the school favours.

Practical ways of supporting children's development in handwriting

The teacher's role

When teachers write underneath children's writing in the early stages of developmental writing or when they work with children on spelling corrections or in shared writing sessions, they should make sure that their writing provides a good model for children. They should ensure that children have the opportunity to see well-formed, clear handwriting as it is produced. Good models provide examples that children can see and imitate. The purpose of well presented and correctly formed writing should always be explained to children so that they understand why they need to produce correctly formed handwriting. They should be told that good handwriting helps the reader to read what has been written and helps the writer to write more quickly.

Individual teaching

It is best to teach handwriting individually to pupils as they write rather than in formal whole-class lessons. During class handwriting sessions it is not usually possible to observe whether children are forming their letters correctly and there seems to be very little transfer from handwriting sessions to handwriting used at other times. Instead it is good practice to match the teaching of handwriting to individual children's needs and to correct errors with the child as one observes them occurring in their everyday writing. While observing writing look for the ease with which the child holds the pen, the mixed use of lower- and upper-case letters, the arrangement of writing on the page and incorrect letter formation. Problems with handwriting can lead to tense and uncomfortable posture and grip, reluctance to write, slow writing and difficulties with cursive script. The aim is for children to start in the right place and move in the right direction. In the early stages this is more important than the look of the letters that are produced. Suggestions for correction should only be made about one or at the most two mistakes in one piece of writing, and the teacher should focus on poorly formed letters or incorrect joining strokes. Having identified the errors the teacher can demonstrate the correct formation of these letters and ask the child to practise making them correctly. The child may be asked to produce a line of correctly formed letters and then to rewrite the word in which the mistake occurred. The best time to emphasise careful presentation of written work is probably just before the child is making a final draft when corrections that have been made should be included. It is at this time that children can see the point of making writing legible and attractive since others may read what has been written.

Developing handwriting across the curriculum

The skills needed for handwriting – hand and eye coordination, muscle control and visual sensitivity – develop through play activities, art activities and exposure to displays and writing seen in school (Whitehead, 2004). Handwriting can be practised in all areas of the curriculum. For example, in art children can produce patterns using letters, print with letter shapes and produce patterns when finger painting. Close observation drawing can be particularly helpful in developing children's visual discrimination and attention to detail (Sassoon, 2003). In mathematics children can use plastic and wooden letters for matching and sorting. To extend play activities children can make labels for the home corner, shop, office, etc. They can also make labels for their models, giving the name of the model, their own name and a message.

Computers and handwriting

There are a number of computer programs that can be used to give children practice at letter formation. They usually show children how to form letters. Word-processing programs can be useful in removing the pressure from children who find handwriting difficult and all children gain a great deal of satisfaction from seeing their stories printed out in a professional way. Typed script can be an excellent way of producing public documents such as class books and posters. Computers can speed up the process of producing first and second drafts of written work and encourage children to correct and change their writing using the editing procedures. Very young children can be invited to play with the keyboard or to try to write their names as a way of helping them to recognise the connection between upper- and lower-case letter forms.

Left-handed writers

Left-handed children may have particular difficulties with handwriting because as they write their writing hand tends to cover their writing. It may help if teachers consider the following points:

- Light – ideally left-handers need the light to come over their right shoulder so that they are not writing in the shadow of their own hands.
- Paper – left-handers need to have paper on the left side of the centre of the body. The paper needs to be tilted to the right so that they can see what they are writing.
- Pencil hold – encourage left-handed writers to hold the pencil or pen a little further from the point than right-handers so that the writing is not obscured. It can be helpful to give children a pencil grip to find the right place for their fingers.
- Position – make sure that left-handers are not sitting too close to the right of right-handers when writing. This will avoid their arms colliding.
- Speed – allow for slower writing until competence increases.
- Teaching – demonstrate to left-handers with your left hand whenever possible.

Punctuation

Punctuation marks such as full stops, question marks and commas help readers to interpret sentences and help writers to express their meaning more clearly. The correct use of punctuation helps to decrease the possibility of ambiguity for both the writer and the reader and for this reason it is an important part of the writing system. We are all amused by signs and sentences which remind us of the role of punctuation such as:

> PRIVATE. NO SWIMMING ALLOWED.
> PRIVATE? NO! SWIMMIMG ALLOWED.

> A woman without her man, is nothing.
> A woman: without her, man is nothing.

We might be able to see ambiguities or errors but understanding how to use punctuation correctly is not easy. Even deciding where to put a full stop can be difficult. To understand where full stops should be positioned it is necessary to know what a sentence is and to understand what characterises the group of words that occur between one full stop and another. 'Although in one sense educated adults all know what a word like sentence means, there is no denying that linguists find it exceptionally difficult to produce a watertight definition of even such a common term' (Perera, 1987: 38). Although adults might have an intuitive grasp of what a sentence is, this does not necessarily make it easy to explain to others. In the Kingman Report (DES, 1988a: 21) a sentence is described as 'what it is that is enclosed between a capital letter and a full stop', but this still leaves the problem of what should be enclosed. Smith (1983: 84) echoed the sorts of conversations that must be familiar to every teacher when he wrote:

'Begin every sentence with a capital letter.'
'What is a sentence?'
'Something that begins with a capital letter.'

He goes on to suggest that the 'rules' of punctuation and capitalisation, although seemingly obvious, tend to be very difficult to explain simply. When adults try to explain what is meant by a sentence and therefore where to place a full stop, they may use phrases such as:

'a complete thought'
'a group of words that make sense'
'where you stop'
'where your voice falls'
'where you take a breath'

Complete thoughts and groups of words could refer just as well to phrases as to sentences, and stopping places, particularly during the composing process, may occur virtually anywhere. Some readers may be familiar with the 'rules' – 'never begin a sentence with and' or 'you can't start a sentence with because' – but this is not always true. For example, one could write, 'Because of the difficulty involved in explaining grammatical rules to children one wonders why we try to teach them to very young children and why we expect children to be able to use them competently in the early years of schooling.'

Punctuation is a way of marking meaning but until children can confidently create their own meanings through writing they cannot clarify what they want to express. They have to know what they intend to mean and be aware that it might be misunderstood before they can knowingly apply punctuation marks to indicate how what they have written should be understood. This entails having a sophisticated level of awareness about grammar, about one's own use of language and about the requirements of an audience.

The development of punctuation

In order to discover how young children use and learn about punctuation, Cazden et al. (1985) analysed samples of writing from a class of 22 first grade (six-year-old) children collected over a period of nine months. They found that children begin to incorporate full stops, question marks, commas and apostrophes into their own writing when they become aware of punctuation in the writing of others. At first children place punctuation marks in the wrong places in their writing, but as they experiment more and receive feedback on their attempts its use becomes increasingly correct. Cazden et al. found that direct teaching about punctuation did not hasten its development. Their research showed that on the way to using punctuation appropriately children passed through six stages of experimenting with the positioning of full stops. Figure 5.8 gives some examples of the stages children go through when learning how to use full stops. They commented that the last two examples, between phrases and correctly, are particularly significant since they show children using their intended meaning to guide their decisions about where to place the full stops. They show children on the way to understanding what a sentence might be and consequently where to position full stops correctly.

Between each syllable in words:

DN. USOS dinosaur
RAS.ING racing

Between each word:

I. AM. WOKEING. MY. BIKE. AP. THE HEL.
I am walking my bike up the hill.

At the end of each line:

WE PRT ON THE.
FORTH FOR.
We parked on the fourth floor.

At the end of a page:

Between phrases:
ON THE WA HOME. MI CAR IT SPLODID
On the way home my car it exploded.

Both between phrases and correctly:

WE ARE SILE [still] DRIVING TO NEW YORK.
WE TOK MY GRRMS CAR. MY DAD MY MOM AND
MY BROTHER MY GRAMY AND MY GRAPY. WAT
TO NOW YORK WITH ME.

Figure 5.8   Children's use of full stops

The examples show that young children's use of punctuation is rarely random. They suggest that children try to discover the appropriate unit of meaning which should be demarcated by a full stop. Just as with the development of oral language or the development of spelling, children use what they know so far of the system to play with the rules, experiment, overgeneralise and discard guesses as they learn more about punctuation. When children start to use full stops to make the meaning of what they write clear the teacher can begin to have productive discussions with them. Prior to this their interest in punctuation is more likely to be in its appearance and decorative function rather than its use.

Practical ways of supporting the development of punctuation

Using books
Young children's awareness of punctuation precedes production. Even very young children comment on the use of punctuation in picture books. Many books for young children contain punctuation marks that are prominent and integral to the meaning of the book. Teachers and children often comment on these non-alphabetic marks on the page as they discuss the illustrations and stories. These early discussions enlarge children's understanding of how and when punctuation marks are used in writing and may begin before there is any expectation that children will incorporate punctuation marks into their own writing. However, young children often surprise adults with their understanding and observation of textual features and may begin to use full stops, question marks and speech bubbles earlier than expected, as the example in Figure 5.9 by Jay, aged four, demonstrates.

Figure 5.9   Jay: speech bubble and punctuation

It is important to give explanations about punctuation in the context of experiences that are meaningful and familiar to children. Teachers can introduce the topic as children comment on and discuss a story after a book has been shared with the class or an individual child. Comics are another good source of punctuation marks.

Using children's writing

The child's own writing may act as a starting point for a discussion about punctuation, particularly if the child has incorporated but misused punctuation marks in his writing. Before discussing the punctuation the child has used the teacher might consider:

- How has the child used punctuation?
- What has the child done well?
- At this stage in the child's development as a writer, what could he do better?

Initially it is important to discover what the child knows about the use of punctuation and ask why the child decided to use the punctuation marks as he has. Then by referring to what the child has written and remembering that the role of punctuation is to clarify meaning the teacher might comment on what the child has done. The teacher might next explain about the correct use of punctuation marks.

Figure 5.10 is a second draft of a description of a healthy meal by Nelson, aged six. It was written to accompany his meal picture and displayed in a class book about food. The content and spellings had been commented on after the first draft had been written, and on his own initiative Nelson included full stops in his final draft. This could have provided a good opportunity to discuss punctuation. The teacher could have begun by finding out what Nelson knows, asking questions such as: 'You've put some full stops and capital letters into your writing. Where did you get that idea from? Why did you decide to put the full stops

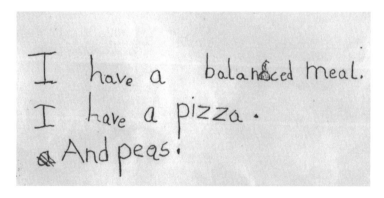

Figure 5.10   Using full stops

here?' After listening to the child's responses the teacher might have suggested that full stops do not need to occur at the end of each line of writing. She might have explained that full stops are used by the writer to help the reader make sense of what has been written and asked Nelson where he wanted the reader to pause as the description was read. Nelson could have been asked to follow up this discussion by looking at print in a picture book to reinforce the point that full stops are not always placed at the ends of lines.

Providing models

As teachers write comments about children's writing they are showing children how to use punctuation, as Figure 5.11 illustrates. They can also draw attention to the use of punctuation during shared writing sessions or when they scribe for pupils. Modelling provides an opportunity for teachers to make explicit the specific thought processes involved in deciding where to place punctuation marks in writing. This may enable children to understand and see the use of and reasons for punctuation.

Writing activities

With older children the teacher might follow modelling episodes by asking the pupils to undertake a writing activity that encourages them to use an aspect of

Figure 5.11 Modelling punctuation

punctuation. The children could be asked to compile a list of questions about a mysterious object that the teacher has brought in. These might then be displayed around a collection of unusual objects. Or, again, using an object as a starting point, the children could be asked to write statements about it to form part of a display.

Writing a class or individual book based on *Where's Spot?* (Hill, 1980) could encourage the children to use question marks and full stops, as in the example in Figure 5.12. Making and publishing books encourages children to pay attention to all aspects of transcription as there is a real purpose for care and effort. After completing their writing the children could talk about their sentences and explain their use of punctuation to others. This would give children the opportunity to learn from each other. Other writing for public audiences, such as making posters for the book or imaginative play areas, encourage children to think about punctuation.

As well as set activities that encourage children to incorporate punctuation into writing the children should also be free to experiment with punctuation in the writing that they do. Correct use of punctuation does not develop quickly or in a strictly linear fashion. The teacher will need to be patient, and

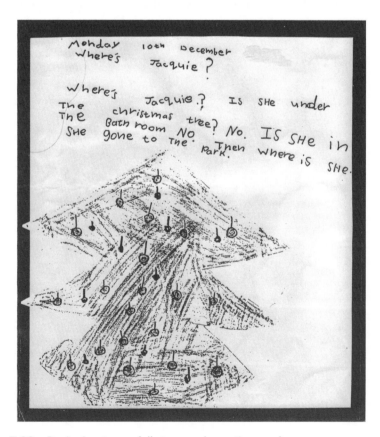

Figure 5.12   Beginning to use full stops and question marks

continue to demonstrate, discuss and respond to children's attempts as their understanding and use of punctuation develops.

Layout

The layout of a text contributes to how we read it and to its overall appeal to the reader. Publishers, authors and illustrators of books for children are very aware of this and together they produce some very imaginatively designed books that entice readers. Different types of texts have their own layout. Prose is continuous. Poets split their writing into lines or shapes as in George Herbert's poem *Easter Wings* where the shape and meaning are linked (see Figure 5.13).

Lord, who createdst man in wealth and store,
   Though foolishly he lost the same,
      Decaying more and more,
       Till he became
        Most poore:
        With thee
       Oh let me rise
      As larks, harmoniously,
   And sing this day thy victories:
Then shall the fall further the flight in me.

My tender age in sorrow did beginne:
   And still with sicknesses and shame
     Thou didst so punish sinne,
      That I became
       Most thinne.
       With thee
      Let me combine
     And feel this day thy victorie:
   For, if I imp my wing on thine
Affliction shall advance the flight in me.

Figure 5.13 *Easter Wings*

Recipes have their own format which helps us to read them easily as with the recipe for scones given in Figure 5.14

Children need to learn how to set out their writing so that it looks attractive or follows an established tradition. They need to be shown how to do this and to be given opportunities to experiment. Examining advertisements, comics and picture books and becoming visually literate helps children with this aspect of transcription. Figure 5.15 shows Marina experimenting with design. She is beginning to use the layout of a letter and matching her illustrations to the content of her letter.

Ingredients

- 2 $\frac{1}{2}$ teaspoons baking powder
- $\frac{1}{4}$ teaspoon salt
- 2 cups of flour
- 5 tablespoons of butter
- 1 egg
- $\frac{3}{4}$ cup of milk

Method

Heat the oven to 200°C.
Mix together flour, salt and baking powder.
Add the butter until the mixture is crumbly.
Whip the milk and egg and add to mixture.
Stir until a soft dough ball is created.
Knead gently on a lightly floured board.
Roll out dough into half-inch thick circle.
Slice into wedges or use a shaped cutter.
Bake for approximately 15 minutes or until golden brown.

Figure 5.14   Recipe for scones

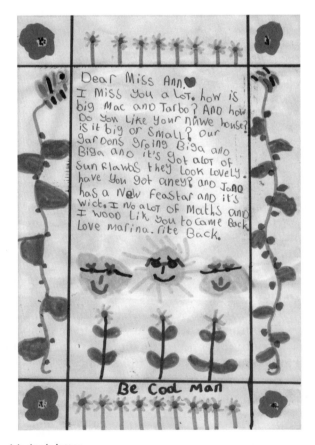

Figure 5.15   Marina's letter

Classroom example: correcting transcription errors

When children show their teacher a piece of writing the first step for the teacher is to respond to what has been written, the content, language, structure and style, and then to respond to the transcription elements of spelling, handwriting and punctuation. Before giving feedback on corrections to be undertaken she needs to consider how the child has presented the writing and whether this represents an appropriate response to the task for this particular child. If she decides that the child and the writing would benefit from comment about and changes to the transcription aspects of the piece she should limit her suggestions and advice to what the child is likely to remember, probably no more than two or three comments overall. The teacher's interventions should teach the child something that he will remember for next time. The comments about Figure 5.16 show how to respond to transcription errors in children's work. There are no hard and fast rules. Teachers will make their own judgements about what to correct based on their knowledge of their own pupils. They will also, unlike in the example that follows, analyse and comment on content as well as transcription.

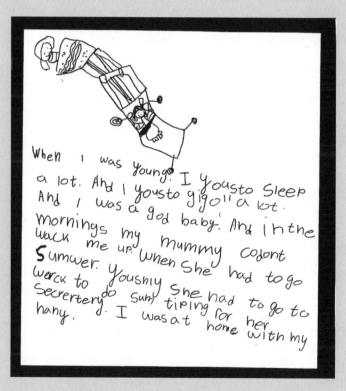

Figure 5.16   Lana's writing

(*Continued*)

(*Continued*)

The context for the writing

The children had discussed some of their early memories in preparation for a piece of writing for their individual personal history books. The opening phrase had been written on the flip chart. Before beginning her writing, Lana had jotted down some of her ideas about what she was going to include. She wrote in pen and after finishing her writing, mounted it herself and stuck it in her book.

Teacher response

Many words in this piece of writing are spelt correctly. Lana has not been deterred from being adventurous in her choice of words by being over-concerned with correctness, although it is clear that she has thought carefully about her spelling. *Codont* shows Lana drawing on her knowledge about English and her understanding of how words are constructed in quite a sophisticated way. The majority of spelling errors arise from Lana's use of phonic strategies and indicate that she needs continued help with strengthening her visual strategies. Lana could be asked to read her writing through, looking for any misspellings. If she recognised that she had omitted an *o* from *good*, she could correct this herself. After her rereading, the teacher and Lana might work on two mistakes that Lana had identified. If Lana had not recognised any errors the teacher could work on the words *some* and *somewhere*, using the look, cover, write, check strategy. The connection between these words means that Lana might learn how to spell two words correctly.

Lana's handwriting is clear and all her letters appear to be formed correctly. She writes fluently and quickly. The long tails on many of the *y*s show that Lana is beginning to develop her own individual style of writing and suggest that she might be ready to begin cursive writing. The tendency for Lana's writing to slope down the page could be helped by reminding her to use line guides.

Lana has incorporated full stops and capital letters into her writing. Their use shows that Lana is well on the way to understanding that punctuation is used to separate ideas. The teacher and Lana might discuss whether the full stop between *young* and *I* in the first line of her writing is necessary.

Lana's transcription skills are developing well. Targets to develop her transcription skills further are for her to:

- proofread her writing;
- begin to use joining strokes in her writing;
- use full stops instead of, not as well as, *and*.

Standard English and language study

Opportunities to develop children's understanding and use of standard English and to study language are part of the English curriculum. The requirements for these run through each aspect of English and are present at each Key Stage. Helping children to learn about the conventions of writing is one way in which teachers can help to fulfil the requirements of the standard English and language structure sections of the National Curriculum for English (DfEE/QCA, 1999a).

Thinking about spelling, handwriting and punctuation can extend children's understanding of how language works. As teachers talk to children about transcription they are using the vocabulary and terminology of language study, as well as introducing children to the 'characteristic language' associated with writing. Words such as letter, word, capital, small, lower case, upper case, direction, full stop, question mark, position, sentence and space will be presented naturally and in context. Discussions about the surface features of writing will involve references to the differences between spoken and written language, the rules and conventions of grammar, spelling and punctuation and the characteristics and features of different kinds of texts. Many of the activities that develop children's writing skills involve them in reflecting on and discussing language and may stimulate children's interest in language.

Teachers can develop this incidental learning through a project on written language. This might begin with an examination of the particular features of different forms of writing, such as diaries, letters, postcards, records, lists, comics, newspapers and advertisements. Different ways of spelling children's names could be considered, for example Ann and Anne or Jon and John. Why certain spellings are chosen might lead to finding out about the origins of words, their meanings, language change and famous people in history. Within the project teachers might like to look at scripts and handwriting in different cultures and the way in which the presentation of writing has changed over time. An investigation along these lines might interest children in language and its conventions and stimulate them to take more care with their own writing.

 Summary

When teaching transcription we need to:

- teach skills in context;
- let children experiment;
- provide demonstrations;
- provide examples in books and other resources;
- respond positively to children's efforts.

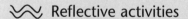 Reflective activities

1. Look at a comic or magazine written for young children and find examples of common words that are difficult to spell such as *there*, *one* and *you*. Can you think of a way of using comics to teach spelling? You might write a word on a card and ask children to circle instances of the word in the comic.

(Continued)

(*Continued*)

2. Collect some samples of children's independent writing. Identify how the children have used punctuation. How many types of punctuation are the children familiar with? How accurately do they use punctuation? Are any of the children at one of the stages described by Cazden et al. (1985)? What could you do to help the children understand more about punctuation?

3. To help children remember frequently misspelled words make a pairs or a snap game for use in school using words that the children need to know.

4. Consider how you can maintain a balance between correcting transcription errors and encouraging children to feel confident at expressing themselves in writing.

Suggestions for further reading

Hall, N. and Robinson, A. (eds) (1996) *Learning about Punctuation.* Clevedon: Multilingual Matters. In this book a number of authors examine how children develop an understanding of punctuation and how teachers can teach it.

O'Sullivan, O. and Thomas, A. (2007) *Understanding Spelling.* Abingdon: Routledge. This book, based on a longitudinal research project, contains guidance on teaching spelling in the primary school.

Sassoon, R. (2003) *Handwriting: The Way to Teach It,* 2nd edn. London: Paul Chapman Publishing. This is a guide to the teaching of handwriting. It covers all aspects of the subject from whole-school planning to classroom management and from initial letter forms to joined writing.

Bilingual learners

Introduction

This chapter covers:

- activities to support the acquisition of English as a second language;
- activities for reading;
- activities for writing;
- creating a multicultural curriculum.

Terminology

The children who are referred to in this chapter may be bilingual, trilingual or multilingual. The term bilingual is used to mean a speaker who is developing competence in more than one language. The exact definition varies as each bilingual child's proficiency in and use of two or more languages depends on the context in which they are using the language, the audience and their experience.

Throughout this chapter the term first language is used to describe the language used at home or in the child's community. It is used in a broad sense to describe the language the child has most competence in when starting school and may not always accurately reflect the complex language repertoire of any one child. For example, at home one or more first languages, including English, may be understood and spoken if members of the household use different languages.

The context

Languages such as Arabic, Bengali, Cantonese, Greek, Gujarati, Hindi, Italian, Panjabi, Portuguese, Spanish, Turkish and Urdu are familiar to and used by a significant number of young children in Britain today. In 2007 13.5 per cent of children in primary schools in England were learning English as an additional language (DCSF, 2008) and it is estimated that 75 per cent of primary schools have bilingual learners (Conteh, 2006). Some schools may have substantial numbers and others may have small groups or individual bilingual pupils. Developing bilinguals who enter school in Britain may be:

- British-born children who speak varying amounts of English at home;
- children who are joining their families in Britain;
- children whose parents have come to study or work in Britain for a few years;
- children arriving as refugees or asylum seekers.

Each child's circumstances will vary. Some children may have previously lived in rural communities; others may have lived in towns or cities. They might be from poor, privileged, middle-class or educated backgrounds. Some will have been to school, others may not.

Language development in two or more languages

Knowledge of a first language is a valuable support for learning an additional language. Children who have learned one language are already skilled listeners and competent users of language. They are aware of the uses of language and they know that its use and form change in relation to audience, context and purpose. They are able to apply their understanding of how meaning is conveyed through sounds, structure and intonation to their learning of spoken English. From their learning of a first language children are intuitively aware that a language is made up of separate words and has a special word order and grammar. When they were learning their first language this took some time to discover, but as learners of a second language they are already aware of the way in which oral language works and are able to apply this knowledge when learning a new language.

Young children who begin to develop a second language at playgroup, nursery or school have another advantage as learners of language. They are old enough and physically mature enough to engage with others in meaningful activities that require the use of a common language. The activities and the contexts within which they take place support the development of the new language. Crystal (1987) suggested that 'If the language environment is natural, consistent and stimulating, children will pick up whatever languages are around.'

The learning of a second language can be advantageous to the learner. Speakers who are proficient in more than one language have a greater linguistic awareness than monolingual speakers (Cummins, 2001). Learning to speak an additional language gives people an analytical awareness of language and linguistic patterns. This is because a first language is acquired unconsciously but a second language is acquired with 'conscious realisation and control' (Vygotsky, 1962).

It is now accepted that acquisition of a second language is not affected if the first language is maintained and supported. Supporting children's home languages helps them to feel valued and gives them the confidence that they will need in order to take the risks and make the mistakes which are necessary when learning and using another language. Indeed there is evidence to suggest that children who feel that their home language is rejected will make less satisfactory progress in English (ILEA, 1990a) and when the first language is suppressed or seen as an obstacle, the linguistic and cognitive gains, outlined earlier in this section, do not occur (Cummins, 1979).

Children do not use language only to communicate. They also use it to clarify their understanding and express ideas. This is another reason for encouraging or allowing children to use their home language in school. In the early stages of learning English, the children's understanding and use of English may not be sophisticated enough to enable them to think and learn across the curriculum. If possible bilingual support should be provided to explain unfamiliar concepts in children's home languages. If adult support is not available other children may be able to help.

> Where several children speak the same language they should be encouraged to use their preferred language for talking through ideas. It does not confuse the children; on the contrary they are able to move in and out of their home language with an obvious understanding of the needs of their audience. (Norman, 1990: 25)

Providing for bilingual learners

Britain is a multilingual society and provision for all learners, whether bilingual or monolingual, should reflect the diversity of languages and cultures found in Britain today. However, schools with bilingual pupils will make extra arrangements for them and their particular needs as learners of English. Arrangements should exist, first, at the level of the school as an institution and, secondly, within the classroom. The National Curriculum (DfEE/QCA, 1999c) makes a strong statement about inclusion and access to the curriculum for all. It describes how teachers should create effective learning environments, consider the appropriateness of their teaching methods and secure children's motivation and concentration so that all pupils can achieve.

School structures and routines

Schools in which the needs of bilingual pupils are taken seriously have a number of procedures in place to make starting school easier and to cater for their needs. These will be reflected in the school language policy and policies that deal with equal opportunities which are likely to stress sensitivity towards social, cultural and religious issues.

Bilingual learners are not a homogeneous group. Linguistically, socially, culturally and politically their lives and experiences are diverse and individual. They may operate along a continuum of language competence in the home and the community. With approximately 300 different languages spoken (Baker and Eversley, 2000), a significant proportion of the school population of Britain is going to bring a wealth of diverse linguistic experience to school. When bilingual children start school it is important to find out what each one knows, has had experience of and can do in languages other than English. This helps schools to accommodate the children's individual needs. The information concerning the languages and dialects that are spoken at home, any previous schooling they may have received either outside or inside Britain and any additional schooling that they are receiving should be entered on their school record and consulted by all the staff who work with the children. It is important that children's names are spelt accurately and that staff know how to pronounce those names correctly.

Good home–school links are important for the English language development of bilingual children. When parents understand and see the way in which bilingualism is welcomed in the school, they can support their children more effectively. So wherever possible information about the school, its policies, the curriculum and links between home and school should be available in community languages and given to parents when they first visit the school. The school will also have considered the way in which arrangements can be made for interpreters when meetings with carers are arranged. When parents register their child at school they can be taken on a tour of the school and given a video which shows different aspects of school life. This is helpful to parents who may not be familiar with the way schools operate in Britain today.

Bilingual parents can become involved in children's education at home and at school. Although the child's parents may not speak English fluently, they will be able to listen to a child as he reads a book and will be able to offer encouragement. They will also be able to tell or read stories to the child using his first language. In school parents may be willing to translate stories, rhymes, signs, labels, letters, notices and children's writing. They may share stories with children by reading, telling, writing or recording them. Some parents might like to teach songs to children or to record these on to tape. They might teach traditional forms of dance, sewing or games. In school parents might also write recipes, cook with the children, help in the home corner, work with children who are writing in community languages and accompany children on school visits. HMI (1990) commented that the help given by parents in producing bilingual resources for schools 'is important not only as a resource for learning but also for recognising the value of children's first language'.

Staff who work in schools in bilingual communities may take the opportunity to learn some of the languages that are used in school. Teachers and parents might organise a language club at lunchtime where the children could speak, read and write in their home languages. Children who attend could teach each other and teachers might use the club to learn from the children. All these structures will help to develop self-esteem among bilingual children and encourage all children to respect and appreciate the diversity of languages.

The school environment
Reflecting a real commitment to multilingual and multicultural education by representing the home, community and cultural experiences of children in the locality and in Britain today is perhaps the most straightforward aspect of provision. The availability of resources means that teachers can make careful

selections of resources and use materials which positively reflect social and cultural diversity.

Home corners and role-play areas should contain resources that reflect different cultures and different home backgrounds. This might include a selection of dressing-up clothes from different parts of the world, including shorts and T-shirts, which are universal forms of clothing, and dolls with the skin tones and features of a variety of ethnic groups. Each classroom should contain games, jigsaws, books and other equipment with multicultural images. Positive images and artifacts from other countries and cultures should form part of displays around the school, as should alphabets, number charts, notices and posters in community languages. Teachers might normally include a repertoire of songs and games from other cultures in classroom activities and give children paints and crayons in all skin-tone colours to use in art sessions. School and individual teachers' curriculum planning should contain reference points which recognise the cultures and histories of all the children in the school.

Attitudes

The attitude of staff to young bilingual learners is critical. For bilingual children, the teacher is a symbol of the majority group and so the way in which a teacher acknowledges a child's first language is of crucial importance if children are to feel positive about their identity and their ability to learn language. If teachers dismiss pupils' home languages they are denying an important part of children's identities. Children's first languages are part of their history, their relationships, their home, their community and their life experiences. It is a powerful part of each child and must be accepted and welcomed by schools and teachers. If adults show respect and interest in children's first languages, children will feel that these are valued in the classroom.

Children who are fluent in the use of one language at the age of four or five have accomplished a great deal and have demonstrated an amazing capacity to learn. Some children's knowledge of language will be even greater than this. Many children who begin school able to speak Turkish or Gujarati, for example, will also be aware of English. They will have heard it spoken in shops, on the television, in songs and on the radio and they may have noticed it in its written form in the environment. They may also be able to use more than one language at home depending on the person they are talking to or the situation they are in. This is a remarkable achievement and one that should be respected. Remembering this may help adults to avoid holding any unconscious lowered expectations about young bilingual children's potential as learners.

The classroom context

Teachers know that regarding and supporting a child's home language is not enough to ensure that bilingual learners achieve at school. They are aware that it is important to develop bilingual learners' abilities in all aspects of English because it is:

- a legal requirement for schools;
- the entitlement of every child attending school in Britain;
- the main medium of learning in school;
- the way of gaining access to the National Curriculum;
- the means by which learning is assessed in the National Curriculum;
- a means of socialising with peers;
- a vehicle for operating in a wider society;
- vital for accessing institutional power and achieving social and political rights in later life.

Teaching English to young children takes place within the context of good early years practice. This is based on an understanding of what the learner brings to the task, giving children the self-confidence necessary for future learning, planning for each child's needs, building on each child's own interests, motivation and strengths, creating meaningful learning situations and helping children to develop their own purposes and strategies for learning. Working with these principles means that the teacher of bilingual pupils has three tasks: first, to recognise that knowledge of a language other than English is an asset; second, to support and value children's home languages; and, third, to induct children into the fluent use of oral and written English.

Classroom organisation

Successful teaching depends upon careful organisation. Each class needs to provide a positive, secure environment for language learning. The teacher will be sensitive to and aware of the children's linguistic and cultural backgrounds and will create a climate of respect for all languages among the children. She will actively promote community and other languages by encouraging the children to use their first language in class, either in groups or individually, and allocating some children to act as interpreters. The normal organisation of the class will include activities that provide opportunities for the repetition of words and structures of English, practical activities and group work. The learning and teaching of bilingual pupils will be integrated into the normal routines of the class.

Group work is particularly important for children who are learning English. The practical nature of group work generally presents children with contextual and visual support which helps them to understand what they are required to do. Working with English-speaking children presents bilingual learners with a significant opportunity to learn English, as the English speakers in the group provide language models and act as role models for participation. Children want to interact with others and to do this they need to share a common language so, when they are working in groups with children who are using English, they will need, want and begin to develop a language that enables them to participate fully in the group. They will be encouraged to use language for expressing their understanding of activities they are involved in as well as for listening and responding to the contributions of others. The experience that children gain in using language in small groups may give them the confidence to talk in more formal settings such as class discussions. Teachers can support communication in groups by:

- allocating sociable and helpful children to work with new children and initiate them into classroom and school routines;
- seating newcomers with others who share the same first language;
- introducing and explaining tasks clearly before assigning children to groups;
- making the expected outcomes of collaborative work clear before children begin to work;
- ensuring that children often work in collaborative groups or pairs, particularly on activities that require children to talk and to use simple repetitive language;
- arranging for compatible personalities to work together;
- sometimes having adults working alongside pupils to support their contribution to the group.

Teachers can prepare for new arrivals by finding out as much as possible about the child's language and culture. If the child is new to England the teacher and the class can research details about the child's country of origin. One child in the class might be asked to be a buddy to the new entrant and to support the new entrant as he settles in. Teachers can also prepare a chart like the one in Figure 6.1 containing pictures of items or aspects of the school day that the child can use to communicate with other children and adults.

Figure 6.1 Picture chart

An 'All about me' book can be made for the child to complete during his first days in the new school. The teacher or teaching assistant can help the child to fill in the pages. The pictures and the activities provide a focus for talk between adults and children and enable the child to make connections between what he hears and the pictures in the book. Completing the book also helps the teacher to find out something about the child and the child to find out about school. The book can be given to the child to take home when it has been completed and may be a source of information for parents about the school. Three pages from the book are reproduced in Figure 6.2 and the whole book can be seen on the website that accompanies this book.

All about Me by	My Name is This is a picture of me. I am years old.	This is a picture of my friend. My friend's name is My friend is years old.

Figure 6.2   'All about me' book

Speaking and listening

Competence in oral language is signified in two ways: first, through understanding the communicative uses of language and, secondly, through knowing and being able to use the vocabulary and grammatical structures of a language. Bilingual speakers are familiar with the uses and purposes of language from their first language, but will have less familiarity with the system of the new language. Cummins (2001) suggested that it may take two to three years to acquire face-to-face, context-supported basic oral communication skills and between five and seven years to develop the proficiency necessary to use oral language competently in more abstract situations. Conversational skills are important but it is the more abstract use of language, called 'cognitive and academic language proficiency', that is necessary for educational success. This is the language for classifying, analysing, hypothesising and generalising. It is the language that supports thinking and learning. There is more about this aspect of language in Chapter 1.

As with first-language acquisition, bilingual learners need lots of experience of listening as they learn the vocabulary and grammar of English. They may pass through a silent period while they focus on listening to and understanding what they hear. Although this is a silent period, it is an active time, since the words and word order needed for participation in conversations and discussions are being heard and absorbed. The silent period is perfectly normal and should not be interpreted as the child having language problems or learning difficulties (Ervin-Tripp, 1978; Krashen and Terell, 1983).

The production of the second language emerges in stages. First, children respond to others through non-verbal communication. Next they communicate with single words such as 'OK', 'me', 'come' and 'see'. Gradually they begin to combine two and three words, saying such things as 'where go?', 'where go you?' and 'stay here'. These utterances will gradually become longer and show increasing understanding of the accepted word order of the second language, for example 'where you go?' Eventually children begin to use complete sentences and increasingly more complex discourse fluently. Throughout each stage the speaker is expressing meaning, but exact grammatical accuracy takes time to develop. Inaccuracies do not need direct correction – errors and misunderstandings need to be accepted as the prelude to greater accuracy which will develop as the learner listens and speaks more. Teachers may repeat and expand utterances as adults do with young children who are acquiring a first language. In this way they are signalling that they have understood and are presenting the learner with correct models.

Activities to develop spoken language

In order to acquire the full range of skills that competent and confident language users have, the listener needs to understand what is being said and the teacher needs to ensure that the child understands. She can do this by providing visual and contextual support, concrete referents and practical demonstrations and by using eye contact, gesture and repetition in her own conversations, instructions, requests and questions. Understanding is supported by the setting or the context, it does not just depend on hearing what is said. Speaking an unfamiliar language involves taking risks, risks of getting it wrong, of being misunderstood and of one's attempts being dismissed or ridiculed. Therefore the learner's confidence and motivation are crucial and depend on the teacher creating a positive learning environment.

For children at the initial stages of learning English, simple, structured and supported oral activities are helpful. Later, children will be increasingly able to participate in all the daily speaking and listening activities in the classroom such as discussions and plenaries, as well as offering opinions and making suggestions as they work with other children. The following list provides some examples of structured oral activities that can be used with children in the early stages of learning a second language:

- games such as 'Simon Says' involving action and imitation;
- imaginative play with others including dressing up, the home corner and role play based on familiar stories;
- collaborative games involving naming and counting such as 'Pelmanism', sorting, matching and labelling activities;
- describing activities such as using a feely box;
- working with others on practical tasks;
- carrying out tasks with others in the sand and water;
- listening to stories in English;
- joining in retelling stories in a group;
- listening to and joining in with songs and rhymes;
- listening to class discussions;
- becoming acquainted with school routines by participating in social activities such as answering the register and accompanying others as message takers;
- participating in all the regular activities of the school.

Classroom example: developing a child's grammar

Teachers should look for opportunities to work on particular aspects of language with bilingual children. For example, it is quite common for inexperienced English users to say 'me like' and 'me no like' rather than 'I like' or 'I don't like'. Noticing this one day, a class teacher spent some circle times with the class talking about things they liked and things they did not like. After the discussions the children had a turn to name something they did like and one thing that they did not like. Each named item was preceded by the words 'I like ...' or 'I don't like ...' The teacher followed up these oral sessions by making two class books with the children. On each page she wrote the child's name followed by likes, or doesn't like. Every child then drew a picture of the appropriate item which they stuck into the book and this was labelled by the child and the teacher. The process of making these books and the use of the books were a way of teaching children about the structure of English.

Although teachers tend to focus more on oral language development for the child who is new to English, because speaking, listening, reading and writing are all closely related many of the activities that are used to develop oral language will also support the development of reading and writing. Listening to stories at story time or during shared reading is a very productive oral language starting point for bilingual children as the illustrations provide visual support for understanding and hearing stories familiarises children with word order, vocabulary and pronunciation. In addition, seeing the text and watching an adult read helps children to learn about the visual aspect of letters and words. Hester (1983) suggested a number of ideas for language activities suitable for bilingual pupils that can follow on from a story. These will support the development of speaking as well as reading and writing. The following list is based on some of Hester's suggestions:

- listening to familiar stories while looking at the book and using story visuals in the listening area;
- making and labelling models arising from the story;
- making and labelling collections of items related to the story such as a collection of clothes to accompany *How Do I Put It On?* (Watanabe, 1977);
- recreating the sequence of the story using pictures, oral retelling or writing;
- retelling the story using a set of sequencing cards;
- making and playing a bingo game based on the story;
- listening to the story again and following an illustrated and simply labelled map of a book such as *Patrick* (Blake, 1968);
- making puppets of the characters in the story;
- making story visuals to accompany a retelling of the story;
- making a dual-language book of the story;
- creating a new ending for the story;
- making a book based on a simply written text such as *Opposites* (Harrison, no date) or *The Baby's Catalogue* (Ahlberg and Ahlberg, 1982);
- following up one aspect of the story such as investigating floating and sinking after hearing *Mr Gumpy's Outing* (Burningham, 1978).

All these activities are similar to those suggested in Chapters 3 and 4 and could be undertaken by all the children in the class.

Stories that are used as a basis for further investigation and work will be shared and used regularly. For this reason they need to be sufficiently interesting and of a high enough quality to be returned to and read many times. Besides offering a way into language, stories also provide children with personal and emotional experiences that are important for their social development and for their learning in its widest sense. For this reason bilingual learners benefit from access to stories in the language they understand most easily. If possible this should be provided through bilingual story-telling sessions and taped stories in home languages.

Reading

The majority of bilingual learners, like their monolingual peers, will already have some understanding of written language before they start school. Literacy will be an established part of the home experience of most children and others may be receiving some instruction in the written form of their home language at a community school. This will have given them insights into the purposes of reading, what it means to be a reader, the way in which written text works and the connection between oral and written language, and these understandings will provide a means of entry into reading in English. This view is endorsed in the Primary National Strategy (DfES, 2006b: 29): 'Bilingual learners bring a range of experiences and understanding to their reading in school. They are aware of and may be able to read texts written in their own language; they know that reading has a range of different purposes.' Verma (1984) found that many teachers did not realise this and commented: 'There is a general tendency to adopt a narrow view of literacy as the ability to read and write in English.'

Research into reading attainment suggests that bilingual pupils are helped as readers when their home or community languages are valued and promoted in the classroom (ILEA, 1990b). The linguistic and cognitive gains that may develop from learning to speak more than one language are particularly enhanced when literacy learning takes place in two languages (Cummins, 1984). One of the findings of the LINC (Language in the National Curriculum) Project was that children's linguistic awareness makes an important contribution to their development as readers and writers. So, wherever possible, children's reading development should be encouraged in their home language as well as in English.

In Chapter 2, I described the reading strategies that children need to use in order to read. In summary these are word recognition and comprehension. Both these aspects of reading may be more difficult for bilingual children than for children who have English as their first language. Phonic work may pose particular challenges. Readers use grapho-phonic information to complement the other strategies that are used when reading. With an alphabet of 26 letters representing about 44 distinct sounds and with its comparatively complex spelling patterns, English has a grapho-phonic system which can be difficult to learn. Some bilingual learners, for example those from Spanish-speaking backgrounds, may have too great an expectation of the alphabetical consistency of written language, while those familiar with ideographic text, such as Chinese-speaking children, may initially have a very limited awareness of sound–symbol correspondences. Emphasising individual letter sounds and sound combinations when the child is just acquiring an oral vocabulary of common words and an awareness of pronunciation and intonation in English could be particularly confusing to bilingual learners. For this reason it may take them longer to develop phonic skills.

The grammatical structure of the English language helps readers to predict words as they read. Inexperienced users of English may only have a partial understanding of the syntactic structure of the English language. For example, they may be more familiar with a subject–object–verb sentence pattern, which is used in Panjabi and Urdu, than with the subject–verb–object structure commonly found in English. Children who are unfamiliar with English grammar will only receive limited support from sentence structures. They might also be unable to judge the grammatical correctness of their reading and this will restrict their ability to correct their mistakes.

Readers use their prior knowledge of how texts work in order to make meaning. Their previous experience of stories, books and other written material helps them to recognise the significance of the phrases and words that are read and to make predictions about what they are reading. Bilingual learners may not always be familiar with the vocabulary that they encounter in books and they may need additional preparation and discussion before and after they read to help them with the meaning of unfamiliar words.

Despite the language challenges, bilingual pupils' ability to recognise words in print develops ahead of their ability to understand what they read. They can be proficient at saying the words on the page yet not understand what they are saying. Both word recognition and comprehension need to develop together as both elements constitute the act of reading. So bilingual learners may need focused support in developing their comprehension. Some of their comprehension problems arise from their lack of familiarity with spoken English and the meaning of words. But their different cultural experiences may be another source of difficulty. Readers draw on the cultural familiarity of beliefs, knowledge, feelings, attitudes, behaviour and events expressed in a text when they read. In order to do this and to reconstruct the author's meaning the reader needs to be familiar with the culture in which books are set (Halliday and Hassan, 1985). British-born English speakers usually take western cultural contexts for granted when reading and since most books for young children are set in these contexts, adults are often not aware of the difficulties this may cause to children with a different repertoire of culture awareness and different levels of familiarity with British culture. In order to avoid the problems that might be caused by unfamiliar settings and cultural assumptions the teacher might sometimes provide children with books that are set in a British context but have been written by bilingual writers as the experiences of these authors might match those of young bilinguals. Books that portray experiences that are common to all children such as starting school and family life are also suitable. Teachers can make books for young readers using photographs of shared experiences. They can also use the children's own stories and experiences to produce books. Some addresses for specialist sellers of children's books suitable for bilingual children are given on the website that accompanies this book.

Bilingual learners approach learning to read, and learn to draw on the same strategies for making meaning, in much the same way that monolingual children do. However, their experience of another language system and their developing competence in English may influence the way they use these strategies. Teachers may need to be aware of this in order to provide appropriate help and support and in order not to judge bilingual learners hastily or harshly as their ability to read in English develops.

Activities and resources to develop reading

There is no evidence to suggest that specially designed language and reading programmes or resources are more effective than the best of good practice when teaching young bilingual learners to read (Merchant, 2001). The authors of *Excellence and Enjoyment: Learning and Teaching for Bilingual Children in the Primary Years* (DfES, 2006b) suggest that bilingual learners will derive full benefit from the literacy hour. They suggest that shared reading which gives children the opportunity to revisit texts and see demonstrations of reading is particularly helpful. Shared reading can be preceded by warm-up sessions where key vocabulary and ideas can be introduced or visual aids or artifacts can be used to illustrate key themes in the book. Guided reading is also helpful because the teacher can explain reading strategies and pay attention to the needs of individuals. Groups should include children who are able to provide bilingual learners with good role models of English. In addition, as part of the reading curriculum, the following list of activities may be useful when planning for the needs of bilingual learners:

- providing access to stories in home languages and in English through the use of dual-language texts, including dual-language dictionaries, to develop the children's awareness of language, stories and early reading material;
- developing familiarity with the sight and sound of the English language through looking at names, talking about print, playing language games, playing with words and sounds, singing rhymes and songs, listening to taped stories and listening to and watching story videos;
- building up a sight vocabulary of words through reading and rereading familiar stories;
- making simple books containing repetitive language structures such as 'I like …' and 'I can …', writing counting books, individual dual-language dictionaries and books based on simple, familiar stories;
- recognising and valuing children's knowledge of other languages;
- providing a rich and exciting reading environment;
- emphasising reading for meaning and enjoyment;
- using materials that match the children's experience and understanding.

All the teaching methods and activities described in Chapters 2 and 3 are also suitable for use with bilingual pupils.

Selecting books for the multilingual classroom

There are many advantages in using real books rather than reading scheme books with bilingual learners. The range, diversity and relevance of picture books are much greater than that available in scheme books, as are books which use natural oral language patterns. Well-selected real books are more likely to contain stories that are rich enough to be told and listened to frequently and to be explored in detail. Some good-quality story books are also available in dual-language versions. The following criteria may be helpful when selecting books for bilingual learners.

- The books should contain positive images of all children.
- They should contain an interesting story and be worthwhile in themselves.
- The text should be predictable, contain repeated sequences of words and be easy for children to retell.

- The illustrations should enhance the understanding of the text.
- Children should be able to identify with the events and characters in the books.
- They should contain simple grammatical patterns and an accessible vocabulary making them easy to read independently.
- They can be used as models for the children's own writing.
- Bilingual versions are available.
- The books can be used for cross-curricular activities.
- The books respect the cultural and linguistic experiences of the children.

Writing

Bilingual children's writing follows the same pattern of development as that of monolingual writers. If there are differences these may be a result of children using their knowledge and experience of writing systems other than English and incorporating features of these systems into their writing. Data collected by Harste, et al. (1994) from three- and four-year-old children from three different language backgrounds showed that children are very observant of their own orthographies. The writing in Figure 6.3, produced by a four-year-old, reflects

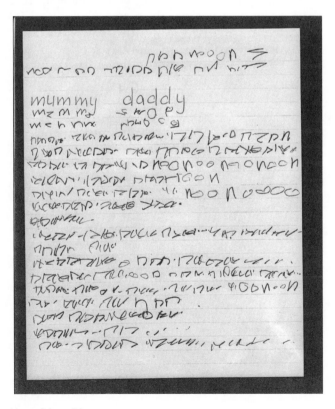

Figure 6.3 Noorah's writing

the child's familiarity with Bengali, a language he would have seen at home, and it demonstrates his understanding of the need to use a particular set of symbols and shapes when writing.

Classroom example: a bilingual child's writing development

The samples of unaided writing that follow represent the development of one bilingual pupil's writing during one school year in a Year 2 class. In September Sezgin had been in England for six months and had spent one term in the Year 1 class. Before coming to London he had attended school in Turkey. At first Sezgin was reluctant to write, his spoken English was developing slowly and he was unable to read alone either in Turkish or English; however, by December he began to produce long pieces of writing. He drew on his memory of words that had been introduced to the class through shared reading and shared writing sessions and incorporated these into his writing. At this stage his writing was difficult to read and, although Sezgin was willing to read his writing back, his spoken English made it hard for the teacher to understand what Sezgin was trying to communicate. The teacher praised all Sezgin's efforts at writing and always commented on any words that she recognised. This gave him greater confidence in his ability to write and he began to write long stories using his reading books as a source for spelling. The example in Figure 6.4 is a story he

Figure 6.4 Visit to a friend

wrote in February about a visit to a friend's house. Although it is not easy to read it indicates how Sezgin incorporated words displayed around the classroom into his writing. He was also experimenting with some spellings on his own, such as 'HES' for 'his' and 'WES' for 'was'. These reflected his own pronunciation of English words and showed his use of phonic strategies when spelling. At this stage he was mainly using capital letters in his writing.

Through shared reading and shared writing sessions Sezgin became very aware of the features of text and words. The example in Figure 6.5 shows Sezgin using lower-case letters in speech bubbles as he introduces his three sisters to the reader. This piece of writing is much easier to understand. It reads, 'I am the first sister and I am the second sister and I am the third sister'.

Figure 6.5   Sezgin and his sisters

Figure 6.6 shows Sezgin following a simple format to produce a piece of writing. Each sentence begins with 'Babies like' or 'Babies need'. The structure meant that some of the work was done for Sezgin so he was able to concentrate on the ends of his sentences. He found words in books and on displays that he thought would make suitable endings to his sentences and also included some full stops.

The example of Sezgin's writing shown in Figure 6.7 was written in June. The class were writing their own school reports. These were to be put in a booklet and

(Continued)

(Continued)

Figure 6.6   Structured writing

Figure 6.7   Sezgin's maths and English report

were to be sent home along with the teacher's report. This extract contains Sezgin's comments about his learning in mathematics and English. This was a first draft. Sezgin was clear about the task and communicates his feelings very effectively. Most of his spelling is correct and again he referred to books to find the correct spelling for many words. The writing shows the influence of Sezgin's spoken English on his writing; he omits some words such as 'and' and 'at' and inserts others such as 'a'. For words that he found difficult to write, such as 'addition' and 'division', he has used the mathematical notation but the meaning is clear. Sezgin was aware that the main purpose of writing was to communicate to an audience.

Throughout the year Sezgin had been included in all the literacy and language activities in the class. His teacher had expected Sezgin's oral competence in English to grow and she had encouraged him to read and write in English. Her interventions, discussions and suggestions had ensured that after spending just over a year at school in England Sezgin was well on the way to becoming a competent writer. Sezgin is not unusual. This case study typifies the sort of development one might expect from a confident child who understands the purpose of literacy.

Activities to develop writing

Bilingual children do not need tightly structured or special writing experiences in order to develop as writers. Like all beginning writers they need opportunities to write independently for a real purpose and for a real audience and so should participate fully in the writing curriculum in the class. All the activities described in Chapter 4 are suitable for bilingual learners. The list which follows contains some suggestions for writing that may be particularly useful for teachers working with young bilingual pupils in the very early stages. Simple, structured writing activities include:

- writing collaboratively with an adult or with another child as this provides support and models of writing in English for the child;
- participating as a member of a group in shared writing sessions;
- writing in their preferred language as this enables the teacher to see what they know about the form and function of writing and enables the child to explore the act of writing;
- writing stories based on familiar story books which provide a simple structure for them to copy;
- writing accounts of personal and class activities which follow a simple structure such as *I went to ..., I saw ..., I bought ...*;
- using the writing area in the classroom;
- being given help and guidance by adults writing beneath their pictures and writing and through discussions about writing.

Exploring language diversity

Examining the oral and written forms of different languages can help children to explore how languages work and the purposes for which language and different forms of language are used, and be a starting point for work on knowledge about language and language study. Bilingual pupils' own languages and their implicit understanding of how language is used in different situations and with different people provide a valuable resource for exploring language, written and spoken, with all the class. The experience and understanding of language that bilingual children have can contribute to raising the linguistic awareness of all the children in the class.

A project on languages has many benefits as it will:

- support bilingualism in the school setting;
- enhance self-esteem and self-image;
- generate respect for all cultures and languages;
- support the cognitive, social and emotional gains of maintaining a first language;
- enhance the linguistic awareness of all pupils.

Work on a language project might begin by exploring the languages, accents and dialects that are used by and familiar to all the children in the class. The children can investigate and make an oral and written collection of greetings in all the languages of the class. They may then try to discover others. The collection could be recorded on tape and in written form and displayed in speech bubbles alongside photographs of the children. The children might select a language for the day or for the week and use the greeting of that language at registration time and at the end of the school day. Looking at community newspapers, posters and writing done by children and adults might result in a collection of written scripts which could be examined and compared. A collection of number systems might also be made. The children might each compile a language history profile to show how they use different languages and different forms of a language with different people. This might contain statements such as 'I speak to my brother in …', 'I speak to my teacher in …'. The class might design a questionnaire to be used with other children in the school including items to elicit information about the different uses and purposes of language. Questions might include such things as 'How do you speak to a shopkeeper?' or 'What language do you use with your grandmother?' When all the information has been collected it can be presented and displayed as a flow chart, poster, spider web or graph. A collection of songs, rhymes and games in different languages and from different cultures could also be made and used by the class. The children could teach these to one another. Bilingual speakers could be invited into school to share their language with the children and to teach them some words and phrases. They might also be able to add to or comment on the collections of greetings, songs, rhymes and games begun by the children. Books written in various languages and scripts could be examined and the information contained in all books, such as publisher, ISBN and date, compared. Traditional tales from different cultures and countries could be shared with the children and compared in order to discover common themes. Other books and stories could be examined for their portrayals of people, events and locations in the text and in the illustrations.

Describing a six-week language project in a West Midlands primary school, Mills (1993) showed how an apparently monolingual staff revealed themselves as a valuable language resource and were able to offer the pupils a number of valuable experiences of language diversity. The staff were able to teach the children:

- classroom commands in Bengali;
- Bengali greetings;
- French greetings and counting;
- German greetings and counting;
- songs in Glaswegian dialect;
- Polish greetings and counting;
- Urdu phrases;
- Welsh phrases and songs.

The staff were able to offer these language experiences to the children from their own experiences in the home, community, school, work and further study. While not exaggerating the command of languages that monolingual speakers have, it is likely that the majority of adults will have some knowledge of accents, dialects and European if not other languages as a result of friendships, holiday and work experiences as well as the other life experiences. By drawing on these and making them public it is possible to discuss with children the positive aspects of knowing languages other than English, some similarities and differences between the forms of languages and when, and in what ways, different languages may be used.

The assessment of bilingual children

The assessment of bilingual learners can be an area of concern for teachers. Some teachers feel that they may not be able to develop bilingual children's full potential since the children's lack of English may prevent the teacher having full access to the pupil's thinking and understanding. They may also be concerned about recognising speech and language disorders, such as language delay and deafness, in children who are developing fluency in English.

Teachers are very aware that bilingual children are expected to reach the same levels of attainment as monolingual English speakers in their use and understanding of oral and written English and in all other areas of the curriculum. Achievement in the National Curriculum for English is assessed through English so children who are developing fluency in English at the age of five or seven may not do as well in end of key stage assessments as children who began school with a fluent command of English. While language support staff may provide translations of the Key Stage 1 tests and tasks for other subjects, not every school has access to an adult who speaks the language of the children to be tested. This again might interfere with the assessment of bilingual children's learning.

To help teachers monitor bilingual children's English development, The Qualifications and Curriculum Authority developed detailed assessment scales (QCA, 2000a). These help teachers to recognise the small steps that children take as they are acquiring a new language. The scales show the characteristics of children's language which will emerge as they progress towards level 1 of the National Curriculum and move beyond this.

For day-to-day continuous assessment teachers should follow the principles of effective assessment that they use with all pupils. They can recognise what pupils can do and reward achievement. They can base their judgements on evidence from a variety of sources including what children do, what they draw and what they make, as well as what they say and write. They will, however, have to tease out what pupils understand from what they can communicate. When teachers are making their assessments of children's learning, particularly at the end of a key stage, they might reflect upon their considerable experience and ability at observing and interpreting children's learning. This should give them some confidence as they collect evidence of children's language development and learning.

Summary

When teaching bilingual children we need to:

- create a multicultural and bilingual ethos in school;
- plan for collaborative and practical tasks that encourage talk;
- acknowledge the different strengths and difficulties children will bring to learning to read;
- teach writing in developmentally appropriate ways;
- enable children to participate fully in the language and literacy curriculum.

 Reflective activities

1. What do you think are the key issues for children who are learning English as an additional language?
2. Consider how young bilingual learners are supported in school. How are specialist support staff deployed? How do staff liaise, plan and assess? How is the child supported during sessions without specialist help? Could more provision be made?
3. Review the resources, posters, artifacts, books, videos, CDs, games, play equipment, etc. that are available in school. How well are ethnic and language diversity represented? Can you suggest any resources that would add to the provision?
4. Look around a familiar classroom and imagine you are a bilingual learner in this environment. Are there images of children like you? Are resources or activities that will interest you available and accessible to you? What would you ask your teacher to change to make the classroom more welcoming and more inclusive for you?

📖 Suggestions for further reading

DfES (2006) *Excellence and Enjoyment: Learning and Teaching for Bilingual Children in the Primary Years.* London: DfES. This publication contains a great deal of practical advice for teachers. The booklets are accompanied by a DVD which shows teaching sequences and a CD-Rom which contains materials for practical activities.

Flynn, N. and Stainthorp, R. (2006) *The Learning and Teaching of Reading and Writing.* Chichester: Wiley. This book includes a number of case studies of literacy teaching in classes where there are bilingual learners. The examples are analysed to identify successful teaching strategies.

Gregory, E. (2008) *Learning to Read in a New Language: Making Sense of Words, and Worlds,* 2nd edn. London: Sage (1st edn, 1996). In this book Eve Gregory examines the theory and practice of learning to read. It is ideally suited to teachers of children in the early years of schooling.

Kenner, C. (2004) *Becoming Biliterate: Young Children Learning Different Writing Systems.* Stoke-on-Trent: Trentham Books. In this book the author traces the writing development of a number of young children. Each chapter gives suggestions about teaching bilingual pupils.

7

Language, literacy and gender

Introduction

This chapter covers:

- **gender differences in language and literacy;**
- **reasons for the differences;**
- **practical suggestions to enable boys and girls to achieve their potential.**

Why gender is an important issue

Acquiring a gendered identity

The world outside school affects children's perceptions of what is expected of them as girls, boys, men and women. The hopes and expectations that adults have for children and the way that they treat and interact with them are often determined by a child's sex. Young children may be dressed in gender-specific clothing which indicates the type of behaviour that is expected of them as a girl or as a boy. For example, trousers and trainers give far more access to energetic play and physical pursuits than do skirts and flimsy sandals. Children are presented with models of appropriate play and other behaviour from TV advertisements, comics, magazines and books. The way adults act in the media, their communities and at home presents children with role models which influence their aspirations both in and out of school.

This may have a long-term effect on young people's lives and the choices they make. Although in recent years girls have become more flexible in their choice of subjects at secondary school and more of them now study subjects that were once thought of as traditionally male, boys have not shown the same flexibility. They still avoid English, humanities, music, PSHE and RE. English, and its counterpart in the primary school, language and literacy, is less attractive to boys because it is often thought of as a feminine subject.

Schools cannot be held accountable for producing gender-specific behaviours but, as microcosms of the world, they may contribute by reflecting sex-stereotyped practices. School staff are role models for the children. Their expectations, attitudes, interactions and judgements about children may be linked to stereotyped beliefs about boys' and girls' learning and behaviour and their own particular views about gender. School routines such as lining-up and rules about uniforms may distinguish between children on the basis of their gender. The organisation of children within the classroom, the type and length of attention that is given to pupils, the choice of themes and the selection of resources may indicate regard for equality of opportunity for girls and boys or may reinforce the differences in behaviour and attitudes that are being learned outside school.

Achievement

There is a growing body of evidence which shows that achievement in language and literacy are gender differentiated. More boys than girls experience difficulties with reading and writing. Girls seem to read more books, particularly fiction, and to produce longer and more effective pieces of writing than boys in early years classrooms. The results of the teacher assessments made at the end of the foundation stage (DCSF, 30 August 2007) show that even at age five most girls achieve better than boys in communication, language and literacy. The percentage of children achieving six or more points, a measure of working securely within the Early Learning Goals, is shown in Figure 7.1.

	Language for communication and thinking	Linking sounds and letters	Reading	Writing
Girls	83	70	74	67
Boys	74	59	64	50

Figure 7.1 The percentage of children achieving six points or more in 2007 on the assessment scales for Communication, Language and Literacy

The results of the national tests for seven-year-olds in 2007 given in Figure 7.2 also show a significant gap between the percentage of boys and girls who reach the expected level for their age.

The QCA report on the 1999 National Curriculum assessments in English at Key Stage 1 (QCA, 2000b) described how boys were doing less well in English than their female counterparts. The analysis of the SAT results showed that in reading girls used inference to good effect, particularly when making judgements about motivation and feelings. Girls were better at structuring their writing, wrote at greater length, used correct punctuation more often and were able to spell better than boys. The gap in achievement in tests at ages five and seven continues and gets wider as children progress through their school careers. While not all girls succeed at English and not all boys underachieve

	Speaking and listening	Reading	Writing
Girls	90	88	86
Boys	84	80	75

Figure 7.2 The percentage of children reaching level 2 or above in 2007 Key Stage 1 teacher assessments

the difference in their overall performance has given rise to concerns that boys could do better and has prompted a great deal of discussion about the best ways to organise and implement an English curriculum that allows boys to fulfil their potential as learners. However, we cannot ignore the needs of girls and so the material in this chapter explores the needs of boys and girls and suggests ways in which we can cater for both groups.

Speaking and listening

Gender differences in speaking and listening

Women and men and girls and boys use language in different ways. In comparison with men's women's vocabulary is characterised by a greater use of words related to domestic interests, of empty adjectives such as 'cute' or 'charming' and of intensifiers like 'It is *such* a good book' (Lakoff, 1975). Trudgill (1974) suggested that women use more tentative and apologetic phrases than men including, 'Is it possible ...?' or 'I was just wondering if ...': They tend to avoid outright statements or, if they do state an opinion, accompany it with tag questions, such as 'Don't you agree?' In general women ask more questions and use language to maintain social interactions and keep conversations going rather than to interrupt or argue (Crystal, 1987). They tend to use the more polite forms of language and tend to speak less in mixed-sex groups (Montgomery, 1986).

These differences in language use are significant for teachers of young children. By the time children come to school they have already learned how to speak in different ways according to their gender and to use language in the classroom in different ways. They speak differently as a boy or as a girl to boys and to girls and about boys and about girls. When they start school, many girls already seem to have learnt to expect to participate less than boys in classroom discussions, whereas many boys expect to be listened to, to hold the floor and dominate during discussions (Jarmany, 1991). It has been suggested that teachers may reinforce this pattern by giving more attention to and interacting more with boys than with girls and as a consequence give boys more opportunities to participate in teacher-organised talk at school (Swann and Graddol, 1988).

Children's gendered identities and their experiences and interactions in and out of school have implications for the way in which girls and boys continue to learn about language, the range of purposes for language in which they engage and their growth in confidence as users of language. Since the teacher's aim is to encourage all children to participate equally in speaking and listening activities she will need to take account of gender differences in oral language when planning the content and organisation of the speaking and listening curriculum.

While there are always exceptions – some boys are quiet and diffident and some girls are confident and articulate – a number of differences between the oral language use of boys and girls in school have been identified.

Boys:

- are more outspoken, assertive and confident;
- are more likely to be openly disparaging about others' contributions;
- interrupt more;
- are unhelpfully dominant;
- make longer verbal contributions;
- may recall anecdotes in order to hold the floor;
- use language to vie for status;
- are less likely to build on the contributions of others;
- like to propose ideas;
- use language dramatically;
- move on rather than develop ideas.

Girls:

- defer to the ideas of others;
- tend to gain more practice at listening than boys;
- signify that they are listening to others;
- respond to what has been said;
- take turns;
- speak tentatively and need approval;
- take longer to become involved in discussions;
- use language to draw out and include others and develop ideas together;
- are happy to collaborate.

Research evidence from the National Oracy Project (Norman, 1990; Swann, 1992) suggested that even teachers who are aware of these issues help to maintain and reinforce gender differences in language use by:

- making distinctions between boys and girls for disciplinary or administrative reasons;
- giving more attention and more time to boys' talk in discussions;
- not noticing the disparity in number and length of oral contributions from girls and boys;
- being more tolerant of behaviour such as calling out by boys, which helps them to learn how to take and hold the floor;
- asking boys more demanding questions;
- selecting topics that appeal to the interests of the boys;

- permitting or arranging working groups which reinforce gender distinctions in behaviour and language use;
- accepting rather than challenging the differences that exist in pupils' use of language.

The characteristic ways in which boys and girls speak and listen may affect their ability to achieve the objectives in the speaking and listening curriculum. Each group will have strengths in and difficulties with some of the objectives. Figures 7.3 and 7.4 show some of the objectives for speaking and listening for Year 1 (DfES, 2003). Some characteristic aspects of girls' and boys' talk have been mapped onto the objectives to show how their natural inclination might influence their achievement.

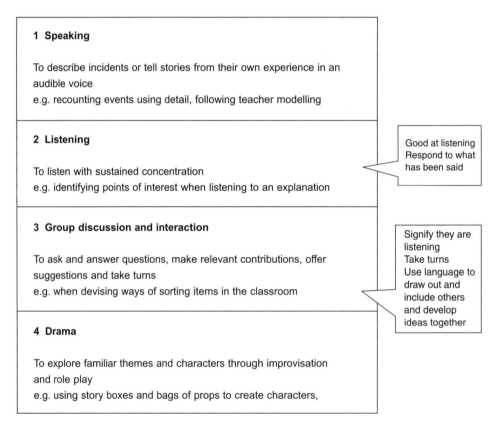

Figure 7.3 Girls and the speaking and listening curriculum

Tackling gender issues in speaking and listening

Girls and boys have different strengths and weaknesses as users of language. This becomes obvious when children work in single-sex groups. In all-girl groups the children are often keen to complete the task. They listen and respond to each other's contributions, are willing to negotiate and compromise and often manage to conclude with proposals that the majority agree with. In all-boy groups there can often be disagreement and argument rather than a real consideration of other children's opinions. It is clear that girls and boys could learn a great deal from each other. Girls could learn to become more assertive and boys could learn to be better listeners and respondents. Before actively intervening with the children, teachers might want to observe the oral behaviour and strategies that children use in a number of different situations. It is likely that different combinations of children, different contexts, different topics and the presence and interactions of adults will affect the children's contributions and participation. Teachers might want particularly to observe how boys and girls communicate, collaborate and behave in groups, noting how they support and respond to one another. Teachers may also wish to reflect on their own use of language and their own behaviour. After observing the children and reflecting on practice, teachers might then wish to make some changes in their teaching style and classroom management in order to develop the aspects of speaking and listening that the children lack.

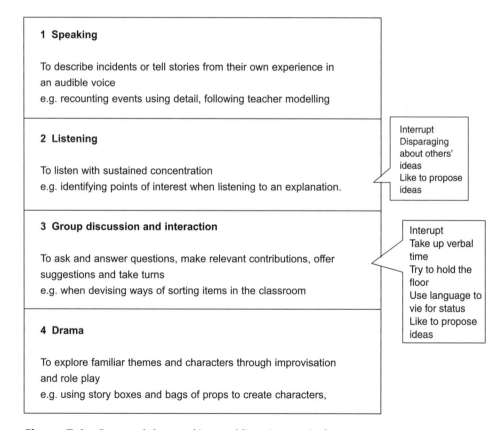

Figure 7.4   Boys and the speaking and listening curriculum

Teachers have found the following strategies useful when seeking to change established gender patterns in speaking and listening:

- selecting themes, resources, activities and organisational strategies carefully so as not to reinforce gender differences;
- supporting girls when they contribute to classroom discussions;
- supporting boys as listeners in classroom discussions;
- modelling non-stereotyped interactions in play situations such as the home corner, the hospital and the cafe;
- intervening in mixed groups to counter stereotyped behaviour and allocating children to non-stereotyped roles, such as scribe for a boy and leader for a girl;
- challenging stereotyped labels or behaviour and discussing this with the children;
- ensuring that boys have the opportunity to engage in activities that will enable them to use the quiet, sensitive, caring aspects of their natures;
- intervening when children regularly choose to work in single-sex groups by allocating children to mixed groups using sets of well matched single-sex pairings;
- organising all-girl groups or pairings in curriculum areas where girls appear to have less confidence, such as IT, science and construction, to ensure that girls experience success and to give them the confidence to hold their own in mixed-group settings;
- establishing rules that allow equal access to resources for play, science and maths;
- choosing girls to make oral presentations to the class and in assembly.

When appropriate, teachers can discuss group work and the pupils' use of language with the class. Talking about talk and encouraging children to reflect on their own roles during small and large group discussions will heighten their awareness of language and may lead to the children compiling a set of rules for discussion times, such as 'Everyone needs to listen and to talk', 'Everyone has something interesting to say' and 'No one needs to shout'. Negotiating the ground rules for talk gives children the opportunity to consider the different ways in which girls and boys use language and can make a positive contribution to effective group work.

Reading

Gender differences in reading

Girls seem to find books and reading more interesting and easier than boys. In the main they learn to read more quickly, and with greater success. Boys read less from choice, have more problems in attaining fluency in the initial stages of learning to read, and form the majority of children with statements of special educational need related to literacy. Far more boys than girls read at a level below that expected of someone of their age and general ability and this impedes the overall learning of many boys.

A number of possible explanations for these differences have been suggested. General expectations about the behaviour of girls and boys may mean that reading is viewed as a more suitable leisure activity for girls than for boys. Girls are expected to read and to enjoy reading because it is a quiet, introspective pursuit rather than an energetic, physical activity. In the early years the reading curriculum is largely constructed around stories and although boys may enjoy stories as much as girls, the emphasis on stories may alienate some boys. Girls' and boys' reading interests and habits are affected by the models of adult readers they see and it is known that women read more fiction than men and that adult male readers tend to read information texts, often linked to their work or their hobbies. If boys do not see men reading fiction this may influence their interest in a story-based reading curriculum. Boys are more likely than girls to read comics and hobby magazines. This type of reading is not always valued in school and this may mean that boys' reading abilities are underestimated. A study of nursery classes and nurseries in Cleveland (Hodgeon, 1984) found that girls' interest and ability in reading is supported by the predominantly female culture of early years settings. The girls in the nurseries spent more time near their teachers and as a result had more access to stories and literacy activities and gained more experience of reading and books than the boys.

Examining the reading experiences of boys reveals implications for the reading curriculum for all children. The gender differentiated models of adult reading that children encounter and the emphasis on story in the early years has disadvantages for girls as well as boys. For both sexes, much of their learning in their later school careers will depend a great deal on their ability to read a wide range of texts and to use information material successfully. Both boys and girls might benefit from an earlier introduction and greater use of information and other texts. The differences in attitudes to and success at reading manifested by boys and girls seem to be linked to a number of cultural and societal expectations and norms which are beyond the control of the teacher. However, whatever the external causes for the differences in attitudes and achievement in reading, there is good reason to consider making some changes to some aspects of the reading curriculum.

Tackling gender issues in reading

In order to enhance the achievement of boys and girls there are a number of practical strategies that teachers may wish to consider using. These include:

- ensuring that there is a greater balance between fiction and information books in the reading material that is shared with and offered to children in the early years;
- using single-sex pairs or groups for group reading in order to support children in their least preferred choices of reading material, for example boys might read stories together and all-girl groups might read information texts;

- keeping lists and records of the books that children read and reviewing their selection with them in order to provide books that match or extend their choices;
- helping children to select non-fiction related to their interests;
- using and displaying books which contain images of boys and men as readers;
- involving older boys, male teachers, fathers and male visitors in reading activities in the classroom;
- inviting male story tellers to school;
- creating play areas that have a literacy focus and where reading and writing are used by both male and female workers, for example a post office or a library;
- using ICT as a resource for reading;
- giving children purposeful outcomes for their reading;
- addressing gender issues with parents and making a positive effort to involve male carers in parent–teacher discussions about reading and in the home–school reading programme.

Writing

Gender differences in writing

Research in this area has shown that boys and girls hold very different attitudes towards writing (Millard, 2001). Girls often enjoy writing, particularly imaginative and personal writing, while boys feel less competent at writing and prefer factual and technical writing. As they continue in their school lives many boys, although good at writing, dismiss it, along with reading, in favour of mathematics, science or technology. They begin to pay less attention to what and how they write and produce carelessly presented writing that does not do justice to their abilities. Girls are often expected to be better at all aspects of writing including handwriting and presentation. Many teachers still expect girls' writing to be neatly written and long and boys' writing to be untidy, brief and exciting. When children are planning and drafting their work, teachers often expect the boys to spend far less time perfecting their writing, while girls are expected to pay more attention to detail and take a greater length of time to complete their work.

As well as differences in attitude and presentation skills children's writing also reveals differences in content and style. Examining the content of what children write can reveal how gender differences are rehearsed and reinforced through their own written words.

Look at the two samples of children's writing in Figures 7.5 and 7.6. Which of these was written by a boy and which by a girl? How do you know?

Figure 7.5 was written by Robert, a six-year-old boy, and Figure 7.6 was written by a girl, six-year-old Laura. The content and the style give us some clues about the identity of the authors. Robert's letter contains a direct request. It is

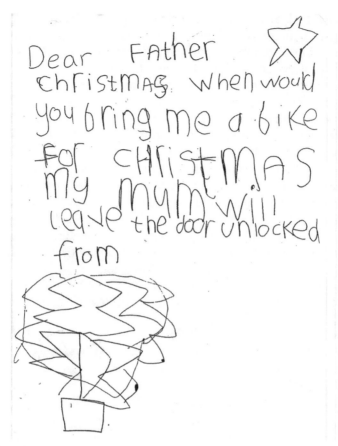

Figure 7.5   R's letter to Father Christmas

Figure 7.6   L's letter to Father Christmas

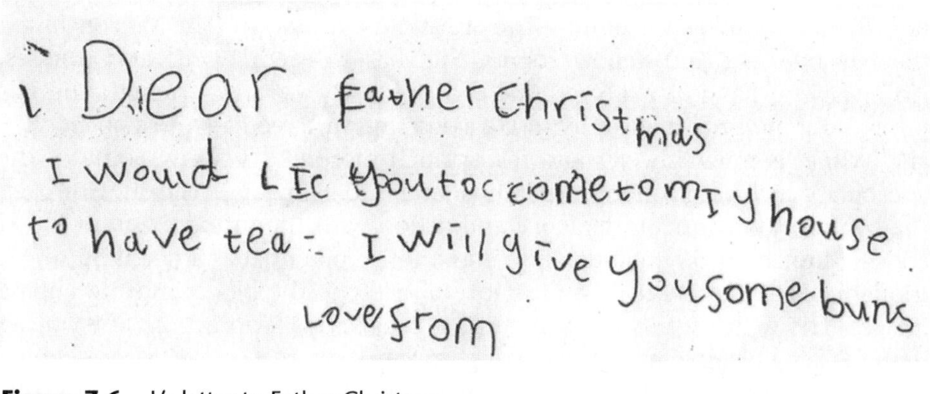

straightforward and to the point, almost abrupt, as it simply ends 'from …'. Interestingly it also refers to the mum as the one who remembers to do the social and domestic jobs at home. Rather than containing a request, the second letter proffers an invitation to tea. It portrays a cosy domestic scene with the writer engaging in cooking and caring for others. Laura has not accomplished the task that was set. She appears to have become so involved in her traditional female role that she is more concerned with writing about social niceties than with the purpose of the activity which was to tell Father Christmas what she wanted for Christmas.

Both letters are well presented. It is clear that Robert is a good writer, but it is also clear that he is less concerned with correct letter formation, consistent use of lower-case letters and letter size than he could be, given his apparent ability. Laura's writing seems to be much more carefully presented. These two samples of writing illustrate the gendered characteristics of children's writing and show why teachers need to consider content, style and transcription when they are thinking about how to meet the needs of boys and girls. The content of what is written and the way in which ideas are expressed reveal a great deal about the children's perceptions of themselves as well as their writing abilities.

Look at the next two pieces of writing, Figures 7.7 and 7.8. These are poems that were written by two six-year-old children. As you read their writing answer these questions.

- Which poem was written by a girl and which by a boy?
- How do you know?
- What do we learn about these two children from these pieces of writing?
- How far has each child succeeding in writing a poem?
- What advice would you give to each child to improve the transcription and composition of their writing?

You might have guessed that 'Yellow and Black' was written by a girl and 'Red and White' by a boy. The girl has tried to incorporate some features of a poem in her writing. She has tried to copy a literary style by missing out the verb in the line 'Black and yellow the bumble bee or naughty little wasp'. She has contrasted the feel of black and yellow rooms. She has repeated words and phrases. However, she has not really produced a poem. By writing at length she has produced something that is a hybrid of a description, a recount and a poem. 'Red and White' is much shorter and reads much more like a poem. Some of the vocabulary such as 'glittering', 'sparkling' and 'squiggling' is excellent. However, the content soon turns to violence and action with the introduction of blood and the fire engine. 'Red and White' has a lot of potential as a poem but more thought needed to be given to the introduction of the blood and fire engine images. The writer seems to have become caught up in an action story rather than focusing on how to craft a striking image.

These examples of children's writing were found in classes taught by thoughtful and aware teachers who were leading children enthusiastically towards the

Black is a black coulour my favourite colour.
Yellow is the sun up in the sky shines
Brown down on my head it makes me feel as
happy as can be. Black and yellow the
bumble bee. or nayty little wasp. the
wasp is nasty and stings my foot.
Black rooms are dark and spooky. Yellow
Rooms are light and bright.

Figure 7.7   'Yellow and Black'

Red and white

Red is a fise glittering bright.

White is Snow falling down Sparkling all around.

Red blood coming out squiggling all about.

Suddenly a fire-engine roaring down the

Street.

Figure 7.8   'Red and White'

goal of control over the writing process. However the samples show the children reproducing the attitudes and values they had learned as they grew up in a world that still differentiates between appropriate behaviour for girls and appropriate behaviour for boys. In their writing the children were expressing these values and, by committing themselves to paper, reinforcing these stereotypes both for themselves and for other children who might read what they had written. In their writing the children revealed something of their attitude towards writing and the way in which they write. The boys' focus on action and speed and the girls' interest in domestic pursuits and their focus on length has affected their ability to produce successful pieces of writing.

In general girls enjoy sustained, open-ended tasks that are related to realistic situations and that require them to think for themselves. Boys seem to prefer time-limited, purposeful tasks that are clearly right or wrong and benefit from feedback that is clearly focused on what they did well and what they need to improve. These different approaches to learning have implications for teaching writing. Writing is a thoughtful, time-consuming and sedentary activity. Success at writing requires concentration, reflection and perseverance.

Figure 7.9 summarises some of the differences that are found in the writing of boys and girls and their general preferences which might explain why they write in this way. In order to develop their writing further it would be helpful to offer boys some of the experiences that have a positive influence on girls' writing and to offer girls the experiences that influence boys' writing. This would help both groups of children to write in different ways and to explore a greater variety of styles, language and content.

Boys	Girls
Prefer non-fiction	Prefer fiction
Concise	Longer writing
Untidy handwriting, inaccurate presentation	Spend a great deal of time on
Include fantasy and action in stories	presentation
Ideas, plots and character underdeveloped	Include domestic or everyday activities
Draw on film and comic influences	Shows literary influences
Preferences	*Preferences*
Read non-fiction	Read fiction
Engage in active play involving single words	Develop stories in play
and noises	Like to please the teacher
	Use dedicated writing areas
	Discuss feelings and personal
	experiences

Figure 7.9 Summary of the differences in boys' and girls' writing

Tackling gender issues in writing

When considering how to create a writing curriculum that will offer equal opportunities for girls and boys to achieve in all aspects of writing, the teacher should first observe the children as they write. At the same time she might ask herself the following questions. Do boys spend less time on writing and do they consider it to be less important than other subjects? Do they rush the work and give less attention to style and detail? Are girls spending more time writing and concentrating too much handwriting and presentation? Do girls spend more time writing creative and imaginative pieces rather than technical or scientific scripts? She might want to reflect on the content of what the children produce to see if it reflects stereotypical ideas and values and to consider how these might be altered and perspectives widened.

If there are aspects of the writing curriculum that might benefit from change teachers might like to employ some of the following strategies.

- Emphasise to all pupils that writing is an important part of the curriculum and that high standards in all aspects of writing are expected from all the children.
- Praise the boys for well-presented writing.
- Encourage the girls to take a chance with their ideas rather than allowing them to spend a long time on presenting a perfect copy.
- Create a balance between imaginative, personal and factual types of writing in the writing curriculum.
- Plan shared writing sessions to give girls and boys the opportunity to discuss suggestions and to challenge and justify ideas that are to be included in a piece of writing.
- Organise groups so that boys and girls get equal turns at suggesting ideas and making notes.
- Select starting points for writing that challenge gender stereotypes and allow for the exploration of new perspectives.
- Positively discriminate when setting writing tasks by asking the boys to write a story that requires the central male character to be gentle and thoughtful and the girls to write a science-fiction adventure.
- Organise different writing activities for each sex so that each group can respond differently. For example, the girls may write the more powerful and controlling parts of the story and the boys the more descriptive and emotional parts.
- Integrate writing into indoor and outdoor activities.
- Become involved in boys' play to model and support story-making.
- Use an active approach to writing by incorporating collaborative writing, response partners, writing linked to play and drama.
- Consider all the messages that are contained in familiar stories that are read to and used with the children, for example discussing the intelligence that Red Riding Hood displays when she outwits the wolf.
- Monitor what is written and analyse children's choices with them, raising gender issues where necessary.
- Provide feedback that is clearly focused on the learning objectives and success criteria.

- Ensure that 'real' writing activities are planned for.
- Make the boys aware of the purpose of each writing task.
- Ensure that the audience for writing is made clear and that, wherever possible, this audience goes beyond the immediate classroom environment.
- Build on boys' enjoyment and motivation through using ICT, film and visual texts as starting points for writing.

Classroom provision and actions

Being aware of language

We might be aware of how boy and girl pupils use language differently and we might be sensitive to the use of sexist language by pupils, but educators, as models for young children, may also need to be alert to their own and other adults' use of language. It is very easy to use words in a way that portrays girls as immature and incompetent and boys as rational or assertive. Adults can sometimes refer to boys who are behaving unacceptably as being like 'silly little girls' and boys may be moved to sit or stand with the girls as if this were a punishment. These references and actions serve to highlight the distinctions between boys and girls and encourage boys to see female behaviour and company as incompatible with being a boy. Adults sometimes talk about children in ways that define the type of behaviour and characteristics that are considered to be the norm for each sex, labelling children in different ways according to gender. Quiet girls may be described as shy; quiet boys may be described as strong, silent types. Children who organise others may be called bossy if they are girls and leaders if they are boys. Girls' talk may be labelled as chat or gossip and boys' talk as loud or noisy. It is still common to hear references to 'the milkman', 'the postman' and 'the policeman', or to hear doctors spoken of as 'he' and nurses as 'she'. Some adults choose to use the word 'lady' rather than 'woman' because they consider it to be more polite, although it is very difficult to discover why they think this. One might ask why it is necessary to be more polite towards women than to men who are very rarely referred to by the equivalent 'gentlemen' or 'lords'. It is easy to fall into this misuse of language when talking to children about the 'lollipop lady' or the 'dinner lady'. If adults' other efforts to reduce gender stereotyping in the classroom are to be convincing and effective then adult models of language use and behaviour must support them.

Resources

Over the past 20 years a great deal of attention has been paid to the stereotyped portrayal of female and male characters in children's books. Researchers have consistently found that, in both text and illustrations, women and men, girls and boys are depicted in stereotyped and limiting roles. Because the visual and written images of books are part of the cultural patterning of children's lives and because readers are directly affected by and will reproduce in their own speech and writing what they see, hear and read, teachers need to continue to be aware of the influence that books may have on pupils. Fortunately there are now many authors and illustrators who are producing excellent books for young children that highlight the achievements of women and girls and illustrate the more creative, caring, responsible and sensitive qualities of men and boys. This makes the selection of new books that complement an anti-sexist approach to education much easier.

However, there are two areas where it is still not easy to find good resources. These are picture books that portray boys as readers and writers and information texts that represent and value the achievements and experiences of women and girls. Because classrooms do not just contain new resources it is often wise to read and appraise existing book stock and remove any material that may impede the aim of enhancing all children's learning. Changing the book provision in school does not necessarily change the attitudes and assumptions that people or children have and will not reverse the powerful process of socialisation, but the careful selection of resources and awareness of the issues will prevent schools from reinforcing limiting stereotypes and open up avenues for potential change.

Themes

The English curriculum presents teachers with many opportunities for pupils to play an active role in exploring equal opportunities in general and those aspects of equal opportunities that may impede their success in English (Tilbrook and Grayson, 1990; Minns, 1991). The teacher might initiate a project where the children investigate the portrayal of women and men, girls and boys as readers, writers, workers and family members in books, resources and in the media.

Classroom example: investigating gender roles

Discussing equal opportunities with children in relation to the language of books, pictures, TV programmes and advertisements can be a useful way of helping children to reflect on gender and language. Brierley (1991) gives a helpful account of a project intended to investigate children's perceptions of gender differences. Although this work was undertaken with ten- and eleven-year-olds, the activities would be suitable for much younger children. She began by using some of the activities suggested in the *Working Now* pack (Development Education Centre, 1989) which help children to examine their own perceptions of male and female roles. She then went on to ask the class to identify toys that would be appropriate for girls and boys. All the work was carried out in groups and ended with a class debate. Throughout the project the teacher was able to observe the oral behaviour and the attitudes of the children and these were discussed with them. This was a very productive way of examining gender-related behaviour at a level that was relevant and interesting to children and could make a good starting point for other practitioners.

(Continued)

(Continued)

Investigating books, reading and writing presents children with another opportunity to investigate gender. The children could devise questionnaires and interview pupils and adults in the class and school about their perceptions of appropriate types of reading and writing for females and males. They might survey the reading material that is looked at and read by each sex in the class. They might also ask adults about the reading materials and writing tasks that they engage in most.

This activity might reveal whether there are gender differences in literacy beyond the classroom. Another activity might involve analysing the topics for writing chosen by their own and other classes to see whether there are differences between the writing of girls and boys and, if so, to find out what form those differences take. Analysing classroom and library books is a straightforward but often revealing activity. The headings listed below were used by one class to compile a useful database of information about the books in their school:

Title
Author
Publisher
Year published
Main character – girl, boy, woman, man
The girls in the story are – brave, intelligent, kind, sensible, other
The boys in the story are – brave, intelligent, kind, sensible, other
The girls in the story are – silly, helpless, cowardly, other
The boys in the story are – silly, helpless, cowardly, other
Other comments

Examining and comparing old and new versions of fairy tales can often highlight aspects of gender stereotyping and encourage children to read and evaluate books attentively. The traditional Cinderella story might be compared with *The Paper Bag Princess* (Munsch, 1980) and *Prince Cinders* (Cole, 1987). As a result of their investigations the children might write letters to publishers, authors and advertisers informing them of their findings. They could rewrite the stories changing the sex of some of the characters or describing different roles for the male and female characters. They might act out the changed fairy tales, giving *The Three Little Pigs* an all-female cast or portraying Mother Bear in *The Three Bears* as the biggest and the strongest of the bears and Goldilocks as a boy. The children could then be asked deliberately to change the way in which they portray female and male characters in their own writing. Such investigations and analysis might result in a more informed and conscious change in the children's own use of written language and awareness of literacy and gender issues.

Even if one does not choose to focus on a language and literacy theme such as the one described above, it is important to consider the scope of any theme that is selected and to avoid choosing themes that are obviously gender biased. Good themes are those which enable the teacher to present a balanced view of boys and girls, and men and women, provide for a balanced diet of imaginative and factual reading and writing activities and for which the available resources support non-stereotyped portrayals of both sexes. A theme such as 'Conquerors and Invaders' might be quite limiting, whereas themes such as 'Change', 'Patterns' or 'Ourselves' can be planned to have more immediate appeal to the interests of all pupils and provide more opportunities to explore issues of gender.

Classroom example: the hidden curriculum

The two examples which follow show how gender can affect the learning of young children. In the first example the teacher is unaware of the issues; in the second example the teacher has thought carefully about how he might avoid the potentially damaging effects of gendered responses and behaviour.

Example 1

A Year 2 teacher was discussing possible titles for class books with the children. The children were all sitting in the book area of the classroom and the teacher was noting down the children's suggestions on a flip chart. He began the discussion by asking the children what their favourite television programmes were. A host of hands went up, mainly those of the boys. They suggested *Turtles*, *Thundercats* and *Batman*. The teacher praised the children for so many suggestions and told them that these would be good starting points for their own stories. The mainly boy group that had volunteered the answers began to shout 'yeah' and raise their fists into the air. The teacher quietened the class down and then asked one girl what she would like to write about. The child did not answer and was questioned further by the teacher. Eventually she said *Blue Peter*. The class burst into laughter and one boy told her that *Blue Peter* was not a story and that it was boring. The girl said nothing. The teacher told the girl that *Blue Peter* might be a difficult starting point for a story and invited her to think again. The girl said nothing.

This example shows how one teacher attempted to stimulate his class into writing imaginatively. He believed that by beginning the class discussion with a mention of television programmes he would hold his pupils' attention and motivate them into wanting to write. The teacher succeeded in catching the attention of many of the children but the topics that were identified and the behaviour of some of the pupils excluded many other children. When the teacher encountered shouts of *Batman* and *Thundercats* he saw this as a discipline problem, not as an assertion of the boys' power and competitiveness. The teacher's attempts to include the girl within the discussion led to her feeling isolated and threatened, hence her silence and refusal to answer any more questions. The teacher did not deal with the boys' response to *Blue Peter*. Instead he allowed the boys to intimidate her with their comments, therefore isolating her even more. This example was not a deliberate attempt by the teacher

(Continued)

(*Continued*)

to differentiate between pupils according to gender. He had merely wanted to identify a starting point for writing that was relevant and familiar to the children. However, he had not thought carefully about his starting point and even when many of the class were alienated by the discussion he did not rethink his strategies, stop the discussion or explore the issues with the class.

This example shows how and why teachers need to be aware of the content they select and the way in which they interact with pupils in the classroom. If teachers praise certain ideas and behaviour they are 'telling' the class what they feel to be good, commendable, exciting, important and so on. Similarly if teachers ignore or avoid particular issues that arise they may be silently reinforcing what the pupils already know.

Example 2

A class of Year 1 children were discussing the care of babies as part of the their class theme, 'Ourselves'. A parent had come into school to bathe her new baby and both the boys and the girls had been excited by this event. During the follow-up session, the teacher had organised the class so that all the children could participate equally in the discussion. During the discussion the teacher put equal numbers of questions to the boys and the girls. She was careful to ask boys questions that involved thinking about the care of babies and to ask the girls about the more technical aspects of childcare such as temperature and nutrition. As the discussion continued one boy put up his hand and said that he was fed up with letting everybody talk when he knew all the answers. He continued to complain, saying that it was not fair that everybody had to have a turn at answering when they didn't know what they were talking about. The teacher responded to this child by asking the rest of the class what they thought about his opinion. They told her that it was fair that everyone had a turn to speak. Later, when the children were asked to write about the discussion, the teacher made sure that the boy who had expressed his personal discontent worked with a group of children who sat with her. She made sure that each child in that group had an opportunity to speak and to make a written contribution to the class book. This example demonstrates careful and sensitive teacher intervention, rigorous planning and structuring of the oral discussion and attention to the organisation for writing, all of which resulted in a productive and positive session for the class.

Summary

When teaching to raise the achievements of boys and girls we need to:

- acknowledge the different strengths and weaknesses children bring to language and literacy;
- challenge boys and girls to do better in ways that are individual to them;
- present children with a view of the world which frees them from the constraints of gender.

〰️ Reflective activities

1. Reflect on your own teaching and consider how both girls and boys are encouraged to participate in all language and literacy activities in the classroom. What strategies do you use?
2. Look at some TV adverts for children's toys and games or look at the toys section of shopping catalogues. Can you tell if the adverts are being targeted? How do you know? Would playing with these toys encourage behaviour that is compatible with reading and writing?
3. In a classroom observe how many times girls or boys ask questions and answer questions. How many times does the teacher respond to girls or boys? Are there differences in the ways that the teacher speaks to girls and to boys? If you notice any differences, how might this affect boys' and girls' learning?

📖 Suggestions for further reading

Barrs, M. and Pigeon, S. (eds) (2002) *Boys and Writing*. London: Centre for Literacy in Primary Education. This is a collection of articles which explore ways of raising boys' achievements in writing.

Baxter, J. (2001) *Making Gender Work*. Reading: National Centre for Language and Literacy. In this booklet the author looks at gender and policies for the teaching of language and literacy, differences in the ways girls and boys speak, listen, read and write, and the different needs of girls and boys, and suggests ways of helping underachieving boys.

Moss, G. (2007) *Literacy and Gender: Researching Texts, Contexts and Readers*. Abingdon: Routledge. This book focuses on the links between literacy, gender and attainment.

8

Special educational needs

Introduction

This chapter covers:

- catering for children with difficulties in language and literacy;
- dyslexia;
- self-esteem;
- catering for gifted and talented children;
- programmes for helping children with difficulties.

Individual needs

Teachers know that all children have individual learning needs and are aware that they need to provide personalised teaching and learning opportunities so that all the children that they teach have the opportunity to reach their potential (DfES, 2005a). However, some children have needs that are in addition to those experienced by most children. Two types of additional needs have been discussed in Chapters 6 and 7 which looked at the needs of bilingual pupils and the separate needs of boys and girls. Other groups of children have additional needs either because they find learning difficult or because they are very able. Both these groups have special educational needs but it is customary to identify children with difficulties as having special educational needs and the more able group as being gifted and talented.

Special educational needs in language and literacy

In England in 2007 more than 19 per cent of children in primary schools had special educational needs:

- 17.7 per cent of children of primary age were on the special needs register without a statement;
- 1.6 per cent of children of primary age had a statement of educational need;
- one in every five boys and one in every eight girls was identified as having special needs;
- one in 40 boys and one in 100 girls had a statement;
- the most prevalent type of special educational need among pupils with statements of SEN was Speech, Language and Communication Needs in primary schools (around 23 per cent).

(DCSF, 26 June 2007)

The National Curriculum (DfEE/QCA, 1999c) offers some guidance to teachers who are catering for children with difficulties. It emphasises the importance of differentiated planning and careful classroom organisation in order to cater for the cognitive and physical needs of all pupils. It also states that teachers may select material from earlier or later key stages where this is necessary to enable individual pupils to progress and demonstrate achievement.

In order to provide for children who need help with communication, language and literacy it is suggested that teachers can make use of the following:

- using texts that pupils can read and understand;
- using visual and written materials in different formats, including large text, symbol text and Braille;
- using ICT, other technological aids and taped materials;
- using alternative and augmentative communication, including signs and symbols;
- using translators, communicators and amanuenses.

(DfEE/QCA, 1999c: 34)

In this chapter difficulties in language and literacy are discussed under the headings of speaking and listening, reading and writing. This division is not meant to obscure the interdependence of these four processes. Oral language development supports literacy learning. If children lack reasonable proficiency in oral language it is often harder for them to achieve success in reading and writing. Children who find reading difficult may also encounter problems in their writing since their experiences with print may be limited.

Speaking and listening

Fortunately many of the oral language difficulties that children present are linked to development and are outgrown as they mature. Others, such as hearing loss, can often be helped by technical means and thoughtful organisation in the classroom. This section examines some of the more common oral language difficulties and considers how the teacher can cater for these in the ordinary classroom.

Poor language

The problem of 'poor language' is one that worries many teachers. Teachers who describe children as having 'poor language' are not usually referring to children with sensory impairments or severe language disorders but are describing those children who, when they are at school, seem to find it difficult to:

- listen attentively;
- follow instructions;
- articulate responses to questions;
- speak clearly;
- use standard English.

Teachers may refer to children identified in this way as having 'no language' or as 'hardly able to talk' and they may describe the home language experiences of such children as limiting.

In the 1980s there were two significant surveys of young children's oral language use at home. The first by Wells (1984) investigated the home language of 128 children between the ages of 15 months and five years; the second undertaken by Tizard and Hughes (2002) examined the home language of 30 girls attending nursery school or nursery classes. Both groups of children were drawn equally from middle- and working-class home backgrounds. Neither study found any evidence of the existence of a language deficit in working-class children. Out of the 158 children surveyed in the two studies, 154 were found to be using language for a wide variety of functions and were exposed to a variety of language at home. Tizard and Hughes (2002: 160) concluded: 'The children who are said to enter school hardly able to talk are almost always children who can talk perfectly well at home, but are initially too ill at ease to display the full range of their verbal skills when they enter school.'

Some children may appear to be less articulate and attentive than is desirable but, before making such an assessment, the teacher might want to discover how the child uses oral language in a number of situations and with a range of conversation partners. They could do this by observing the child in a number of contexts and talking to parents about the child's language use at home. Where there is evidence that the child's competence in oral language is poor in relation to normal development, then activities which enable children to use language in purposeful contexts and with real and supportive conversational partners should help to remedy this. The suggestions for group and paired work in Chapter 1 should form the basis of any oral language curriculum and will help all children to develop their competency in speaking and listening. In addition, reluctant talkers might benefit from the following strategies:

- enjoying the right to be quiet;
- working and playing with a friend or partner with whom they seem to communicate easily;
- talking about a topic that they are really interested in;

- recording oral contributions prior to group discussions which can be played back for others to listen to;
- using puppets, toys, masks, role play and drama to enable them to speak on behalf of someone else.

Adults often say that children cannot listen and they frequently blame this on television viewing. There is no evidence to suggest that children listen less well than they used to; they rarely seem to have a problem with hearing things that they want to or that adults would rather they did not hear. Children may have problems concentrating and listening in large groups for long periods of time. They may also stop listening if they do not understand or are not interested in what is being said. Teachers need to make sure that they do not speak for too long or about things that are removed from the experience of young children if they expect children to listen carefully. Teachers in the National Oracy Project (Norman, 1990) found that children were more attentive in classes where teachers limited their talk, did not repeat instructions and provided a good model of listening. Reluctant listeners benefit from:

- discussion in small rather than whole-class groups;
- discussions that are relevant to their interests and experiences;
- clear, brief teacher instructions;
- compiling questions they want to know the answers to and asking these;
- listening to taped stories;
- seeing models of good listeners.

Hearing loss

Hearing losses vary from those that are severe and only treatable by the use of a hearing aid to slight losses attributable to ear infections, impacted wax or glue ear. Children with undiagnosed hearing losses are sometimes labelled as inattentive or lacking in concentration. They do not appear to listen or to understand what they have to do and may withdraw into their own world or become troublesome in class. If a child manifests these sorts of behaviours or if the teacher suspects that a child is deaf, she should look for the following signs which are characteristic of those with a hearing loss:

- does not respond when called;
- hears name but little else;
- misunderstands or ignores instructions;
- frequently asks the teacher to repeat instructions;
- watches faces closely;
- frequently asks neighbour for assistance;
- reluctance to speak;
- speaks very softly;
- speaks very loudly;
- speech defect;

- orally poor;
- appears dull and is not making expected progress;
- appears uninterested in class activities;
- complains of ear ache;
- discharging ears;
- persistent colds and catarrh.

(Adapted from Fraser and Chapman, 1983)

If a hearing loss is confirmed then the teacher needs as much information as possible about the impairment. It is helpful if she knows how severe the loss is, how much the child can utilise lip-reading skills and how the hearing aid works. She should also make a realistic assessment of the child's natural ability so that she neither under- nor over-expects from him. All the staff in school who come into contact with deaf children need to be aware of them and need to be given basic guidelines for their interactions with them.

Deafness affects both communication and comprehension, but careful classroom organisation may help the child with both these aspects of language. A quiet classroom will help the child to hear more easily. When the teacher is speaking the child should be close to the teacher and able to see her lips, face and gestures. The teacher will want to encourage the child's oral contributions and may need to re-explain tasks and instructions to the child. Children can also demonstrate their understanding through visual or written means rather than orally. Other children in the class can work with the hearing-impaired child, giving explanations and repeating instructions, and the teacher can plan paired work for some tasks so that the child benefits from listening and speaking in a small group.

Speech disorders

Wade and Moore (1987) write that 75 per cent of speech disorders are articulatory, that is they involve the inaccurate production of phonemes. As an example the child might say 'tome' instead of 'come' or 'cool' instead of 'school'. Articulatory disorders may be linked with hearing disorders, physical abnormalities such as a cleft palate or immature development. Misarticulation frequently occurs as part of the normal pattern of speech development, with most but not all children acquiring 'normal' pronunciation by the age of five or six. About 1 per cent of six-year-olds continue to have difficulties with accepted pronunciation and may benefit from the intervention of a speech therapist (Wade and Moore, 1987). When children continue to have problems with articulation they may begin to avoid speaking and miss out on the practice they need to develop their speech. They may also encounter problems with aspects of spelling and reading that draw on accepted pronunciation and phonic awareness. Intervention should help the child to learn and practise the sounds that are mispronounced. It is helpful to the child if the teacher is aware of the programme that the speech therapist devises, so that she can help the child practise the relevant sounds and offer praise when these are pronounced correctly. Other speech disorders are largely those associated with language fluency and rhythm. Probably the most common of these is stammering, which is the involuntary distortion of speech rhythms.

For all children who have difficulties with speaking and listening the teacher should:

- give the child plenty of time to speak;
- not interrupt or finish what the child is saying;
- create safe situations in which the child feels comfortable about speaking aloud;
- encourage the child to relax when he is speaking;
- focus on the content of what is being communicated rather than the way the child speaks;
- accept and at times encourage brief responses;
- never force the child to speak.

Significant difficulties in speaking and listening

Children with enduring speech, language and communication needs have difficulties with one or more of the following:

- speech – clarity and fluency of speech;
- expressive language – vocabulary and combining words to make sentences and longer sequences of language;
- receptive language – understanding the meaning of words, sentences and longer sequences of language;
- functional and social use of language – understanding the use and rules of communication.

These children may need to communicate through the use of body language, gesture, facial expression, eye-pointing, communication aids, photographs, pictures and symbols, print and signing. The teacher will need to plan carefully so that the children can participate in lessons. She might have to prepare some special resources and will need to work closely with the child's learning support assistant and with the school's special needs coordinator. *Speaking, Listening, Learning: Working with Children with Special Educational Needs* (DfES, 2005b) provides detailed guidance for teachers working with children with significant communication difficulties. It provides examples of how children can participate in all four elements of the speaking and listening curriculum: speaking, listening, group discussion and interaction, and drama.

Reading

Children's failure to make good progress in reading is probably the area which causes the teachers of young children the greatest concern. Even with high-quality teaching some children do not make sufficient progress in reading to enable them to gain satisfaction and success with books. These difficulties manifest themselves in a number of ways and some children may have several types of difficulty.

Identifying the causes of reading difficulties

Before deciding that a child has a reading difficulty it can be helpful to consider what factors can cause difficulties with reading and see if any of these apply. These are listed in Figure 8.1. Some of the causes can be tackled quite easily and this might be sufficient to improve the child's reading. Identifying where the problems are located can help us to move away from a 'these-kids-cannot stance' to a 'what-do-I-need-to-do-so-that-these-kids-can stance' (Comber, 2007: 129).

Physical factors	School factors	Home factors	Personal characteristics
Visual impairment Hearing problems Language delay or disorder Ill-health resulting in prolonged or frequent absence from school	Irrelevant materials Teacher expectations too high Teacher expectations too low The purposes for reading not clear to the children Poorly organised reading programme Teachers responding negatively to children who are slow to start reading	High adult expectations and pressure Absence of books at home Unfavourable home circumstances	Anxiety Lack of motivation Short attention span Poor self-image Not understanding what reading is for General learning difficulties

Figure 8.1   The common causes of reading difficulties

Some causes may be corrected easily. For example, physical factors can often be corrected or helped by referring the child for a sight or hearing test. Physical problems do not mean that the child cannot or will not read, just that there are tangible reasons why the child is experiencing problems. When the physical difficulties are severe the child may need a statement of special educational need so that they get additional support and resources.

Some children do not learn to read because of the way that literacy is presented rather than a deficit in themselves (Comber, 2007). If the teacher suspects that some aspects of the teaching programme are not helping the child to learn to read she can change these quite easily. She can ensure that all the children in the class are aware of the purposes for reading by her demonstrations of reading and her explanations about the uses of reading. Reading specially written repetitive reading material and activities which are intended to teach children letters and words out of context do not always make the purposes for reading clear to children and might not convince them that becoming literate is a worthwhile pursuit. The teacher might want to make sure that her reading programme consists of meaningful, intrinsically interesting activities which relate to literacy in the world outside school. She will want to provide the child with books that are motivating, that are linked to the child's experiences and interests and that contain vocabulary and grammatical structures that match the reader's own use of language.

Talking to children to find out how they feel about reading, books and school can be helpful in allaying children's anxieties. The teacher can act on what she finds out in order to give the child activities which help him to feel successful. Emotional trauma such as a bereavement can cause a child to become anxious and lack concentration. For most children this interruption to their learning is temporary and the child will be helped by a teacher who takes account of and is sympathetic to such circumstances.

There is increasing interest in the effect of home circumstances on children's literacy development. Research suggests that poverty, low aspirations, social class, ethnicity and the difference between literacy practices at school and at home can contribute to reading difficulties (Bird and Akerman, 2005). The most significant is thought to be poverty and it is when poverty is combined with the other environmental indicators that children are most at risk. The government uses free school meals as a measure of poverty and the DCSF (26 June 2007) figures on the incidence of special needs in primary schools show that children with special needs were twice as likely to be receiving free school meals. Lack of money may adversely affect the number of books and other resources for literacy, such as computers, that are available for children in the home. The absence of books at home need not prevent the child from learning to read as other forms of text, such as newspapers or environmental print or comics, can introduce the child to reading and writing. However, without books children may not receive as much practice at reading as children who do. Because the amount children read is a major contributor to their achievement (Bird and Akerman, 2005), teachers who work in areas of deprivation will encourage parents and children to make use of local libraries and ensure that children regularly borrow books from school. They will also need to make sure that such children gain as much practice at reading as possible at school.

Environmental difficulties may be helped by discussions with parents about their expectations for the child and their own interest in reading. Schools can also set up parental school programmes. When these focus specifically on reading they can be very successful (HMI, 2004). In the same report HMI also suggested that schools should do more to build on the literacy experiences of the home and use the range of materials children use at home in order to improve children's motivation and interest in reading. Some suggestions about working with parents are given in Chapter 9.

Some children from ethnic minorities may be at risk when learning to read. The ethnic group that seems to be most at risk is Gypsy Traveller pupils. On average they achieve less well than other pupils and many significantly underachieve. The DCSF (26 June 2007) figures show the following.

- The proportion of pupils with SEN with statements was greatest among Traveller of Irish Heritage (around 26 per thousand in primary schools) and Gypsy/Roma (around 25 per thousand in primary schools.
- The proportion of pupils with SEN without statements was greatest among Traveller of Irish Heritage (around 56 per cent in primary schools) and Gypsy/Roma (around 49 per cent in primary schools).

Education authorities have outreach programmes to cater for the particular needs of Gypsy Traveller pupils. They also provide training for teachers, and resources that such pupils can use. These are helpful when considering how to make provision for them.

Identifying the type of reading difficulty

Before designing a teaching programme for a child with difficulties with reading it is important to explore the sort of difficulty the child has. Any action that is then taken will be of most benefit to the child because it will be linked to what is wrong. The child might:

- not want to read;
- not understand what he reads;
- think he can't read;
- not read the texts provided.

To identify the nature of the difficulty teachers need insights into children's attitudes towards reading and the strategies that they can use. Talking to children about their reading can reveal how a child feels about reading and what reading material they enjoy. Some children are simply not interested in the books that the school normally provides and so they do not engage with reading as an activity. This can result in them not understanding what they read and not wanting to read. To rectify this, the teacher can find books that will appeal or encourage the child to select his own reading material. Alternatively poor readers try to avoid reading and may use the books that are provided as an excuse.

Children with difficulties often draw on a limited range of strategies when they are reading. They may overuse phonic strategies and pay little attention to the meaning of what they read. Sometimes they make guesses about words using initial letters or the pictures as clues and these guesses may have little relation to what the text actually says.

Carrying out a miscue analysis where a child's use of reading strategies is analysed in detail can help the teacher to pinpoint where the child's difficulties lie. It can show which strategies the child makes use of and those that he does not use. As the child reads the teacher can ask herself, is the child reading for meaning? Does he go back and reread when he encounters difficulties? Does he self-correct? Can he use phonic strategies? Does he have a sight vocabulary? Can he talk about the book in a way that shows he has understood it? A detailed example of a miscue analysis can be found in Chapter 10.

The results of a miscue analysis can show which sight words the child knows and which he cannot read. They can indicate how the child uses phonics. He might be able to use phonics to sound out initial letters of words but may not be able to use phonics to work out the sounds produced by combinations of letters. This information can help the teacher to plan sessions that will meet the child's needs. The results of a miscue might lead her to alter the way in which she plans for individual or guided reading sessions. She might give the child time to prepare the text before reading with an adult. She might make sure that reading sessions are long enough to spend time discussing the text both before and after the reading. She may institute paired reading sessions for the child with adults or more experienced readers in school and at home.

Activities to help with reading development

Not all poor readers benefit from an intensive phonics programme or special reading books; they need to develop at all aspects of reading. What they require is regular, systematic and sustained reading sessions and reading activities which cater for their weaknesses. These activities will include those described in Chapters 2 and 3 and will be carefully selected to meet the child's needs.

> There is no special mystique or methodology for pupils who have difficulties with reading. Time and effort spent with such pupils are the only factors likely to be repaid with increased interest and competence. Thus we can help best by diagnosing children's differing needs in reading and by adapting the strategies *we normally use* to meet them. (Wade and Moore, 1987: 95)

The lists that follow suggest activities that are particularly suited to developing different reading strategies.

Activities to develop understanding

- Reading taped books
- Cloze procedure
- Preparing texts and talking about the book – what it might be about and what will happen – before reading it
- Talking about what has been read
- Encouraging the guessing of words using the context
- Encouraging prediction when reading – ask what might happen next
- Setting questions before the child reads
- Making a story board
- Reading plays
- Guided reading
- Reading with a partner
- Using text disclosure programs such as Developing TRAY (http://www.2simple.com) alone or with a partner

Activities to develop phonic strategies

- Playing Snap, matching and Lotto games using single letters
- Talking about words after shared reading or individual reading sessions

- Encouraging the child to look at the ends of words as well as the beginnings
- Playing oral word games, such as 'I Spy', 'Odd One Out', etc., to develop phonic awareness
- Using the books that are shared with the child to hunt for words that begin with or end with …
- Building up a repertoire of rhymes and jingles, songs and jokes, which are enjoyed and learned by heart to develop awareness of language and sounds
- Sharing entertaining books with simple rhyming texts such as those by Dr Seuss

Activities to develop a sight vocabulary

- Helping the child to make a book containing personally important words such as his name, family names, names of favourite toys or foods, and using this as a reading book and as a dictionary when writing
- Making and playing word and picture games such as pairs, lotto or dominoes using words from familiar and popular books
- Hunting for the word that says … in books and comics
- Writing out familiar rhymes and jingles for the child to read
- Reading familiar books that contain simple, repetitive text, such as *Peace At Last* (Murphy, 1980), *How Do I Put It On?* (Watanabe, 1977) and *My Cat Likes to Hide in Boxes* (Sutton, 1973)

General

- Demonstrating the purposes of reading through displays of print and noticeboards and by reading a variety of material in the classroom
- Providing plenty of opportunities for listening to stories
- Using extra helpers to listen to reading
- Matching books to the child's reading ability and interests
- Providing opportunities to retell and reread familiar stories using story visuals and tapes – the children can make their own story visuals and word labels for these
- Following up silent reading times with a short discussion of books children have enjoyed

Success at reading for the child who has experienced difficulties

Success at reading will be different for every child and may be linked as much to a positive attitude towards reading as to successful performance. The child who is interested in becoming a reader and who feels that he is a reader will make progress when his interest and efforts are supported. Teachers will have a number of particular aims for those children who experience difficulty at learning to read and their progress should be evaluated using these aims. The statements that follow are important for all children but have particular relevance to children who are not finding the path to reading easy.

Successful readers:

- make meaning from written texts;
- read with intelligence, enjoyment and economy;
- turn to books for information and enjoyment;
- know how to select books for their own purposes;
- use their knowledge of language and of the world when reading;
- have developed reading strategies that with further practice will enable them to grow in competence as readers.

Writing

Children who have difficulty with reading are often those who find writing difficult. The fewer experiences children have with print the less they will learn about its use and its conventions and the less they will benefit from the reciprocal benefits that occur when learning to read and learning to write develop together (Clay, 1991). For those children with combined literacy difficulties all the reading activities described in the previous section will also help to alleviate their writing difficulties. As difficulties with recording may affect the assessment of children's learning across the curriculum, it is helpful to remember that speaking and listening can provide an alternative means of learning and demonstrating learning for those children with literacy problems.

Motivation

Less successful writers often feel little enthusiasm for writing. Writing is slow and painful and as a result they do less writing than their more successful peers. Because they engage less in the process, they receive less practice, less help and less positive feedback and begin to think of themselves as unable to write. This can fuel their unwillingness to write.

Children who have a negative attitude to writing spend a great deal of time writing the date and the title of the piece of writing but little else, rarely complete a piece of writing or regularly produce one or two poorly transcribed sentences which even they have difficulty in reading back. With difficulties such as these it is first of all important to check that the child is aware of what writing is for, that he knows that it is a lasting means of communicating important, interesting information to an audience.

Some classroom practices can conceal the true nature of writing from children, and teachers may want to check that they are not giving pupils poor messages about the nature of writing before they identify the child as having a problem. Classroom practices that may result in poor attitudes to writing include overemphasis of the transcription aspects of writing, 'one-chance' writing, the teacher as the only audience for writing in class, starting points for writing that are not relevant to the children, writing activities that regularly lack an audience other than the teacher and writing tasks in the classroom that are divorced from writing purposes in the real world. Often, if these are changed and children can see that writing has a purpose and an audience who responds to what they have to say rather than what they do, they will begin to write interesting and sustained texts. One way of demonstrating this to children is to find out what the child wants to say and scribing this for him in order to produce a text that he and his audience can read and respond to (Smith, 1994).

Composition

Difficulties with composition may be seen when children refuse to write, produce very short, incomplete or repetitive pieces of writing and writing that is poorly structured. If children have heard and participated in story sessions at school and shared stories at home they should be able to make up oral stories of their own. They will have some familiarity with the pattern and language of stories. Their reluctance to write may arise from lack of confidence in their own ability or their anxiety about spelling and handwriting. There are a number of ways in which the teacher can help children who have difficulties with composition. Writing which is modelled on known texts provides children with a familiar starting point and simple structure for them to follow (Smith and Alcock, 1990). Using stories containing a journey can be a particularly good starting point since these contain an easily recognisable and memorable structure (Smith, 1994). Children can first draw a sequence of pictures, a time line or a map which represent the events in the book and this pictorial representation can then be used to sequence the writing. Stories like *Rosie's Walk* (Hutchins, 1970) and *Patrick* (Blake, 1968) make useful starting points for this activity. The teacher may set a limit on the number of events that are included in the retelling, asking the child to write about four things which Rosie passed on her walk. As children gain confidence in planning and rewriting known stories they can gradually be encouraged to work towards creating their own stories or relating their own experiences. Telling the child that he can make a tape to accompany a story can also be a great incentive for reluctant writers.

Other starting points for children who feel that they have no story to tell might include using a set of photographs of play resources in the class. These can be incorporated into a book along with a brief written description by the child. The child might also make a catalogue of his toys using photographs or illustrations cut from mail-order catalogues (see Figure 8.2).

Asking a child to write an ending to a story that has almost been completed in a shared writing session provides another means of support for the child who feels daunted by writing. The conclusion can be quite brief and may draw upon words that have been used during the shared writing episode so these will be familiar to the child. The example in Figure 8.3 was written by six-year-old Calum, a reluctant and careless writer, in collaboration with an

Figure 8.2 Toy catalogue

adult. Seeing Calum playing in the writing area, the teacher suggested that they write something together. Calum had previously spoken about his stay with his Aunty Pat and the teacher proposed that they write a thank you letter to her. As the teacher and Calum shared the writing, Calum was impressed by the length of the letter, talked about his writing and asked about his spelling. He was eager to make some corrections as the writing shows. The next day Calum copied out this draft and the letter was sent. Collaborating on a piece of purposeful writing had been very motivating for Calum.

If children write at great length and cannot always read back every bit of their writing, or if the length simply leads to repetition, the teacher will need to put a limit on the child's writing and work with him on planning and organisation. Children who write too much also benefit from spending more than one session on writing, perhaps using the first session to plan their writing and then returning to the plan later to write their extended version. This helps children to structure their writing and not just write for the sake of it.

Figure 8.3 Calum's thank you letter

Transcription

Becoming a mature and confident user of the transcriptional elements of writing takes time and few children will move easily and speedily through the process. It takes over four years for children to become fluent, if incomplete, users of oral language and it would be reasonable to assume that it will take at least as long for children to become successful, albeit apprentice, users of the written language system, a system that can pose difficulties for many adult users. However, some children may appear to be making very slow progress and need extra encouragement and help.

Spelling, handwriting and punctuation should always be taught in a meaningful context. As far as possible work on improving writing conventions should take place using writing that the child has produced. If transcription skills are very poor or if the child is too reluctant to write because he feels inhibited by his transcription skills, scribing may provide the answer. The child will learn a great deal about how words are written, how letters are formed and how punctuation is used by watching an experienced writer. He will begin to understand the demands of writing such as planning, composing, drafting and taking the reader's role, all of which are useful for composition and transcription. The teacher's main aim should be to get the child to write. Once the child is writing something, the teacher will be able to see the nature of the child's difficulties and work with him on these.

Spelling

Difficulties with spelling may affect the content of what is written. Slow and less confident writers may be limited to short words and simplistic ideas. They may be unable to catch their ideas in writing and put them on the page because they avoid unknown spellings. Scribing, brainstorming with the teacher to provide a short collection of words, using the word processor or introducing children to drafting may help with this difficulty as will general work on spelling.

Some children seem to get stuck at the phonemic stage of spelling development and may only use sounds to help them write the initial letters of words producing, for example, *cad* for *cat*. For these children the teacher may first need to check that they do know the sounds and names of all the letters of the alphabet. Next she might, when writing, correct versions of words, emphasise the ends of words by underlining these and discussing them with the child. She might also limit all her spelling interventions to a small, frequently used group of short words. Strategies which encourage children to see and remember important and often-used words, including the look, cover, write, check approach, should also be used regularly.

If the child writes at length but his spellings are bizarre and the child himself experiences difficulty in reading back what he has written, the teacher may ask the child to limit what he writes to a couple of lines, but to think carefully about what he writes and to remember what he was writing about. The teacher can make a small word bank for the child to refer to when he is writing. The teacher can help by talking to the child about the content before and as he writes. She may attend to this child as soon as the writing is finished, before he has time to forget what he wrote, and provide a correct model immediately underneath the child's writing. This should be discussed and compared in detail with the child's writing. Asking the child to draw a picture depicting the content of the writing before he writes will also remind the child about the content and give the teacher an idea about what has been written. If the teacher wishes she can discuss the picture with the child and together they can provide labels for some of the items in the picture. This provides the child with a spelling bank which is another source of help for the child and information for the teacher.

Although good readers will have the advantage of having more experience of print than inexperienced readers, they may need just as much help with spelling as poor readers. Good readers can be poor spellers since confident readers tend to read quickly focusing on the meaning of a text rather than the letters contained in each word.

Handwriting

For children with poor handwriting it is worth checking for any physical factors such as posture, pencil grip, tension, space to write and paper position which may be inhibiting their writing. It may be that by changing these the child's difficulties will be eased. Some children with motor control problems or those who persistently reverse letters may need additional practice in handwriting. Activities such as pattern-making incorporating letter strings and words, and drawing and painting using finger paints, big brushes and bold felt-tips, may help. Computer programs that encourage children to form letters on the screen are available and these may be helpful for persistent reversals and difficulties with letter formation. Introducing children to the cursive forms for *b* and *d* may help when these letters are consistently reversed or confused as the cursive form emphasises the differences between them far more than the print script does. Letter and letter-order reversals are not always indicative of a problem with writing since they are common in very young children's writing and they tend to disappear after two or three years at school (Brown, 1990). Children who find handwriting particularly difficult may be motivated by using a word-processing package on the computer.

Punctuation

By the age of eight it is probably too early to say whether a child is experiencing real difficulties with punctuation or whether he needs more time for his understanding and the correct usage to develop. However, many children do seem to get stuck at the stage of connecting large sequences of writing with *and*. Discussion about the limited use of *and* in published texts, identifying alternatives and asking children to substitute full stops for *and* may help.

Carelessness and overcorrectness

Some children, particularly boys, may grow careless in the presentation of their writing and others, often girls, produce pieces that are perfectly presented but very short. The teacher can address this issue by making sure that girls understand that a draft can be untidy and by emphasising that content is more important than presentation in writing. The teacher may also want to make it clear to children who are habitually untidy, without good reason, that careless final drafts are unacceptable even if the content is good, since they are difficult for others to read.

Classroom example: a child making little progress in reading and writing

The following case study illustrates one child's literacy difficulties, the possible causes of these and the individual programme that was drawn up for him. It demonstrates how early systematic and thoughtful intervention can help to alleviate literacy difficulties.

John, aged six, seemed not to be making progress in reading or writing. Although he appeared to be interested in books and was willing to write, he was not showing any inclination to read alone and took a long time to complete any writing. When he shared books with adults he did not always seem to be paying attention to the overall meaning of the book, although if the book was read to him he was happy to talk about it after hearing the whole story. When he read alone he seemed to be concerned to read every word and used initial letters to help him make a guess at words that were unfamiliar. In writing he was able to use some letter sounds to begin words, but often his spellings, apart from the initial letters, were very difficult for others to read. He was always able to read back his own writing. This plateau in literacy had lasted for some time and when no progress had been made for nearly a term, was starting to cause the teacher some concern. John was slowly beginning to fall behind his peers in reading and writing and was not improving in line with his apparent ability.

The sorts of literacy difficulties that John was experiencing were limited motivation for reading and writing and not understanding what was read. There was no obvious physical, environmental, school or personal cause for these problems. The teacher concluded that John's lack of motivation was the problem and that this might have arisen because John did not appreciate the place of literacy in his life. Her aims for the reading programme she devised for John were to:

- enable him to see the relevance of reading and writing;
- give him more control over the selection of reading material and topics for writing;
- work on visual strategies for word recognition and spelling;
- provide frequent and varied opportunities for him to gain practice at reading;
- ensure success and to praise any independent successes he might show.

The teacher knew that John had a good sense of humour and very much enjoyed drawing so she decided to use these as her starting point for working with him. She read a number of amusing books to the class, such as the 'Happy Family Series' (Ahlberg, 1988) and various joke books. She had made tapes of some of these books and placed them, along with copies of the books, in the listening area. She offered the books she had read to the children to read for themselves and particularly asked John if he would like to read some of the joke books. The whole class were invited to make a large book retelling the story of *Mrs Jolly's Joke Shop* (Ahlberg, 1988). John was asked to contribute some written and illustrated jokes to the book. These were short pieces of writing and because they were to be used for a class book it was important that the words were spelt correctly. As part of their research for the project the joke-writing group read and listened to the tapes, asked other members of the class for their favourite jokes and asked family members to write down jokes for school. The jokes that were written at home were read to the class, and since the humour of jokes very often depends on how they are delivered, they had to be read accurately and quickly. Any jokes that were not included in the class book were used to make small individual reading books for the class library.

John became very involved in this project and became an avid collector and writer of jokes. His interest in reading and writing was rekindled and he appeared to see that one purpose for recording is to remember and that reading can recover what has been recorded. As many jokes rely on a simple formula, John encountered many repetitions of simple words, such as 'What

(Continued)

(Continued)

do …?', 'What did the …?', 'Why did the …?', 'I say, I say, I say …', 'Knock, knock, who's there? …', all of which were adding to his reading and writing sight vocabulary. After the project was over John continued to read the individual joke books and he and a friend made a tape to accompany the class version of *Mrs Jolly's Joke Shop*, an activity that required accurate reading and sustained involvement with text. As part of the project, when he was looking for jokes, John had examined a great many of the books in class. When he was asked to select books to read he was able to use his knowledge of what was available to choose books that he thought he would enjoy.

This project gave John's reading and writing development a boost and enabled the teacher to address many of her concerns about his progress. His successes also increased his own self-esteem as he had become an expert at telling, reading and writing jokes. The teacher pursued her aims for his learning during individual reading sessions, encouraging him to focus on the meaning of what he read, to guess at unknown words using the illustrations and meaning as a guide and to compare the words in books with words that he now knew and used in his writing. Through identifying John's needs and gearing her teaching towards her aims the teacher was able positively to intervene in John's reading and writing so that he was functioning at a level that was normal for his age and the class, rather than falling behind at a critical point in his development.

Dyslexia

Dyslexia describes difficulties with words in reading, writing and spelling. It 'is evident when accurate and fluent word reading and/or spelling develops incompletely or with great difficulty' (British Psychological Society, 1999: 18). These difficulties cannot be attributed to:

- poor teaching;
- lack of motivation;
- below-average intelligence;
- lack of opportunity or support for literacy at home;
- abnormal vision, hearing or physical health;
- resistance to normal teaching and remedial help.

Dyslexia is a language-related problem which is found in all ability groups and across a range of environmental circumstances, and affects about 14 per cent of the population (DfES, 2006c).

Children with dyslexia are likely to show some of the following characteristics:

- an inability to recognise and name words;
- mispronunciation and omission of words when reading;

- an inability to integrate visual and auditory information and use phonics;
- omissions, bizarre spellings, reversals, mixed use of upper- and lower-case letters, the right letters in the wrong order in words, words incorrectly ordered in written sentences;
- writing in English produced from right to left;
- an inability to sequence actions;
- left-handedness;
- speech disorders;
- reading and writing failing to develop normally.

In spite of there being a set of tangible traits associated with dyslexia it remains difficult to diagnose. In the first place not all of the characteristics are present in all those who have dyslexia, for example, as many as 50 per cent of dyslexics may be right-handed. The presence of these factors does not automatically impede normal reading development in all children and in fact many of these signs are characteristic of young children's early reading and writing. Finally, the diagnosis of dyslexia may be difficult because by the time the disability in reading is recognised other symptoms and compensatory strategies such as poor self-esteem, lack of motivation or deviant behaviour may have been acquired.

The diagnosis and identification of dyslexia remain difficult and it is a term that should be applied with caution. However, its use can be positive. It can bring relief to parents when they are told that their child's difficulties are not due to laziness or stupidity, but to a neurological condition which demands special help and sympathy rather than pressure and disapproval. Children too can feel relief and welcome the term which appears to recognise their frustrating struggle with reading and writing. Their self-esteem may be restored and they may be in a better position to respond to making a fresh start at learning to read.

The literacy difficulties that children with dyslexia have seem to stem from their problems with processing language sounds. This makes it difficult for them to divide words into syllables, identify the beginnings and endings of words, match sounds to letters and blend letters together. Children with dyslexia benefit from structured phonics teaching which is tactile and kinaesthetic. Activities such as tracing over sandpaper letters, using wooden and plastic letters and making letter shapes out of clay are helpful. They also benefit from opportunities to revisit and reinforce their learning. Because children with dyslexia need to concentrate so much on word recognition they may have difficulty understanding what they read. To help with this they may need to become familiar with books before they read them and benefit from discussions about books before reading. Although teachers will want to see improvements in spelling and writing, because writing is so difficult for children with dyslexia, they can sometimes ask children to represent their learning in ways which do not depend on writing a great deal. Picture sequences, diagrams and labels, mind maps, computer programs and tape recordings can all be used instead of connected prose.

Self-esteem

Readers of this book will probably be very skilled and experienced readers and while 'knowing' that reading failure affects children's personal and academic lives, they may find it difficult to understand the damage to self-esteem that the continued experience of reading difficulties may cause. It is salutary and sometimes illuminating to think of something which we as adults are not good at and then to consider:

- how we feel about that activity;
- why we are poor at it;
- what might make us better at it.

By doing this we might be able to better understand children's difficulties. The following example makes this clear.

Despite being an experienced driver I am not very good at parking my car and even after arriving at my destination after a long, tiring journey can sometimes waste 15 minutes looking for an easily accessible parking spot which may be some distance away from where I want to be.

How do I feel about this?

- I feel angry with myself.
- I feel foolish and stupid.
- I don't want anyone to watch me when I am parking.
- I feel irritated with people who might see me and with those unknown people who have successfully parked their cars.

Why am I poor at parking?

- When I learned to drive I didn't realise the importance of being able to park well.
- I then assumed that I would just learn how to do it.
- Later I began to avoid situations where I would find it difficult to park.
- If I had a passenger who could drive I might ask them to park the car.
- I began to make jokes about my inability to park, to excuse myself and to conceal my frustration.
- I now begin every attempt at parking expecting to fail.

What would improve my parking?

- Practice, encouragement and sympathetic guidance.

There are a number of lessons to be learned from this example. First, whatever I cannot do, in this case park a car, is not as central to my life as learning to be literate is to a young child. All children expect to learn to read, they see success at reading praised by adults in and out of school and know that it is an important activity. When they have difficulty with reading not only may they feel they are failing at reading but also that they are failing as a person. Their failure is public. Children who are poor at reading are known to be so by all the members of the class and their failure is demonstrated every time they are expected to read or when they have to read aloud.

As with the parking example, children who have difficulty with reading will avoid reading. They gain fewer reading experiences and as a result they will accumulate less knowledge about reading than their more competent peers. They will begin to distrust their own reading competence, become anxious about reading and they will not see themselves as readers; their self-confidence will falter. They may begin to withdraw increasingly from situations where they may have to read, not concentrate or attend to demonstrations of reading, appear unmotivated and even become disruptive during reading sessions in order to distract attention away from their reading failure. All this leads to them gaining even less practice and obtaining less guidance and support.

If any remedial programme is to succeed it is important to build up children's confidence and remove the pressure so that they feel they want to learn and are secure enough to be able to take the risks that learning involves. For some children enhancing their self-esteem may be sufficient to enable them to succeed at reading. As Asher (1980) suggested, failure to learn to read often occurs not because children lack the physical or cognitive resources to succeed, but because they lose impetus and belief in themselves.

Ways to enhance children's self-esteem:

- Think through the learning experiences that are offered from the child's perspective.
- Organise activities to facilitate not impede children's success.
- Provide a safe environment where risk-taking is possible and valued.
- Value the process of learning, not just the product.
- Praise and encourage the child, making the reasons for your praise clear to the child.
- Provide learning situations across the curriculum which will result in success.
- Respond promptly and positively to work which the child does.
- Set achievable goals for the child and let the child know when he has achieved them.
- Use language positively. Rather than saying 'You aren't trying', say 'I don't think that that is too hard for you. I think that you can do it.'
- Don't label struggling readers as a 'problem'. Think of them as inexperienced.

Ways to develop a positive self-image through literacy activities:

- Listen to what the child says about reading and texts and take this seriously – the child's views are important and enlightening.
- Make an 'I can ...' book with the child, containing simple sentences and pictures that demonstrate what the child can do.

- Use the child's interests to help him write his own material.
- Let the child prepare all texts before reading.
- Compile reading material that interests the child from books and magazines.
- Provide tapes to accompany books the child enjoys.
- Make tapes based on books the child writes or the adult scribes for him.
- Provide a wide variety of books at a simple level.
- Read books together that children with low self-esteem can identify with, such as *Willy the Wimp* (Browne, 1984) and *Willy the Champ* (Browne, 1985).
- Scribe a book he composes and use this as a reading book.
- Write a simple book for the child based on the child's interests or with the child as the central character.
- Let the child choose his own reading material.

Gifted and talented

Most of this chapter has been concerned with the needs of children who experience difficulties in language and literacy. However, there is another group of children who need careful attention. Gifted and talented children are those who have one or more abilities developed to a level significantly ahead of their year group, or with the potential to develop these abilities, and they make up about 2–3 per cent of the population (Essen and Welch, 1990). 'In England the term "gifted" refers to those pupils who are capable of excelling in academic subjects such as English or history. "Talented" refers to those pupils who may excel in areas requiring visio-spatial skills or practical abilities, such as in games and PE, drama, or art' (DfES, 2005a).

In English gifted pupils may be particularly able in speaking, reading or writing. They may be articulate and able to use a wide range of vocabulary which is unusual for their age. They may speak confidently and effectively in a variety of situations and to a range of audiences. They may enjoy reading and talking about books and other texts that are far more challenging than those normally read by children of their age. Their writing will be well structured and show originality.

Gifted children may need personalised support to reach their full potential. They need to be presented with work that challenges, stretches and excites them on a daily basis and given opportunities to further their particular talents outside school. The sort of tasks that will benefit gifted children include:

- open-ended activities;
- activities which involve analysis and evaluation;
- challenging texts;
- opportunities to work at their own pace;
- extension work which allows them to broaden or deepen their learning;
- appropriately challenging targets.

Classroom example: analysing a sample of writing by a gifted child

The story in Figure 8.4 was written by Alex, a seven year-old boy. Alex begins the story in an unusual but striking way by using dialogue. The opening sentences also introduce the reader to the two characters, rat and mouse. As the story progresses Alex builds up the tension between events. He gives us an insight into what the main character is feeling, his fear, his relief and his attempts to be brave. He concludes by bringing back one of the characters he introduced at the beginning of the story and attempts to use a surprise at the end with the final word 'Boo!' He uses a range of vocabulary like 'peeped' and 'gobbled' and instead of 'said' he uses 'laughed' and 'chuckled' which add to the reader's enjoyment. The internal monologue and dialogue are an integral part of the story. Alex understands when to use speech marks and at times he uses full stops and commas. This is a piece of writing by a child who knows how to tell a good story and how to include literary devices to very good effect.

It can be difficult to know how to stretch a child who is writing as well as this but there are some areas where he could improve. Although his idea for the ending was good he does not quite get it right. Perhaps he could think again about how he could get his desired effect. Rereading his writing might help him to see what he could improve. It might also help him to see where he could insert full stops. Alex obviously enjoys writing and could be asked to write some extended stories on screen so that he could alter and improve his stories over time.

The Literacy Framework and children with special educational needs

All children are expected to participate in the literacy hour and be taught according to the objectives in the Primary Framework for Literacy (DfES, 2006a). While the aim is to teach children using the objectives that match their year group some children may need to work at earlier or later levels. In order to select the objectives for children who have difficulties or who are gifted the teacher needs to read through the Framework and identify what they can do. This will enable her to see which year group the child is working in. The teacher can then select relevant objectives from years below or above the child's chronological year group. Work that is planned to remediate difficulties or stretch the more able can be undertaken during the group and independent work. It might be possible for the children to work with an adult at this time. The introductory part of the literacy hour includes demonstrations of reading strategies and explanations about texts. This is likely to benefit all children but the teacher's questions can be differentiated according to need and ability. Plenary sessions may also benefit pupils whose needs in literacy are different from the majority of the class. Here the emphasis is on reviewing, reflecting on and consolidating earlier work. The repetition that is involved in the plenary can help to reinforce learning or

14th of June   A Scary Story night come to

"Bob do you read and scary storys give my

house and mouse it's a windy night and I

thanks might go to bed early"

Said to

when rat got home he read

himself "I just when he started

myself" and to read Scary Storys

Tap tap tap who "thats" help a birds

come to carry me to it's nest he hid

under his bed covers) rat peeped from

'under his bed

He went down stairs "I am "laughed rat.

Hole what 'idea I think I'll read the

another scary Story and he closed the

curtains) bang bang bang helo a hunter has

come to shoot me) the hid behind the

So they he peeped) ole still me) chuckled

rat "it was only

the shed door."

I don't think I'll read any more scary storys and

he went to the kitchen and got some biscuits.

Gurgle gurgle gurgle he gobld it's a monster come

to eat me up gurgle up all the biscuit's)

Some cake) and four packets of crisp's)

felt much braver after that. Thump thump help

Said rat he hid behind the door

come to eat me up "rat it's only me mouse ok"

"I was getting alone.

"Lucky you) came

"Small I tell you scary storys "yes"

gurgle gurgle "ok it was only

"what was that" said mouse

the rain.

Boo!

Figure 8.4 A scary night story

provide an extra opportunity to understand what has been taught. More able children can ask more challenging questions or offer suggestions about improving work that are expressed in a way that all children can understand but that are insightful and thoughtful.

In order to provide for children with special educational needs teachers are expected to use three tiers or 'waves' of teaching. Wave 1 is normal, good-quality teaching that all children should receive every day. Wave 2 teaching includes tightly structured intervention programmes for children who are lagging behind the expected norms for their age groups. *Early Literacy Support* (DfES, 2007a) for children in Year 1 and *Year 3 Literacy Support* (DfES, 2007b) are the two Wave 2 intervention programmes produced as part of the Primary National Strategy. Both of these programmes take the form of time-limited, carefully targeted, small-group sessions which can be delivered in addition to or within whole-class English lessons. Wave 3 teaching includes highly personalised interventions designed to meet the individual needs of children experiencing significant literacy difficulties. Children who are on the special needs register are entitled to support under Wave 3 provision. Greg Brooks (2007) has produced a useful survey and evaluation of Wave 3 intervention programmes for reading, spelling and writing intended to help teachers to select appropriate approaches. This can be found on the website that accompanies this book.

Summary

When teaching children with special educational needs we need to:

- analyse children's strengths and difficulties and then plan ways to develop their learning;
- provide structured, systematic, intensive, regular and positive support;
- consult other teachers and agencies with particular expertise where necessary;
- make sure day-to-day practice complements any additional work the child undertakes.

 Reflective activities

1. Select one child with reading difficulties. Carry out a miscue analysis with this child and talk to them about reading. Using the results of the miscue and your discussion, identify the strengths and weaknesses of the child's reading and draw up a plan which will address the child's weaknesses.
2. Collect some samples of writing from a child who has difficulties with literacy. Consider how you could respond to the child's needs in writing. What feedback would you give to the child? What are the implications for your teaching?

Suggestions for further reading

Gross, J. (2002) *Special Educational Needs in the Primary School,* 3rd edn. Buckingham: Open University Press (1st edn 1993). This is a practical and straightforward guide to special educational needs.

Porter, L. (2005) *Gifted Young Children: A Guide for Teachers and Parents,* 2nd edn. Buckingham: Open University Press (1st edn 1999). This book contains information about identifying and working with gifted and talented children aged 0–8.

9

Working with parents

Introduction

> **This chapter covers:**
>
> - **reasons for working with parents;**
> - **how parents contribute to children's learning;**
> - **how schools can involve parents in language and literacy learning;**
> - **how schools can build on children's home experiences.**

Reasons for working with parents

Early years educators have a long tradition of involving parents in the life and curriculum of the school and parental involvement is a significant and established feature of early years education, particularly in the area of language and literacy. The part that parents can and do play in developing children's language learning is now widely recognised as beneficial to pupils and is so widespread that involvement in reading has been described as 'unstoppable' by Hannon (1989).

The benefits of active parental interest in education at home and at school have been demonstrated in a large number of studies undertaken over the past 30 years. The initiatives which followed the *Plowden Report* (DES, 1967) such as the Haringey Reading Project (Hewison and Tizard, 1980) and the Belfield Reading Project (Jackson and Hannon, 1981) showed how additional practice in reading given to children at home enhances their competence at reading. In a National Literacy Trust position paper (Bird and Akerman, 2005) the authors found that most children who know adults who read for pleasure take it for granted that reading is a valuable and worthwhile activity and that the strongest predictor of children's early literacy development is provision for children's literacy development at home.

Support for involving parents in their children's education has also come from government bodies such as the DCSF and Ofsted. The Education Reform Act 1988 gave parents the legal right to be involved in their children's education and to have access to information about education, schools and pupils. One of the criteria used by Ofsted for judging the success of a school is the degree of satisfaction that parents feel with the school. This is defined as how much they know about, are involved in and are supportive of the school and its curriculum. In the additional guidance which accompanied the original National Literacy Strategy parental support was described as necessary to the success of the strategy and 'vital if children are to understand the relevance of literacy skills to real life, and get opportunities to practise and reinforce them in everyday situations' (DfEE, 1998: 95).

Recent research concerned with parental involvement in literacy has been investigating the variety of home literacy practices. When these are similar to the literacy practices of the school children are at an advantage in learning to read and write but where there are differences children can be at a disadvantage. For many years school literacy has been privileged at the expense of home literacy. So children who are familiar with alphabet charts, story books and educational games and videos make the transition to reading and writing at school more easily. Home literacy practices such as writing e-mail and text messages or reading computer and video games are far less congruent with literacy practices at school. They are often not recognised by teachers as supports for learning and are often not built on in the school curriculum. An HMI report on reading (HMI, 2004) found that primary schools rarely use the broader range of materials that pupils use at home as starting points to further children's reading at school. The authors suggested that children's motivation could be increased and standards improved if schools found out about and built on home literacy practices.

Currently there are three main reasons for school to work closely with parents. First, parents are recognised as users of the education system and so are entitled to information about the services that are provided for their children. Secondly, when parents actively contribute to children's literacy development children can make greater progress. Thirdly, children's success at literacy and language can be enhanced when schools match some of their literacy practices to those that children are familiar with outside school.

Close cooperation between parents and teachers is beneficial to children because discussion can foster mutual respect, understanding and openness between parents and teachers. The information that parents share with teachers can be used to match the curriculum to the individual needs and interests of the children they teach as they draw on parents' knowledge of their child and find out about the child as a learner outside school. This can help to smooth the transition between home and school. Parents who are informed about literacy learning are in a better position to support their child's learning and can provide opportunities for their children to apply their learning at home.

How parents contribute to language and literacy learning

The results of the work undertaken by Clark (1976), Tizard and Hughes (2002) and Wells (1986) have shown that parents play a powerful and positive role in their children's learning before and outside school without any intervention from school or outside agencies. They provide children with resources, literacy models and opportunities for learning about oral and written language as they involve them in everyday experiences at home. A survey undertaken by Hall et al. (1989) of more than 400 families showed that many parents do help children with writing at home without waiting for suggestions or support from schools – a finding that was probably fairly obvious given the large numbers of reading and writing work books that are published and sold in shops and supermarkets. The research reported by Minns (1990) and Weinberger (1996) give a detailed picture of how parents of very young children spend a great deal of time sharing books with them. Their findings recognised the learning that parents encourage in the home, demonstrated that the majority of parents are keen to participate in children's education and suggested that the informal contribution that parents make to their children's learning can be educationally beneficial.

Many schools have more formal schemes for working with parents. Increasingly these are based on Hannon's (1995) ORIM framework. Hannon suggested that parents can provide opportunities, recognition, interaction and models of literacy at home. The opportunities, recognition, interaction and models framework is also used at school but at home children benefit from a high adult–child ratio and experiencing literacy use in real-life situations. This makes the home a potentially very powerful environment for learning. Not all parents are conscious that the opportunities, recognition, interaction and models that they provide are valuable and this may need to be explained. Schemes such as the Raising Early Achievement in Literacy project (Nutbrown et al., 2005) are intended to help parents understand the benefits of everyday literacy practices in the home. As part of the schemes teachers demonstrate how parents can make best use of literacy opportunities in the home. Parents can recognise and praise children's literate behaviour. They can interact with children by sharing books together, showing children how to write their name on a greeting card, playing games or looking at print in the environment. They can provide children with models of how to read and write and why literacy is an important part of people's lives when they read magazines, newspapers, books, bills and letters or send text messages, complete forms or sign their names.

As well as recognising parental contributions to literacy learning schools may make specific arrangements for parents to continue school learning at home. These can include sending reading books and other school resources home for parents and children to use or through arranging curriculum evenings which provide information about how teachers work on aspects of literacy. Encouraging parents to read with their children, and providing information about school practices creates opportunities for parents to recognise their child's achievements more easily and interact with them more fully.

Making parents feel welcome

When parents visit the school in order to enrol their child, they need to feel welcome. They need to be greeted and put at their ease by all the staff that they meet. Clear notices about what to do when visiting the school, labels on rooms and offices, and a highly visible, attractive and up-to-date parents' notice board give positive messages to visitors. The school prospectus and other booklets that are given to parents should be well-presented, accessible and jargon free.

During their initial contacts with the school, parents can be given information about the ethos, expectations and teaching practised in the school. Their early visits, the information contained in the school booklet and initial meetings with the head will provide some of this information. Parents may have their own expectations of schooling or of this particular school from their own school experiences, older children, friends or the reputation of the school. Initial meetings may be an appropriate forum in which to explore parents' existing knowledge about the school. This can help to avoid later misunderstandings. Early meetings also provide schools with the opportunity to demonstrate the value they place on the learning that children bring to school. When parents are asked about their child's language abilities and interests, staff can make clear why this information is useful and how it benefits pupil learning at school. From the start of the child's school career parents can be given the message that education takes place at home and at school, that children's learning develops in a spirit of partnership between home and school and that it is important for both partners, parents and professionals, to be aware of children's learning experiences at home and at school. Involving parents in this way from the start acknowledges and values parents' intimate knowledge of their own children and signals that, although once children start school there is an important professional input to their learning, the contribution and knowledge of parents are significant.

In order to be actively and productively involved in children's education, parents need information about the school's way of working, what they can do and how they can contribute at school and at home. The more they are aware of this the more confident they will be about participating in the life and work of the school. Information can be given and contact maintained through newsletters, invitations to assemblies and other school events, use of the parents' room and parents' evenings. To make it easier for all parents to attend school events provision should be made for younger children to attend or a school crèche can be provided.

Ways in which parents can be involved in school

There are many ways of involving adults and friends in the language and literacy curriculum at school. The following list suggests ways of employing parents' oral and written abilities to help extend children's language learning:

- run the library;
- run a school book club or shop;
- talk to pupils while supervising activities;
- lead activities such as cooking which involve talk;
- teach games, songs and rhymes to pupils;
- help with school drama productions;
- tell stories to children;
- help bilingual children to read and write in their first language;
- act as a translator for parents and children;
- help children to use the computer for writing and reading;
- make books with children;
- act as a scribe;
- listen to reading;
- act as an interviewee for children's questions.

If parents are to be invited to work with pupils in school guidance needs to be provided by the staff. In order for teachers and parents to work together successfully, it is important that parent helpers are clear about what they are expected to do and that their work is carefully managed and explained by the class teacher. All staff should be familiar with the school's language policy as inviting parents to participate in the language curriculum can lead to questions and queries which will have to be answered consistently by all staff.

Some parents may be able to stay and read to small groups of children first thing in the morning after bringing children to school. Very often these are women, which can, together with the preponderance of female staff in nursery and infant schools, reinforce the idea that boys and men do not read as much as girls and women. To counter this schools might want to make a particular effort to encourage male carers to volunteer. Bilingual parents may be able to read or tell stories in their first language. Some parents may be able to read or tell stories onto tape to help schools to reflect the linguistic diversity of the local community as well as extending the school stock of audio books.

Ways in which parents can be involved at home

In a survey of how parents and teachers listen to children reading aloud Hannon (1995) found that adults do not always make reading a positive experience. When correcting children's errors they sometimes provided negative feedback and insisted on accuracy. Although they paid a lot of attention to helping children use phonic cues to read unknown words they were less likely to draw their attention to the use of other reading strategies. Adults also spent more time on helping children to decode than on discussing the text and finding out if children had understood what they read. Parents may need to be reminded that reading should be a rewarding experience for the child. For example, children can be asked to point out the words that they do recognise rather than being corrected when they make mistakes. The importance of talking to children about their reading can never be overemphasised.

Most schools send home guidance on how parents can share books with their children or listen to them read. This can help parents to do this positively and well. The information given in Figure 9.1 was written for an infant and nursery school booklet and given to all parents on their initial visit to the school and at the start of every school year. It was also explained at termly reading meetings organised by the nursery and reception teachers. It could be complemented by booklets or letters, written by children to their parents, in which they describe the language work that they do in school.

Information about Reading

Reading

All children have a daily reading time in school. They may read books, their own writing or the teacher's writing. They may read alone or in groups, aloud or silently. They also listen to stories. If you would like to know more about reading in school, please come in to see your child's teacher.

Children will bring reading books home each day and we ask all parents/carers to read to, listen to or encourage their child to do some quiet reading at home every day. We feel that the extra attention that parents/carers give to children is very helpful.

Helping children with reading at home

You can help your child with reading in the following ways:

- Read to your child.
- Read with your child.
- Listen to your child read aloud.
- Encourage your child to do some quiet reading.

All children enjoy listening to stories and all children need to have a go at reading. Whatever your child's ability s/he will benefit from a mixture of these activities.

Reading to children

When reading to children talk about the pictures, what is happening, what has happened and what is going to happen in the book. This helps to develop the child's interest in books and understanding of stories.

Reading with children

Sometimes you and your child might read a book aloud together. The child should join in with you when s/he feels confident. If the child attempts a number of words you can stop reading and let the child read alone. When the child stops reading you take over again.

Listening to reading aloud

If the child finds a word difficult there a number of ways that you can help:

- Give the child plenty of time to work out what the word says.
- Encourage the child to guess what the word says.
- Ask the child to guess using the pictures for clues.
- Ask the child what word would make sense.
- Tell the child the word.

If the child uses a word which is different from that in the book, but one that does not change the meaning, don't correct this. The child is understanding what s/he reads and this is good.

If the word does change the meaning, ask the child if that word makes sense. If the child cannot guess the word tell it to him/her.

Quiet reading

All children benefit from looking at books and reading to themselves. Encourage your child to spend 5–10 minutes reading in a quiet place. You may want to ask the child what s/he has been reading about and whether s/he had any problems that you might be able to help with.

If you are not a very confident reader you can still help your child a great deal by looking at books together and talking about the story. The pictures will help. You can also listen while your child reads aloud. The child is still benefiting from practising reading. You may have an older child, relative or friend who can read with the child.

Please take care of books that are sent home, but if a book or folder is lost please tell the teacher so that a new book or folder can be supplied.

We have a bookshop in school every Thursday afternoon. Parents, carers and children are welcome to buy books.

We all want children to enjoy and succeed at reading. If you have any queries about your child's reading please talk to your child's teacher.

Figure 9.1   Information for parents about reading

Some schools encourage parents to help their children learn spellings or work on their literacy targets at home. Other schools remind parents that children benefit if parents provide children with resources such as pencils and notebooks and involve children in the real-life and one-to-one literacy activities that are part of home life.

Informing parents about the school curriculum

Schools often organise curriculum meetings and workshops to which all parents are invited. During literacy meetings the focus could be on reading or writing or both. The aims of these evenings are to provide information about the school's approach to the teaching of literacy and to give advice to parents about how to support their child's literacy development at home. They provide an opportunity to invite parents to contribute to the language curriculum in school, either by coming into school or producing materials at home. Meetings and workshops also provide opportunities for staff and parents to get to know each other better. Some suggestions for activities that could be included in a writing workshop for parents are given in Figure 9.2.

A reading workshop might have two functions. It might help parents to become more aware of the value of the opportunities, recognition, intervention and models of reading that are provided at home. It might also be a way of explaining how they can share books with their children at home. An outline for a reading meeting is given in Figure 9.3.

A Writing Workshop for Parents

How and why do we write?

Ask the adults to make a list of all the writing they can remember doing during the previous seven days. When the lists are complete ask how people wrote some of the things included on their lists. What was it written on? How long did it take to write? What was it written with? Was it written out more than once? If so, what was corrected on the second draft and how was it corrected? The answers to these questions should raise some interesting issues about the factors that affect how we write and the reasons for writing. At this point audience, purpose, style, transcription, composition and any other issues that emerge from the lists that the parents have generated can be discussed. Teachers can compare the range of writing that has been identified by the adults with the variety of opportunities for writing that are offered to children at school and at home.

The writing process

Talk to the adults about the process of writing. Use slides of the children's writing to show how development occurs over time and to explain how writing is learned. Discuss how, when and why teachers intervene and correct children's writing.

Spelling

Give the parents a spelling test of ten commonly misspelt words. This should illustrate the point that spelling is a difficult skill for most people. The teachers can then explain that spelling needs to be learned and taught in a systematic way, not just corrected. The staff might explain the look, cover, write, check approach and any other methods that are used in school. Staff may like to illustrate this by 'teaching' the adults how to spell a word correctly.

Handwriting

Ask the adults to look at all the writing they have done so far during the evening and to consider whether it was uniformly neat, well-formed and legible. Were there any crossings-out in the spelling test? Did the neatness matter? If someone else was to be reading the writing would they copy it out? Follow this by discussing the school's policy on handwriting.

Asking adults to write

The parents can be asked to write a short description of the meeting for the children to read the next day. They should be given a time limit. Observe how the adults approach and carry out the task. Give feedback on what writers do when they write and what they need. Issues such as drafting, making mistakes, the value of collaboration and time should arise from this activity.

Writing a book

If children have been invited to the session ask the parents and the children to work together to write a book. The parents could write a story drawn from their childhood experiences. The children could illustrate the book. Again the adults should be able to see that writing is not straightforward. It calls for planning and drafting and it takes time to produce something for someone to read. The adults might like to continue and complete this activity at home.

Helping at home

Give parents some ideas about how they can help with writing at home in ways that will support the school's approach to writing. Providing children with resources for writing, including notebooks, pads and envelopes and allowing children to join in writing shopping lists, letters and greeting cards are good starting points. Many parents may already provide these activities and resources but it might be reassuring for them to realise how valuable these activities are.

Displays

As a backdrop to the meeting have displays of children's writing and the books that they have made arranged around the school. Display first drafts as well as the final piece of writing. Provide written explanations of the work. Some of these could be written by the children, and if appropriate link the writing that is displayed to the Early Years Foundation Stage curriculum and the Primary Framework for Literacy.

(Continued)

(Continued)

Questions

Questions should be answered fairly and honestly. If teachers can convince parents of their commitment to and interest in children's progress it is likely that the parents will support the approach that is advocated by the school.

By the end of the meeting all the adults present might have remembered how hard writing can be, that it is rarely right first time, that sometimes ideas are hard to find and that neatness is not necessarily the most important part of writing. They might have more understanding about how children's writing develops and gained some insights into the way that the staff of the school help the children to become successful and motivated writers. They may also have become more confident about the support that they give children at home.

Helping at school

Teachers can take the opportunity to invite adults to work in school. They can explain and give examples of how adults can help with writing and ask for volunteers.

Figure 9.2   A writing workshop for parents

A Reading Meeting

Reading pictures

This is a fun yet relevant ice-breaker activity that can prevent the meeting from seeming too serious. Parents can be given a picture and asked to imagine what happened before the picture was taken and what will happen afterwards. This activity helps participants to understand how much information is contained in pictures. It can help them appreciate how helpful pictures are to beginning readers and to understand that spending time looking at pictures helps children to read and understand books.

Reading activities at home

To begin the meeting, teachers can talk about the benefits of involving children in the daily literacy events of the home, such as shopping, using e-mail, reading street names and reading mail such as postcards and letters together. They can talk about the benefits of children joining in literacy activities when there is a high adult–child ratio and where activities are relevant and interesting to the child. Teachers might want to make clear that children learn from siblings, grandparents and other relatives as well as parents.

Explaining the school's approach

To give parents a picture of what happens in school, teachers might explain:

- the way that books are used in school;
- the development of reading in the early stages;

- the procedure for sharing a book with a child;
- the reading experiences that all children receive.

Explaining the home–school scheme

The practical arrangements of the scheme can be explained, including the frequency with which children should take books home, the selection of books to go home, and filling in the record and comments card or booklet. Teachers might refer parents to the school's explanatory booklet about the scheme at home.

Providing guidance about how to listen to reading

The staff can talk parents through a list of guidelines for sharing books with children which could include the following suggestions:

- Sessions should be short – about ten minutes is usually long enough.
- If possible read together about three times a week.
- Let the child sit close to you.
- Give plenty of praise.
- You don't always have to listen to reading aloud, you can read to your child.
- Encourage the child to guess at words that he can't read.
- Look at and discuss the illustrations.
- Talk to the child about the book.
- Do ask for advice if you have any queries or worries.

Videos such as those one produced by the Centre for Language in Primary Education (CLPE, 1999) or the DfEE (2000) are very useful in demonstrating many of the points that teachers might want to make, or schools can make their own video of children reading to adults in school and at home. Teachers can also role play the wrong and the best way to hold reading sessions at home.

Figure 9.3   Outline for a reading meeting

The Reading Connects Family Involvement Toolkit available from the Literacy Trust available on http://www.literacytrust.org.uk/readingconnects/Family_Involvement_Toolkit.pdf contains some excellent suggestions about activities and projects that can encourage parents and children to read together. It has some useful ideas about reaching out to fathers and ethnic minority parents.

Working individually with parents

When working with parents schools can adopt the role of the knowledgeable or senior partner. In this kind of relationship parents are expected to act on the instructions of the school and adopt school literacy practices at home. As more is learned about the proactive part parents take in the education of their children, this relationship is changing. Children benefit most when schools and parents engage in real dialogue about learning and where the sort of help that best suits each child is the result of negotiation (Hancock, 1995; Roberts, 2001). For this to happen parents and teachers need to discuss the specific needs of individual children. Before making suggestions about the sorts of activities that children can engage in at home teachers need to know what help parents already provide and what help their circumstances allow them to give. This more open and flexible form of partnership requires a willingness to listen. It can be beneficial because it allows parents and teachers to learn more about the child and it allows the help that is discussed to fit the child's needs.

Parent–teacher meetings

In *The Primary Language Record*, Barrs et al (1988) suggest that there should be a 15-minute discussion between parent and teacher during the child's first term at school in order for parents and teachers to share their knowledge about the child. They give a clear set of guidelines which are helpful for setting up successful meetings between parents and teachers, suggesting the following:

- Parents should be contacted personally through written invitations, conversations or phone calls.
- Schools should offer day and evening times to suit parents' circumstances.
- Once appointments are arranged they should be adhered to in order to minimise disrupting child care or other arrangements.
- Interviews should take place in a private, comfortable area.
- If necessary the services of an interpreter should be arranged.
- Parents should be clear that the purpose of the meeting is the educational welfare of the child.
- Important and useful points should be recorded.
- Such meetings give parents the opportunity to contribute to children's records.

The discussion should focus on the child's speaking, listening, reading and writing experiences out of school, including his attitudes, language opportunities and interests. As well as finding out more about the child, the meeting provides the teacher with an opportunity to clarify any queries that the parent might have. These early meetings with new entrants are the first of many regular meetings that take place between parents and teachers.

Parent–teacher meetings are often held yearly or termly and provide further opportunities for teachers and parents to exchange information and discuss children's progress. They should follow a similar format to that for the first meeting. During parent–teacher meetings it is a good idea to have a display of children's reading books for parents to look at. Some parents might find it helpful to see the range of books that are available for and enjoyed by young children.

Ways of bringing home and school learning closer

Working with parents to improve children's reading and writing does not only consist of teachers encouraging parents to support their children's literacy development at home. It can also mean bringing some home and community literacy practices into school. Building on familiar practices means that children do not have to start from scratch when learning to read and write. It can help children to see the relevance of learning and the connection between learning at school and at home. The language and literacy curriculum at school can reflect home literacy practices by using:

- objects and texts from popular culture as a starting point for literacy, play and project work;
- collections of items found in the home as a starting point for discussion and writing;
- e-mail, blogs and websites for reading and writing;
- shops and other businesses in the local area as the stimulus for imaginative play areas;
- members of the community to talk to children.

Maintaining parents' involvement in language and literacy

One-off workshops or booklets might not sustain parental interest or reach every parent, so schools need to continue to send information and requests for help home and to plan a programme of literacy events each year. The school newsletter or website might contain a regular invitation to parents asking for their help in school and might list some of the contributions they could make. Some schools notify parents of the themes that are being undertaken by classes each term and ask for offers of help in relation to the theme, such as talking to children about care of a baby, being interviewed by children about their own memories of school or bringing in items related to the theme for display and discussion. Specific invitations to help with class topics can also be written by the children. Other special literacy events to which parents can be invited, either as participants or observers, are book weeks and sales of second-hand books.

Schools can organise a language open day each year when parents are welcome to observe children at work in class and to look at displays of books and children's writing. They can also be invited to join in with the work in school on that day. Teachers can produce a short booklet containing advice about book selection and the sorts of books to buy or borrow from the public library as well as a brief list of suitable titles. This could be distributed to parents at some point during the school year to encourage and sustain parental interest in literacy.

Some schools encourage parents to read with their children before they start in the reception or nursery class and encourage parents to borrow books for their pre-school children as well as their children who attend the school. Schools can establish a collection of wordless picture books and stories for parents to read to young children for this purpose. This might include the Reading Together series of books published by Walker Books. The stories are simple and enjoyable and each book contains notes on how to make the most of an adult–child reading session. As well as books some schools and nurseries loan language games and equipment such as story tapes and personal stereos and story sacks to parents to use with their children at home. Schools may also wish to loan books or videos about literacy to parents who want to know more. Some useful titles include *Read With Me* (Waterland, 1988), *The New Read-Aloud Handbook* (Trelease, 2006), *Babies Need Books* (Butler, 1982) and *Literacy in Practice* (CLPE, 1999). The National Centre for Language and Literacy (http//www.ncll.org.uk) produces a number of easily accessible books and pamphlets that might be of use to parents.

Summary

When working with parents we need to:

- acknowledge the important contribution parents make to children's learning;
- act on the information parents share with schools;
- keep parents informed about the educational work of the school;
- make links between learning at home and learning at school.

 ## Reflective activities

1. Review your school's procedures for new entrants and their parents. How are parents involved and what systems exist for promoting good home–school links? Can you identify or suggest areas for improvement? How might you do this?
2. Try to build up a fuller picture of one child's language and literacy learning outside school. Ask the child, older siblings, previous teachers and parents what activities they enjoy and take part in and who supports the child's learning.
3. How can schools help parents to feel that they are regarded as equal partners in the education of their children?

Suggestions for further reading

Hannon, P. (1995) *Literacy, Home and School: Research and Practice in Teaching Literacy with Parents*. Abingdon: Falmer Press. The author suggests new ways of thinking about parental involvement. He describes key findings from research into literacy work with parents and suggests a framework to underpin practice in schools.

Nutbrown, C., Hannon, P. and Morgan, A. (2005) *Early Literacy Work with Families: Policy, Practice and Research*. London: Sage. This book provides a review of the research into family literacy initiatives and provides practical examples of work undertaken with parents.

10

Assessment

Introduction

> **This chapter covers:**
>
> - a rationale for assessment;
> - assessing speaking and listening;
> - assessing reading;
> - assessing writing;
> - end of key stage tests.

A rationale for assessment

Why teachers assess

Ideally there should be close links between assessment and teaching. Assessment is 'an integral part of teaching and learning' (SCAA, 1995) and 'lies at the heart' of the process of promoting children's learning (DES, 1988b). Collecting and analysing information and evidence about children's achievements and experiences provides teachers and others with insights into what has been learned and how it has been learned, and enables teachers to understand more about the learning needs of the pupils they work with. This should lead to more effective teaching. As curriculum planning is informed by the learning needs of pupils, the more understanding teachers have about pupils as learners, the more closely they will be able to match planning and teaching to pupils' needs. In short, assessment can help teachers to modify and fine-tune their teaching and improve the quality of pupil learning.

There are other reasons for assessment besides providing teachers with feedback about pupil learning and their own teaching. Assessment can:

- provide a statement of current attainment;
- be used to compare pupils;

- measure progress;
- be used to diagnose or confirm learning difficulties;
- inform schools' long-term planning and the provision of resources.

When assessment takes place

Assessment can take place at the end of a period of learning, for example at the end of a year or at the end of a key stage. Assessment also takes place every day and in every session as teachers make judgements about how well children are succeeding at the tasks that have been planned for them. Assessment at the end of a period of learning is known as assessment *of* learning or summative assessment. It summarises where learners are at a given point in time. Daily, continuous assessment is known as assessment *for* learning or formative assessment. Assessment for learning involves collecting information about the progress and needs of pupils and planning teaching to ensure their continued progress. It directly influences teachers' weekly planning as they consider how to make provision for children who need to revisit learning and children who need to move on. Assessment of learning has a less immediate impact on teaching. Initially it informs the school's long-term plans and whole-school targets and then influences teachers' medium- and short-term plans. For example, if at the end of a key stage many children are underachieving at reading whole-school decisions will be made about how to prioritise reading during the next school year. If a decision is made to arrange booster classes or to invest in new resources this will eventually affect teachers' weekly planning for English, but not immediately.

What is assessed

The aspects of learning that should be assessed are progress in knowledge, skills and understanding and the development of positive attitudes. There should be a match between what the teacher intends children to learn and the criteria for assessment. As most English teaching is planned using the objectives in the Early Years Foundation Stage curriculum (DfES, 2007a) and the Primary Framework for Literacy (DfES, 2006a) these objectives are often used as assessment criteria. Attitudes to learning are not usually specified as learning objectives but it is important to monitor attitudes. Children who enjoy their learning are in a better position to make progress than those who lack motivation or concentration.

How learning is assessed

When teachers make assessments they are making thoughtful, professional judgements about learning based on evidence. To do this they need to collect information. There are a number of ways to collect information about what children can do and understand and their attitude to learning, including:

- observing children as they work;
- analysing samples of work;
- having discussions with pupils;

- noting responses during teaching sessions;
- holding literacy conferences;
- marking children's work;
- talking to parents;
- talking to teachers and other adults who work with the child;
- looking at the results of school, local authority or national tests.

Most assessment is carried out by the class teacher. However, parents and other adults who work with the children may offer further perspectives on children's development in listening, speaking, reading and writing. Parents may talk about when the child chooses to read and write outside school, or if they have noticed a change in the child's attitude towards literacy. Parents of bilingual children may be able to tell the teacher about the child's knowledge and understanding of languages other than English. In Foundation Stage settings all the adults who work there are usually involved in making assessments of children.

Audiences for assessment

There are a number of audiences for the assessments that are made in school. Teachers are perhaps the most immediate audience as they are in a position to act quickly on the results of their discoveries. The immediate feedback that teachers give to children as they read and write is based on assessment. This means children can benefit straight away from the assessments that are made. Teachers share their judgements about pupils with parents, not only through the legal requirement of a yearly report but also at other times throughout the school year. This may be done formally at open evenings and informally if the teacher or parent wishes to ask about or discuss issues related to progress.

Government bodies use the results of assessments to keep a check on national standards and trends. They may use this information to support educational initiatives and research in areas where standards are not as high as is desirable. Local education authorities use the results of assessments to monitor standards in their schools. They may also operate screening procedures in order to identify children who need extra help, often in aspects of literacy. All those who contribute to the life of the school, including governors, will be concerned with the achievements of their pupils. They need to keep track of the progress that children make over time in order to ensure that standards are maintained or that action is taken to improve them.

The assessment of language and literacy

Standards in English are probably monitored more closely than those in any other area of the curriculum, particularly in the early years of schooling. Success at listening and speaking, reading and writing, is considered to be essential for every child. In order to assess each child's development in language appropriately, teachers need a thorough understanding of the way in which competence in speaking, listening, reading and writing develops.

They need to remain aware of the long-term aims of development in language and literacy, which include enabling all children to become confident and critical users of language for their own purposes, and they need to make sure that the shorter-term goals which are assessed indicate progress towards the long-term aims. Assessment should always begin by looking at what children can do and then identifying areas where they could do better. It is where room for improvement is noted that targets for development can be set so that the child will continue to make progress.

Assessing speaking and listening

The aspects of speaking and listening which are monitored
By the time children enter the Foundation Stage or Key Stage 1, the majority of them will already have many skills in speaking and listening. However, their vocabulary, sentence structure and their use of spoken language in social situations and to support their thinking and learning will continue to develop during their time at school.

The DfES (2007a) have provided detailed guidance about what should be monitored during the Foundation Stage. Two main aspects of language should be assessed. These are children's use of language for communication and language for thinking. Within these adults should expect to notice a developing ability to communicate easily with others, to enjoy language and integrate it into play, to listen attentively, to use a more extensive vocabulary, to speak with increasing confidence and clarity and to explore experiences and clarify ideas. The Primary Framework for Literacy (DfES, 2006a) identifies four areas that should be taught and assessed during Key Stage 1. These are speaking, listening and responding, group discussion and interaction and drama. Children are expected to develop skills, such as clarity, fluency and turn-taking. They should also demonstrate a growing ability to match their use of language to the situation and the listener and to use language to think and learn.

The objectives in the guidance for the Early Years Foundation Stage and the Literacy Framework need some unpacking when they are used to assess children's progress. For example, teachers need to assess 'attentive listening' and 'listening with concentration', two statements in the Literacy Framework for listening and responding for children in the Foundation Stage and Year 1. To demonstrate this, children need to show that they can listen in different contexts. This might include listening to each other, to tapes and stories and to adults. To show that they have attended or concentrated they will need to respond to what they have heard by asking questions, commenting, interpreting, relating what they have heard to their own experience or acting on instructions. The appropriateness of their response will also be important and will involve them demonstrating confidence and sensitivity about when and how to contribute. It is also important to be clear about what is not being assessed. It is not children's accent, dialect, length of contribution, opinions, or their confidence and leadership qualities.

How and when speaking and listening are assessed

With speaking and listening, as with every other area of the English curriculum, it is helpful if teachers build up a record of children's achievements and progress over time. This involves observing and noting children's spoken interactions within normal classroom activities across the curriculum. To facilitate this, it is useful for teachers to indicate in their weekly planning the activities that lend themselves to observations of children using talk in a variety of situations, across different curriculum areas and with a range of partners and audiences or where they can have extended conversations with children.

Within their observations teachers may want to record samples of children's talk using notes or a tape recorder as well as noting spontaneous examples of children demonstrating positive achievements as speakers and listeners. By having examples of children's successes over time they will have sufficient evidence to provide information which may help with future curriculum planning and provision for speaking and listening. They will also have the information they will need when they are making a summary of each child's progress and achievements to pass on to the next teacher, share with other relevant adults or use for their assessment at the end of a phase of learning.

Since teachers are concerned with discovering positive achievements they will need to consider a number of factors, not necessarily related to oral ability, that may affect the quality of children's talk when they are undertaking assessments. These include the:

- nature of the audience or listener;
- type of task that has been set to stimulate the use of talk;
- child's interest in and ownership of the task;
- child's previous experience of using speaking and listening during this sort of task;
- child's fluency in his home language as well as in English;
- child's gender and that of his partner or other group members;
- child's personality;
- composition of the group.

Teachers know that assessment is never based on a single activity but on a range of evidence built up over time from a number of different situations in which children engage in different kinds of talk. Evidence from a variety of contexts is particularly important when assessing speaking and listening since it is an area where it is easy to make an unfair assessment by overestimating the confident, loud speaker in a group and underestimating quieter children who may be using speaking and listening effectively.

Because talk is not permanent it is important that teachers have a system in place which will enable them to capture moments which show a child using talk well. They or the teacher assistant can make quick notes as an activity is taking place or very soon after. The notes can be transferred to a record sheet later if this is necessary. Apart from the times when a child makes an unusual or surprising contribution it is most helpful to have criteria for assessment in mind. These may be the learning objectives for the session. Some teachers have a checklist which acts as a reminder of what to look out for. Figure 10.1 is an example of a

---

Things to look out for in children's speaking and listening

Language for communication
Look for:

- clarity, coherence, audibility, detail, pace
- ability to communicate one to one, in small groups, large groups, to known and unknown audiences
- listening skills
- ability to interest an audience
- use of formal/informal language
- range of vocabulary, use of technical terms
- use of standard English, dialect, slang

Language for thinking and learning
Look for:

- explanations
- exploring ideas
- asking questions
- predicting
- reasoning
- giving examples
- making connections
- changing ideas
- challenging

Speaking
Can the child use talk for a variety of purposes and with different audiences? This includes:

- enjoyment
- developing ideas
- explaining
- planning
- investigating
- sharing ideas and insights
- sharing opinions
- reading aloud
- telling stories
- reporting
- describing
- evaluating

Listening and responding
Can the child listen to a variety of speakers in different situations? This includes:

- the teacher
- classmates
- friends
- older pupils
- younger pupils
- visitors
- parents
- videos
- tapes
- assembly
- formal presentations
- drama
- story sessions
- poetry
- whole-class discussion
- paired work
- group work

Group discussion and interaction
Can the child take on different roles and participate in talk with others? This includes:

- willingness to work with others
- their role in the group
- the variety of roles they adopt
- turn-taking
- encouraging others to speak
- listening and responding to others constructively
- making suggestions

Drama
Can the child use drama to create, share and evaluate ideas? This includes:

- role play
- improvisation
- performance
- reciting poems
- presentations

Figure 10.1 Observing speaking and listening

checklist which can be used to assess speaking and listening across the curriculum. It is also helpful to focus on specific children each week so that the speaking and listening of all the children is formally assessed each half term.

Assessing a sample of talk

Even a short extract of children's collaborative talk can provide the teacher with insights into children's strengths and help her to identify what some children might be finding difficult. In the following example three five-year-old children were discussing the character of Mr Gumpy after having read *Mr Gumpy's Outing* (Burningham, 1978) in a guided reading session. The discussion was the follow-up activity to the reading. The children had been asked to consider what they knew about Mr Gumpy and to jointly make a list of words to describe the sort of person he is.

> **A**: Mr Gumpy, right, he's kind.
> **B**: He makes … takes them for a picnic … But they muck about.
> **C**: And … and they all fall in the water and it's the end of the trip.
> **A**: But they get to have something in his house.
> **B**: He's … kind or … good.

In this extract the children demonstrate their ability to:

- communicate in a small group;
- use language appropriate to the task and when communicating with peers;
- cooperate, take turns and not dominate;
- speak with confidence, clarity, coherence and audibly;
- use a varied and appropriate vocabulary;
- make relevant contributions;
- reason;
- summarise;
- listen to others.

The children were discussing something that was familiar to them. This no doubt contributed to the confidence they showed. They listened carefully to each other as B's repetition of 'kind' shows. Yet he was able to alter this to 'good' demonstrating his ability to incorporate different vocabulary into his talk and his ability to think independently. Both A and B provide evidence for their judgements about Mr Gumpy showing their ability to reason. C only made a brief contribution to this discussion and so the teacher might want to observe C talking in another situation to find out how well he is speaking and listening.

Assessing reading

The aspects of reading which are monitored

The aim of teaching children to read is not just to produce children who can read but also children who want to read, who do read for their own purposes and who can learn from and evaluate what they read. To this end teachers need to assess a great many aspects of reading. They assess the child's competence and use of reading strategies, his attitude to reading, his choice of reading material and his understanding of and response to what is read.

As with speaking and listening and with writing, most assessment of reading is formative and informs the teacher's day-to-day actions in the classroom. The teacher learns a great a deal about children's reading through normal classroom activities and interactions. In many situations such as guided and individual reading sessions the teacher is able to give children immediate feedback and guidance.

Ways of assessing reading

Regular reading sessions

Sessions when children read aloud to an adult either alone or in a guided reading session are probably the most common method of assessing pupils' reading. Listening to children read and discussing reading with children can give the teacher a great deal of information about children's reading strategies and their understanding of what they read. At the end of a reading session the teacher should plan appropriate follow-up work that will help the child to make further progress in reading. Teachers should maintain a record of these reading sessions as in Figure 10.2 which shows a record of individual reading sessions and Figure 10.3 which shows a record of a child's reading during guided

Date	Book	Child's strengths	Teacher strategies
12.05.07	*Titch*	Selected the book himself. Remembered the title from when I read the book to the class. Able to point out the word Titch.	Read the book to D. Asked him to tell the story using memory and illustrations. Gave D the tape and the book to read and take home.
19.05.07	*Titch*	Was able to read it with support. Discussed the book well. Recognised some words: bike, little, big.	Read with D. Looked closely at some words and discussed the letters *b* and *l*. Asked D to use and write *big* and *little* in sorting activities.
24.05.07	*I Like Books*	Talked about the pictures. D named a number of favourite books, e.g. the *Little Bear* books.	Looked for the words *books* and *like*. Use this book for guided reading next week for practice and to boost D's confidence.

Figure 10.2 David's reading record

Guided Reading Record year 1: Carly Smith		
Word recognition: decoding	**Understanding and interpreting texts**	**Engaging with and responding to texts**
Recognise and use alternative ways of pronouncing graphemes	Identify main events and characters, and find specific information in simple texts	Select books and give reasons for choices
Identify the constituent parts of two-syllable and three-syllable words to support the application of phonic knowledge and skills	Use syntax and context when reading	Visualise and comment on events, characters and ideas, making imaginative links to their own experiences
Recognise an increasing number of high-frequency words	Make predictions showing an understanding of ideas, events and characters	Distinguish fiction and non-fiction texts and the different purposes for reading them
Read more challenging texts Using phonic knowledge and skills and automatic recognition of high-frequency words	Recognise the main elements that shape different texts	
Read phonically decidable two-syllable and three-syllable words	Explore patterns of language and repeated words and phrases	
	Speaking	**Group discussion and interaction**
	Retell stories, ordering events using story language	Ask and answer questions, make relevant contributions, offer suggestions and take turns
	Interpret a text with some variety in pace and emphasis	

Book	Targets	Book	Targets
Where's My Teddy? Made good use of syllables to recognise some words, e.g. sobbing	To have a go at longer words using sounds, meaning and illustration, e.g. giant-sized, horrible		
Enjoyed the rhyming words and the humour	Help her with these before she begins to read a new book		

Figure 10.3 Guided reading record

reading. In Figure 10.2 the teacher has noted the books that David has chosen, some of his reading strategies, such as his ability to remember some words and stories, his confident attitude to reading and the sort of support and teaching strategies she has given to him during the sessions and will continue to offer to him. In this extract these include working on meaning, word recognition and phonic strategies.

These records, together with the child's home-reading notebook containing a list of books shared at home and comments from other adults, would present a very full picture of the children's reading.

Sharing books will always involve the child in some reading aloud, but fluent readers who have a firm grasp of decoding strategies and who are at the stage of reading silently may spend very little time reading to the teacher. The child might only read a short extract from their current book because the teacher will be able to assess their progress mainly through discussion and their retelling. The aim for these children is to deepen their understanding of what they read and keep them interested in reading by suggesting new authors and books for them to read.

Observations

Teachers can learn a great deal about their pupils as readers from observing them in a number of reading contexts. These contexts include children:

- listening to, telling or participating in stories in sessions led by an adult;
- retelling stories using story props;
- browsing and choosing books to read for pleasure, use in class or take home;
- reading with other children;
- reading silently, either voluntarily or during quiet reading times;
- demonstrating incidental awareness and use of print;
- discussing books and authors;
- incorporating literate behaviour or actions and words from stories into play.

Observations of children in these situations help the teacher to build up a full picture of:

- how the child reads – with independence, with confidence, with interest, out of choice, in English or in another language;
- when the child reads – with others, alone, out of choice;
- what the child reads – published stories, books written by the class, non-fiction texts, dual-language texts; and
- the strategies the child uses when reading.

The teacher can make a note of anything she observes that is particularly striking or that reveals a pattern in the child's behaviour and add this to the reading record. Alternatively she may feel that there is some aspect of the child's reading behaviour that she would like to verify and so deliberately make time to observe the child's interactions with books in a number of different situations.

Reading conferences

Conferences are a means of monitoring children's interests, attitudes and knowledge about reading and provide a detailed picture of children's reading strengths. They can begin in the nursery class and ideally they should take place about once a term. During a reading conference the child will read aloud a whole book or a substantial amount of text. The amount that is read should be sufficient to allow the teacher to note the range of word recognition strategies which the child uses and the balance between them. The teacher can also make notes on the child's confidence, independence, involvement and enjoyment. With less experienced readers, in the Foundation Stage, teachers may be particularly interested in noting the child's use of book language, his ability to read the illustrations and his awareness of print as well as skills such as directionality, one-to-one correspondence and the ability to recognise some words and letters. After the reading the child is invited to talk about his response to the text and this gives the teacher further insights into the child's comprehension and his ability to evaluate what he reads. The child is invited to talk at some length about himself as a reader and the books that he enjoys. He may have prepared for a reading conference by reviewing his own reading diary or looking back at the list of books he has read since the beginning of term. As the child reads and speaks the teacher may make notes which will be included in the child's records. At the end of the session the teacher should read what has been written to the child and ask whether the child wants to change or add to her notes. After the conference the teacher can think about the experiences and support that the child should be given to enable him to make further progress as a reader. She may draw up targets for the child's reading development during the next term. These may be shared and agreed with the child; when this happens it is a useful way of involving children in their own learning.

Reading diaries

Children can keep their own lists of what they read. If these are kept in a personal reading diary there will be space for children to write comments about some of the books or authors they encounter during the year. If reading diaries are shared with adults they can respond to the children's comments. Reading them gives adults a useful insight into the child's tastes, range, understanding and responses to books.

Checklists

As a way of keeping track of children's early development in reading, some teachers like to fill in or refer to lists of signs which demonstrate children's growing competence in reading. They might include characteristics such as:

- demonstrates an interest in books;
- chooses to look at books;
- is able to recognise his own name;
- is able to retell a story using picture clues.

For more experienced readers teachers might want to see signs such as:

- takes over from adult when sharing a book;
- is able to self-correct when reading;
- is able to talk critically about what he reads;
- enjoys silent reading.

Schools very often compile their own lists and make them appropriate to the age and experience of the pupils that they cater for. Even if checklists are not used as a record for each child, they can be a helpful reminder about the sorts of behaviours which indicate progress in reading development.

Miscue analysis

Miscue analysis (Goodman and Burke, 1972) is a detailed and systematic method of listening to a child read. It is a diagnostic assessment technique which can provide the teacher with insights about the reader's strengths and areas for development. The miscues or mistakes that the child makes while reading help the teacher to understand which strategies the child is using. The word miscue is used rather than mistake because miscues reveal strengths as well as weaknesses.

Miscue analysis requires no special materials. Young children can read a complete picture book, more experienced readers can read a passage of text containing about 150 words. This should not be too easy or too familiar but neither is it necessary to make the reading frustrating or unnecessarily difficult. The teacher needs a copy of the text which the child will read on which to note the miscues, although some teachers prefer to tape record the child's reading and fill in the miscues later. Before beginning the miscue analysis the teacher and child should discuss the book and the teacher can support the child as he reads the opening few sentences. The child should be told that for most of this reading session the teacher will not provide the usual support and will only intervene if the child is really stuck. Once the child begins reading alone the teacher notes the miscues that occur using a consistent form of notation. The most common types of miscues and the symbols used to represent these are shown in Figure 10.4.

The possible causes of the different types of miscue are summarised in Figure 10.5. Substitutions are the most common miscues and often the most helpful to teachers. They give the most insight into the strategies that a child uses to decode words.

In addition to noting the reader's miscues the teacher also observes the way in which the child reads, listening for the child's use of intonation, fluency and awareness of punctuation. After the child has finished reading the teacher may ask the child to retell the story and then talk about the child's response to what has been read. The analysis of the miscues, the teacher's observations and the child's summary and comments provide the adult with a full picture of the child's strengths and weaknesses as a reader. They indicate the strategies the child employs and his understanding of reading as an activity. After the analysis the teacher should have sufficient information about the child's reading to plan a reading programme for the child.

Miscue		Symbol
Non-response	The child is unable or unwilling to read a word or part of a word	Underline the word with dashes
Insertion	The child inserts a word or words not present in the text	Use an insertion mark and note the word that was inserted
Omission	The child leaves out a word	Circle the word omitted
Hesitation	The child pauses for some time before continuing to read	Insert a stroke before the word
Repetition	The child repeats a word before reading on	Underline the word
Reversal	The child reads the words in the wrong order	Indicate the words with an arrow or curved line
Self-correction	The child says the word incorrectly at first and then says another or the correct word	Write in the substituted word and then amend with a tick
Substitution	The child substitutes a word for the one in the text	Cross out the word in the text and write the substituted word above it

Figure 10.4   Miscue notation

Type of miscue	Reason for miscue
Non-response	Word or concept outside the child's experience. Child lacks confidence in making predictions.
Insertion	Fluent reading, eyes ahead of voice.
Omission	Fluent reading, when there is no interruption to meaning. Negative omission occurs when the reader does not recognise the word.
Hesitation	Trying to decode the text. Trying to understand confusing syntax, style or meaning.
Repetition	Uncertainty about the word or meaning. Trying to understand confusing syntax, style or meaning.
Reversal	May indicate fluent reading, where the reader is adapting what is written into a form closer to familiar speech patterns, e.g. 'Martin said' rather than 'said Martin'.
Self-correction	Understands that reading involves making meaning. Trying to make sense of the text.
Substitution	The child does not recognise the word but makes a guess.

Figure 10.5   Causes of miscues

Classroom example: miscue analysis

Figure 10.6 is an example of a miscue analysis undertaken with Philip, aged 6, reading *Suddenly!* (McNaughton, 1994).

Suddenly! by Colin McNaughton

Potter
~~Preston~~ was walking home from school one day when suddenly!

Potter/
Peter   re-eme-m
~~Preston~~ remem̲bered his mum had asked him to go to the shops.

Preston was doing the shopping when suddenly!

The disaster   He/remembers   monkey
~~He dashed~~ out of the shop! (He / remembered he had left the shopping ~~money~~ in his
        d-esk
school desk.)

                could/called   the   w-as
Preston ~~collected~~ the money from ~~his~~ desk and was coming out of the school when suddenly!

Peter
~~Preston~~ decided to use the back door.

One   Peter   it have/hear/have
~~On~~ his way back to the shop ~~Preston~~ stopped at the park ~~to~~ have a little play when suddenly!

        b-u-ll shot   p-ast
Billy the ~~bully shoved~~ past him and went down the slide!

Potter   copied
~~Preston climbed~~ down from the slide and went to do the shopping. He was just coming out
of the shop when suddenly!

    P-l-i-m-p sh-op-k-eep-er   Potter
Mr Plimp the shopkeeper called ~~Preston~~ back to say he had forgotten his change.

        Peter a-rr-i-v-ed   a   standing
At last ~~Preston~~ arrived home. "Mum," he said. "I've had ~~the strongest~~ feeling that someone
has been following me." Suddenly!

Peter's   tt   round he   goes   e
~~Preston's~~ Mum t̲urned ~~around and gave~~ him an e̲normous cuddle!

Source: McNaughton (1994) *Suddenly!* Reproduced with permission from Anderson Press.

Figure 10.6   Miscue analysis: *Suddenly!*

Analysis of Philip's reading

Word recognition

Philip used a variety of strategies to help him read this book. His use of phonics was the main strategy. He regularly used initial and the second and third letters to help him when he came across words that were unfamiliar. This often helped. He was able to blend or synthesise groups of sounds which is a good phonic strategy. In the longer words he did not sound out the letters at the end. He tended to sound out or respond to consonants rather than vowel sounds. He might need to revisit some phonic sounds associated with vowels, in particular long vowel sounds and vowel digraphs. His incomplete use of phonics led him to make some inaccurate guesses.

(Continued)

(*Continued*)

He drew on his knowledge of the English language to make grammatically appropriate substitutions. He was generally aware when what he read did not make sense. At these points he looked intently at the illustrations for clues but needed an adult to help him. He is beginning to self-correct but needs to use this strategy more. The miscues Philip made are itemised and explained in Figure 10.7.

Comprehension

Philip was not familiar with the Preston Pig books. However, when he looked at the book before reading it, he was able to read the illustrations and used them to talk about the story fairly accurately. In response to the question, 'What do you think the story is about?' Philip replied, 'A wolf eating a pig, but he's a smart pig, he's the smarter one … look at him in all the pages [he pointed to some of the illustrations] … and look, look what else.' He was very enthusiastic about the book. He had seen that it was humorous and when asked to begin reading he said, 'Now this is going to be interesting.' At the end of the reading when asked to say what the story had been about he said, 'The wolf is always trying to get the pig, but always ends up hurting himself, not the smart pig. He is a silly wolf, really.' When pressed and asked if Preston was really a smart pig, Philip thought for a moment and said, 'No, not really I suppose. He was a bit lucky. He doesn't really know what's happening does he? So really, he's a lot lucky … but … the wolf ended up in hospital. That's definitely not smart.'

Philip had a good understanding of this story. He recognised that it was luck that allowed Preston to escape from the wolf and that Preston was unaware of what had been happening. He recognised that the wolf was a comic figure who came to a bad end. Philip was willing to discuss the story and to reflect on his original impressions. He also enjoyed reading the book.

We now know a great deal about Philip's reading and have a good understanding of the areas where Philip could improve. Using the areas for improvement the teacher can set targets to ensure that Philip continues to make progress. The guidance on raising standards in reading (DfES, 2005c) reminds us that targets should cover a balance of word recognition and comprehension strategies. It is also suggested that the work on targets should be incorporated into the work and the teaching methods that form part of normal everyday teaching. Children's progress towards any targets that are set should be monitored regularly so that the targets can be adjusted to fit their developing needs. Targets should be quite specific and should be accompanied by specific suggestions about teaching strategies and activities which will help the child achieve the targets. Below is a list of targets that could be drawn up for Philip based on his reading of *Suddenly!*

Targets for Philip:

- To continue to enjoy reading
- To use phonic strategies to read the ends of words as well as the beginnings
- To learn to recognise function words such as *to, his* and *it*
- To break words into syllables to help him analyse the sounds they contain
- To self-correct when what he reads does not make sense

Preston	He knew this was a name and used the initial letter to help him. *Preston* is an unusual name so he made 2 good attempts as he was reading. *Potter* was perhaps influenced by the Harry Potter books. The teacher did tell him the word twice at the start of the book and he did remember it twice but then reverted to his original guesses. This may have been because he was trying to follow the story and wanted to know what happened.
remembered	He tried to sound this word out and almost used syllables. The teacher supplied the word.
he	He misread this word as *the*.
dashed	Having misread *he*, he needed a noun to follow. He used the initial letter and the *s* to substitute *disaster*. His miscue made sense in itself but not in the sentence and it was not what the author intended.
remembered	He almost read this accurately perhaps recalling it from having been told it earlier.
money	He used the initial letters and the look of the word to substitute *monkey* for *money*. This did not make sense.
desk	He was able to read this word by sounding it out. He ran *e, s* and *k* together which is a good phonic strategy.
collected	He made two attempts at this word using the initial letter as a clue. He realised these were incorrect and the teacher told him the word.
his	Substituting *the* for *his* doesn't alter the meaning of the sentence.
was	Sounding out didn't really help him to read this word but it did buy him time until he remembered *was*.
to	He has substituted one common word for another. The *t* may have been the clue he was using.
have	He originally read this as *have* which was correct but *it have* doesn't make sense so he changed his mind and then, perhaps because he knew it, went back to the correct word.
bully	He sounded out the first syllable to produce *bull*
shoved	*Shot* retains the meaning of the text.
past	He was able to sound out this word and again ran the final three letters together.
climbed	He used the initial letter and substituted a verb, which is grammatically correct, but it doesn't make sense in the sentence.
Plimp	He sounded out the letters and read this word correctly.
shopkeeper	When he put the *k* sound with shop he was able to say *shopkeeper*.
arrived	He tried to sound this word out but said *i* rather than an *I sound* and so the teacher supplied the word.
the	Substituting *a* for *the* doesn't really affect the meaning of the sentence.
strangest	He used the first two letters to help him with this word. *Standing* doesn't make sense.

(*Continued*)

(*Continued*)

turned	He sounded out the first letter but the teacher gave him the word.
around	*round* for *around* does not affect the meaning and often follows *turned*.
and	He was reading the pictures as well as the text and this substitution possibly came from his assumption of what the ending might be rather than the author's words.
gave	*Goes* often follows *He*. He may have been using the first letter as a clue.
enormous	Philip didn't attempt this word. After it had been supplied he said, 'that's a hard word'.

Figure 10.7   Commentary on the miscues that Philip made

Activities and teaching that would help Philip reach his targets:

- To become familiar with a text before reading it to an adult
- To read along to taped stories in order to become familiar with difficult words before reading alone
- To be given help with potentially difficult words prior to reading
- To complete cloze passages to help him find words that retain the meaning of the texts
- To play games which involve matching roots and suffixes to make words
- To play word recognition games
- To be shown strategies which might help him to self-correct, including rereading a sentence and reading beyond the problem word

Guided reading would help Philip as it gives children the opportunity to become familiar with the text before they begin to read it. Difficult words could be identified at the beginning of the session. He would be reminded of the strategies he can use when tackling an unknown word. Finally, at the end he would have the opportunity to discuss the text and reflect more fully on its meaning. Phonic sessions that are a regular feature of the class's literacy work could be geared towards work on long vowel phonemes, vowel digraphs and syllabification.

Miscue analysis is time-consuming for the teacher, but it is truly a 'window on the reading process' (Goodman and Goodman, 1977: 332) and many teachers have found miscue analysis an illuminating experience. By administering one or two miscue analyses with average readers or children who seem to be experiencing difficulties in reading the teacher can gather a great deal of information that she can use with these pupils. She will also learn a great deal about the way she is teaching reading and the strategies she is emphasising. It may be that this will lead the teacher to focus on other strategies with all the children she works with.

Assessing writing

The aspects of writing that are monitored

There are three main aspects of writing to assess. These are composition, transcription and children's attitudes towards writing. The reasons for assessing composition and transcription are clear. These are the skills that teachers teach every day. Despite spending a large part of each school day writing, we know that writing is the aspect of literacy that children do least well in when they are tested at the age of seven. Writing is a difficult skill to master but it may be that children's attitudes also affect their progress in writing.

Children's poor attitudes towards writing at school have been evident for many years. The 1988 Assessment of Performance Unit (APU) survey of language performance revealed that 'not less than two out of ten pupils have developed negative views about writing by the time they are eleven' and that 'such attitudes are established long before pupils reach the age of eleven' so 'It can be assumed that they are established primarily when children are first being taught to read and write' (Gorman et al, 1989: 57). Although poor attitudes may arise for many reasons, children's feelings about writing and their view of themselves as writers are likely to be influenced by the way that writing is taught and the messages that the teacher transmits about writing. Children may become discouraged with writing because they think that they have nothing to say that needs to be communicated through writing. They may not see the purpose of writing. They can become overwhelmed by transcription because the demands that are placed on them to produce neat, correctly spelt writing at the first attempt are difficult to meet. They may decide that writing takes too long if they have to wait for every spelling from the teacher or for the teacher to write their sentence down before they copy it. Writing can become boring because children just do too much of it.

When assessing writing it is helpful to reflect on and evaluate classroom practices. These might not be supporting children's writing development. As well as setting targets for children's development the teacher might want to alter some aspects of her teaching to improve children's learning. Teachers have found the questions in Figure 10.8 useful when examining children's writing and their own practice.

Ways of assessing writing

Teachers make frequent assessments of writing whenever children are engaged in written work. Feedback related to the teacher's assessments is an integral part of the child's learning about writing rather than something separate. As part of the daily assessment process teachers will use a variety of methods including observation, discussion and analysis of the child's writing, involving the child in these procedures whenever possible. Assessing writing in this way provides the teacher with insights into the process of writing as well as the outcome of the activity, providing information about what the child knows as well as about what the child can do.

Composition	About the writing	About classroom practice
	Are the ideas expressed in writing equivalent or nearly equivalent to those expressed orally? Does the child use vivid, imaginative and appropriate language in his writing? Does the child organise his writing clearly? Can the child write in a variety of styles and formats? Is the child able to use longer, more complex sentences?	Do I provide opportunities for children to dictate text to adults? Do I respond to content and organisation first when assessing children's writing? Are a range of writing styles and formats displayed around the classroom? Do I encourage children to 'have a go' at difficult or unfamiliar spellings? Have I given children strategies for collecting ideas for pieces of written work, e.g. brainstorming, listing, etc.? Do I give guidance on ways of organising and planning using drawings, diagrams, headings, etc.? Do I demonstrate all the processes involved in writing through shared and guided writing sessions? Do I encourage children to discuss stories and to base some of their writing on familiar story structures? Do I encourage children to re-read their writing as they write?
Transcription	About the writing	About classroom practice
	Does the child use visual and phonic strategies when spelling? Does the child make use of capital letters, full stops, commas and speech marks in his writing? Is the child's writing clear, legible and correctly formed? Does the child use grammatically appropriate structures in his writing, e.g. sustaining the use of 'he' throughout a narrative written in the third person?	Do I model writing so that children can see spelling in action? Do I encourage children to look at and memorise words as part of my spelling policy? Do I encourage children to notice grammatical features in books during shared, guided and individual reading sessions? Do I encourage children to reread and alter their writing once it is finished? Do I provide opportunities for practising letter shapes in play and creative activities? Do I correct handwriting errors in the presence of the child?
Attitudes	About the child	About classroom practice
	What is the child's attitude to writing? Can the child identify his own reasons for writing? Does the child choose to write freely? Does the child become involved in his writing and sustain his involvement over time?	Am I an enthusiastic writer? Do I convey this enthusiasm to my pupils? Do I provide a range of resources for writing for the children? Do I make provision for writing in play activities? Do I give children a variety of written activities with different purposes and audiences? Is finished writing praised, displayed, published or shared with others? Do I read children's writing so that they understand that writing is an important way of communicating? Do I make use of other ways of recording such as pictures, diagrams and models rather than asking children to write?

Figure 10.8   A framework for examining writing

Observation

Observation involves listening to and watching pupils as they write. Sometimes observations are preplanned and may have a specific focus, or they may occur routinely as the teacher moves around the classroom offering support and checking on children's engagement with the task. Although teachers continually make observations about children's work and progress in the course of daily classroom activities, all children may not be observed equally. Quiet children may receive less teacher attention than children who have difficulties or those who frequently seek the teacher's help. In order to ensure that all children are observed it can be a good idea to draw up a schedule of observations. For instance, teachers may decide to observe one writing activity that will be undertaken by all the children over the course of a few days. The teacher will focus on each group of children as they work at this writing activity. Alternatively the teacher may identify two or three children to observe each day until all the class have been observed as they write. In addition there may be spontaneous and important moments of literacy learning that occur and that are observed. These may represent a significant step in the learning development of a particular child and may be noted or recorded by the teacher.

The two observations which follow are of John and Glen, two Year 2 pupils. Each observation has been analysed to show the value of observational data in adding to one's picture of the child as a learner and in providing evidence for teacher assessments:

2/11/02 John

Tiny writing.

Does not use the page correctly.

Crosses out continually. Can only guess at first letters of words. Little knowledge of letter patterns. Words he knows, 'the', 'and', 'we', 'put'. Writes 'soc' for 'stories'. Does not know letter names. Reverses 'b' and 'd'. Can form other letters correctly.

Doesn't want to write.

Finds it difficult to make the words make sense. Panics about work. Chooses because of difficulties to talk and not complete work.

Needs more opportunities to write for a purpose – short texts.

From this observation it is clear that John is having difficulties with writing and, because he finds it difficult, he does not want to write. The teacher needs to find ways of making writing easier for John. If he is to make progress as a writer he needs to become interested in writing and to understand what it is for. He needs to gain some satisfaction from writing. The observation also indicates that some direct teaching of how to form *b* and *d* would be useful. The teacher might also begin to revise letter names with him and provide some activities that encourage John to look at how words are spelt. He needs to see how writers use the page and how writing is arranged.

The following observation, although primarily about Glen, also features John and gives further information about him as a writer when he is working collaboratively with a more able and enthusiastic child:

12/11/02 Glen and John

Glen asked if he could make a book about *Mrs Plug the Plumber*. Chose John to work with him.

He has now been working on the book for 2 days.

13/11/02

Glen and John read the book to the class today. They are extraordinarily proud of it.

Glen explained how they worked – planning together, writing a first draft together and then each writing a page of the final draft in turn. They also took turns with the illustrations. They needed to refer to the original text to remind themselves of the details of the story.

They worked without any help from me on this project.

More collaborative activities would help John.

Glen needs some challenging, open-ended writing activities where he can research, plan and then write.

Although John has many difficulties with writing, when he is supported by a more able writer, he is able to sustain his interest in writing. Glen is able to work independently for long periods of time and is willing to collaborate with others.

Although these are primarily observations of children writing, because all areas of the English curriculum overlap they also contain evidence of achievement in speaking and listening and reading. The two observations provide a rich picture of both children's strengths, weaknesses and learning styles. They provide the teacher with important information that could be missed if the teacher only referred to samples of work for her assessments. Reflection on these observations gave the teacher an indication of what to work on next with both children in order to meet their individual needs as developing writers.

Writing conferences

Writing conferences may take place when the teacher is reviewing the child's writing profile. This might happen once every term. The child can be asked to select a recent piece of writing to be included in the portfolio or the teacher may ask the child to comment on one or all of the pieces of writing that have already been selected. Teachers can ask pupils how they think they can develop and improve their writing. As the child talks the teacher should note down what is said and include these comments in the profile. These comments may provide additional evidence for assessment and future planning.

Writing conferences involve pupils in the assessment process and provide opportunities for children to reflect on their learning. They enable the teacher to provide the pupil with an input that is directly related to their needs. In this form of assessment the teacher will be asking questions and listening carefully to answers. She may be drawing out ideas and checking understanding. There may be a specific focus for the discussion that enables the teacher to check her observations or to explore an aspect of the child's writing behaviour more thoroughly.

Analysing samples

Teachers can collect and analyse one or two pieces of writing from every child in the class every term. This gives the teacher the opportunity to gain insights into children's progress as writers away from the classroom. The teacher can also add the samples to the children's portfolios and use them as a starting point for discussions with children and parents. It is useful to collect one piece of writing from the beginning of the school year as this provides a baseline from which teaching can proceed and a reference point when assessing how much progress children have made over the course of a term or a year. The rest of the samples that are included should be drawn from a variety of starting points and curriculum areas and represent a variety of styles of writing, for example narrative, poems, notes, records and messages. First drafts as well as fair copies should be included to show how the child revises and corrects his work as well as how he has responded to suggestions from the teacher. Some of the writing may be selected by the child and accompanied by the child's comments. Once a piece of work has been selected it should be dated and then annotated, using headings such as the ones that follow:

- *Context* This section might include notes about how the work arose, the purpose of the writing, the intended audience, the length of time the child spent on the writing and information about the child's previous knowledge or experience in this area.
- *Analysis* This section is concerned with the strengths and weaknesses displayed by the child as a writer. The comments might refer to attitude, content and writing conventions as displayed in the piece of work. If plans and drafts are collected one might note the differences between the drafts and refer to the learning processes that the child has gone through between the first and final copy. It is always useful to look for positive points in children's writing and to ask oneself, what has the child attempted and achieved?
- *Targets and activities* Under this heading the teacher might indicate learning targets and the activities, experiences and work that might help the child to meet the targets.
- *National Curriculum and Primary Literacy Framework requirements* A note could be made here of the Programme of Study requirements covered and the level descriptions reached in this piece of work.

Classroom example: analysing samples of writing

The two samples of writing in Figures 10.9 and 10.10 are taken from the language portfolio of a six-year-old pupil, Imran. Imran's first language was Urdu. At the time of this writing he was able to talk clearly but not fluently in English. He enjoyed writing but tended to rush at his work.

Context

The piece of writing in Figure 10.9 emerged after the children had listened to the story of *William's Doll* (Zolotow, 1972). The children had been asked to think about the sorts of games that both girls and boys like to play.

Analysis

Imran writes easily, confidently and quickly. He had understood the task and responded appropriately. His response is in the form of a list. Imran frequently uses the same letters when he is writing. He does not yet see the connection between sounds and words. He was able to read back what he had written and the teacher wrote the correct version close to his words. Imran and the teacher talked about the letters that were common to both sets of writing. The teacher also talked to Imran about spaces between words.

Figure 10.9   Imran: boys and girls

Targets

Imran needs:

- to think about what he wants to write and how he will write it before he writes;
- to become familiar with the sounds and names of letters;
- to use the initial letters of words when spelling.

Activities to help Imran meet these targets:

- adult demonstrations of thinking before writing during shared writing;
- demonstrations and reminders about planning before writing during guided writing;
- work on letter and phoneme recognition through the planned class work for phonics and spelling;
- involve Imran in letter recognition games such as lotto and snap;
- praise for his positive approach to writing.

Context

The class were working on the theme of 'Homes' and after listening to the story *Charlie's House* (Schermbrucker, 1992) had worked in pairs to make a home for Charlie. The writing in Figure 10.10 was an account of how they had made their model. The children were going to copy out the writing to make explanatory notes for the display of model houses. The title was written on a flip chart for the children to copy. Imran had written:

Friday 6th December
How I made my home
First we got a box
Then we cut the door
Then we put the carpet
Then I me and Kevin finished.

Analysis

This writing demonstrates a vast improvement since September. The writing is organised logically and well. Imran has produced a clear, factual account of his work with Kevin. It includes spaces between words and concludes with a full stop. Imran is beginning to be aware of the features of print. Many of the spellings approximate closely to the correct versions and words such as 'we', 'door' and 'put' are spelt correctly. There is evidence of attention to initial letter sounds and a greater variety of letters than in the earlier sample.

Targets

Imran needs:

- to take greater care with his presentation;
- to proofread his writing;

(Continued)

(Continued)

Figure 10.10 Imran: making a house

- to enlarge his knowledge about a range of writing types;
- to increase the number of words that he can write correctly.

Activities to help Imran meet his targets:

- pair him with a response partner who can proofread his writing;
- draw Imran's attention to the details of print, including the use of upper- and lower-case letters in text during shared and guided writing and when giving feedback;
- focus on word recognition and spelling patterns during shared, guided and individual reading;
- encourage Imran to use classroom resources to find correct spellings of words;
- teach Imran how to try out different versions of spellings when he is unsure;
- provide teaching about different types of writing and audiences through the planned programme of literacy work and writing in other curriculum areas.

Checklists

Some teachers like to include checklists for writing in children's records. These sometimes take the form of a preprinted list of common behaviours seen as children's writing develops. As the child incorporates these strategies into his writing, the relevant box is marked. Some teachers make one mark when the child is beginning to use a strategy and a different sort of mark when the strategy is being used confidently and consistently. A sample version of a checklist for writing development is given in Figure 10.5. The items which have been included in this example are taken from the Primary Framework for Literacy (DfES, 2006a).

Creating and shaping texts	Amy	Billy	Colin	Dan	Emma
Attempt writing for various purposes, using features of different forms such as lists, stories and instructions					
Independently choose what to write about, plan and follow it through					
Use key features of narrative in their own writing					
Convey information and ideas in simple non-narrative forms					
Find and use new and interesting words and phrases, including story language					
Create short simple texts on paper and screen that combine words with images (and sounds)					
Draw on knowledge and experience of texts in deciding and planning what and how to write					
Sustain form in narrative, including use of person and time					
Maintain consistency in non-narrative, including purpose and tense					
Make adventurous word and language choices appropriate to the style and purpose of the text					
Select from different presentational features to suit particular writing purposes on paper and on screen					
Make decisions about form and purpose, identify success criteria and use them to evaluate their writing					
Use beginning, middle and end to write narratives in which events are sequenced logically and conflicts resolved					
Write non-narrative texts using structures of different text-types					
Select and use a range of technical and descriptive vocabulary					
Use layout, format graphics and illustrations for different purposes					

Figure 10.11   Checklist for writing

Peer and self-assessment

Peer and self-assessment can engage children more fully in their learning and help children to become reflective and independent learners. When children are aware of the learning objective for their work they can consider how well they have met the objective. For peer assessment children can work with their response partner. Children need guidance on how to assess their own learning or that of their partner. This was explained in Chapter 4. As well as demonstrating how to work in this way, teachers can sometimes ask children to find one thing in their writing that they are really pleased with and read this to their partner or find one place in their writing that they would like help with and ask their partner for suggestions. Listening to what children say during peer assessment can help teachers to find out what children understand about their work and where they would like to improve.

Immediate feedback

Teachers assess writing when children are engaged in their daily writing activities either independently or in a guided writing activity. At these times teachers are able to provide immediate help and support. Before giving feedback it is important to ask the child to talk about and read back what he has written. When making a response to writing the teacher should first focus on and comment on the content, giving feedback about the positive aspects of what has been written and then provide the child with some form of teaching that is related to his stage of development and his immediate needs. This should relate to the learning objective that was set. For example, do not comment on punctuation if the objective was to write an opening for a story. The teacher's response should be helpful and informative. It is not enough to say or write 'Well done'. The teacher needs to say why the writing is good so that the child can incorporate the good features into his next piece of writing. Similarly, if the writing could be improved the teacher needs to explain how this could be achieved. Ticks, crosses and general comments such as 'good' do not give children the information which they need to develop as writers. The Qualifications and Assessment Authority has provided the following helpful advice on feedback:

- Feedback is more effective if it focuses on the task and is given regularly and while still relevant.
- Feedback is most effective when it confirms the pupils are on the right track and when it stimulates correction of errors or improvement of a piece of work.
- Suggestions for improvement should act as 'scaffolding', i.e. pupils should be given as much help as they need to use their knowledge. They should not be given the complete solution as soon as they get stuck so that they must think things through for themselves.
- Pupils should be helped to find alternative solutions if simply repeating an explanation continues to lead to failure.
- Feedback on progress over a number of attempts is more effective than feedback on performance treated in isolation.
- The quality of dialogue in feedback is important and most research indicates that oral feedback is more effective than written feedback.
- Pupils need to have the skills to ask for help and the ethos of the school should encourage them to do so.

(QCA, 2001)

End of key stage assessments

The Early Years Foundation Stage

Throughout the Foundation Stage, as part of the learning and teaching process, practitioners assess each child's development in relation to the objectives in the *Practice Guidance for the Early Years Foundation Stage* (DfES, 2007a). These assessments are made through observation, discussion and analysis of samples of the child's work as well as through discussions with parents. At the end of the of the Foundation Stage teachers make a summative assessment of the children's learning based on the assessment information they have collected during the year. The summative assessments are recorded in the *Early Years Foundation Stage Profile* (QCA, 2003).

The *Early Years Foundation Stage Profile* is slightly different to the aspects of learning in the *Practice Guidance for the Early Years Foundation Stage* in that communication, language and literacy assessments are made against four scales which correspond to the six aspects of learning in the Practice Guidance. The four assessment scales are: language for communication and thinking, linking sounds and letters, reading and writing. Children can score up to nine points on each assessment scale. The first three points describe a child who is still progressing towards the early learning goals and who is working at the stages which lead up to what is expected at 40–60+ months. The next five points are drawn from the early learning goals. Most children are expected to achieve at least some of the early learning goals by the end of the Foundation Stage. Children who score six or more points are classified as working securely within the early learning goals and have achieved a good level of development. The final point in each scale describes a child who has achieved all the points from one to eight, has developed further both in breadth and depth, and is working consistently beyond the level of the early learning goals. The points on the assessment scale for reading are shown in Figure 10.12.

The profile booklet can be completed periodically throughout the year, using evidence from ongoing assessments, to record the achievement of the items in the scales. Alternatively, schools can use their own recording systems and then summarise their assessments using the scales at the end of the reception year. The profile should form the basis for reports to parents and for information to be passed on to the child's next teacher. If the profile booklet is used throughout the reception year, periodically discussed with parents and completed in the summer term, it can be used instead of a conventional written report at the end of the school year.

Key Stage 1

Children's achievements in English at the end of Key Stage 1 are assessed through teacher assessment supported by national tests and tasks. Towards the end of Key Stage 1, teachers summarise their assessments for children and, using nationally agreed criteria, make a judgement about the level that each child has reached in reading, writing, speaking and listening. Children can

---

Communication, language and literacy: Reading

Points 1-3	Points 4-8	Point 9
1 Is developing an interest in books.	4 Knows that, in English, print is read from left to right and top to bottom.	9 Reads books of own choice with some fluency and accuracy.
2 Knows that print conveys meaning.	5 Shows an understanding of the elements of stories, such as main character, sequence of events and openings.	
3 Recognises a few familiar words.	6 Reads a range of familiar and common words and simple sentences independently.	
	7 Retells narratives in the correct sequence, drawing on language patterns of stories.	
	8 Shows an understanding of how information can be found in non-fiction texts to answer questions about where, who, why and how.	

Figure 10.12   The assessment scale for reading

achieve level 1, 2 or 3. For reading and writing level 2 is divided into 2C, 2B or 2A. Teacher assessment is based on the formative assessments that have been made throughout the year. As these have been collected in a range of contexts using all or some of the methods described in this chapter they provide an in-depth picture of children's strengths and weaknesses.

After making their judgements about the level at which children are working, teachers have to administer sufficient tests and tasks to enable them to make a secure teacher assessment. The tests and tasks are normally given to children in the summer term. There is a range of tests and tasks appropriate to the level that the teachers consider the children have reached. Figure 10.13 summarises the tests and tasks that can be used.

Children working	Reading	Writing
Towards level 1	Optional use of the reading task	Optional use of the writing task
At level 1	The level 1 reading task	Two writing tasks and a spelling test
At level 2	The level 2 task or the level 2 test	Two writing tasks and a spelling test
At level 3	The level 3 test	Two writing tasks and a spelling test

Figure 10.13   Key Stage 1 tests and tasks

For the reading tasks and tests teachers assess the children's reading ability against a number of criteria. At Key Stage 1 these are to:

- use a range of strategies, including accurate decoding of text, to read for meaning;
- understand, describe, select or retrieve information, events or ideas from texts and use quotation and reference to text;
- deduce, infer or interpret information, events or ideas from texts.

For both the level 1 and level 2 reading task a fiction or non-fiction picture book is selected from a list of titles and, after a preliminary discussion, the child reads a section of the book aloud. The teacher makes notes on the child's reading including the strategies he uses, any comments he makes and his understanding of what he has read. In many ways this is similar to a miscue analysis. The results of the teacher's observations should reveal the child's ability to read aloud with accuracy and his understanding of the text. They enable the teacher to award the child a level 1, 2C, 2B or 2A.

The level 2 reading test involves the child reading a specially written booklet containing a story and a non-fiction text. Both texts have follow-up questions which the child has to answer in writing. The level 3 reading test also uses a specially written story and non-fiction text with follow-up questions. The questions for level 3 explore the child's ability to deduce, infer and interpret.

There are two writing tasks. One is to write a piece of fiction and the other a piece of non-fiction. Both tasks are assessed on the following criteria:

Composition and effect:

- Write imaginative, interesting and thoughtful texts
- Produce texts which are appropriate to task, reader and purpose
- Organise and present whole texts effectively

Sentence structure:

- Vary sentences for clarity, purpose and effect

Punctuation:

- Write with technical accuracy of syntax and punctuation in phrases, clauses and sentences

The spelling in the writing tasks is not assessed. There is a separate spelling test of 20 words. Judgements about handwriting are made using the writing from the two writing tasks. Marks are given for composition and effect and sentence structure and punctuation in the two pieces of writing. These are added to the marks given for spelling and handwriting. The total number of marks determines the level at which the child is working. Teachers mark the tasks and tests that children take.

Some children with special educational needs who are working below level 1 of the National Curriculum may be assessed using the P Scales (http://www.qca.

org.uk/303.html). The P Scales should not be used to assess children in the Foundation Stage or those who are learning English as an additional language, unless they have been identified as having a special educational need. QCA has also developed optional reading and writing tasks for children who are gifted and who are working beyond the expected levels for their age.

The end of Key Stage 1 assessment of speaking and listening is based entirely on teacher assessment. This means that teachers have to collect evidence throughout Year 2 in order to make an informed and accurate assessment of the level that children have reached.

At the end of every school year parents are given a report on their child's progress. At the end of Key Stage 1 this includes the level their child has reached in each aspect of English together with a commentary written by the teacher which explains what the teacher assessments show about the child's learning and progress.

Reading tests

Some schools and local authorities administer reading tests in addition to the National Curriculum tests and tasks. These may be given to all children towards the end of a school year or they may be given to individual children, particularly those who are experiencing difficulty in becoming readers. The best tests should be useful to the teacher and so should provide information about why the child is failing and the nature of the child's difficulties and suggest the possible focus for the intervention so that the child can be given specialised help.

Reading tests that are administered to large groups of children generally provide teachers with a reading age, reading quotient or standardised score. These numbers show whether children are reading at an average, below average or above average level for their age. Very few tests provide diagnostic information about strengths and weaknesses that can be used to inform planning or teaching.

Summary

When assessing children's learning we need to:

- see assessment as an integral part of teaching and learning;
- build assessment into planning and classroom organisation;
- monitor progress regularly and frequently;
- use assessment to modify teaching and plan teaching programmes for children.

Reflective activities

1. Think about how you give feedback to children about their writing. Do you address aspects of composition and transcription? Is your feedback clear and does it help the child to understand what they could improve?
2. How is children's progress in reading monitored in your school? How quickly are children who do not seem to be progressing given extra support?
3. Do you have a sense of children's progression in each strand of speaking and listening? This is often the aspect of English in which teachers feel least confident. It might help to read through the objectives and examples in DfES (2003).

Suggestions for further reading

Clarke, S. (2008) *Formative Assessment in Action: Weaving the Elements Together.* London: Hodder Arnold. This book shows teachers how to integrate all the elements of formative assessment into everyday teaching. It includes sections on establishing clear learning objectives and success criteria and encouraging pupil and peer assessment.

11

Planning for language and literacy

Introduction

> **This chapter covers:**
> - the role of the subject leader and the English policy in planning;
> - long-term planning;
> - medium-term planning;
> - short-term planning.

The role of the English subject leader

Subject leaders play a significant role in planning by writing the policy and long-term plans for English. They also do a great deal to promote their subject through organising special events such as a book week or visits from authors, poets and theatre companies. Their knowledge and enthusiasm means that they can have a real impact on the quality of teaching and the success of children's learning. 'In effective schools, subject leaders provide a strong sense of direction ... Weaknesses in subject management ... inhibit progress' (HMI, 2005: para. 71). Their role is to develop the teaching and learning of language and literacy throughout the school by:

- maintaining, implementing and developing the policy;
- monitoring standards of learning and teaching;
- supporting staff in the area of language and literacy;
- identifying staff development needs;

- managing and organising resources;
- maintaining a high profile for English;
- liaising with colleagues in other schools and settings which pupils transfer from and to.

The English policy

All schools are expected to have written policies which cover each area of the curriculum. Policies guide the practice of those who work with pupils in school, providing them and other interested parties with a statement of teaching aims and intentions. Policies articulate the approach taken to the teaching of English and are the starting point for long-, medium- and short-term planning. HMI (1990, 2005) found that clear policies combined with effective curriculum leadership have a strong, positive effect on the quality and standard of pupil achievement in English. They are helpful because they:

- support professional confidence;
- identify agreed ways of working and teaching approaches;
- ensure consistency of approach throughout the school;
- support planning;
- ensure progression and continuity for pupils;
- provide guidance and starting points for new members of staff, students and supply teachers;
- help with the management of the curriculum;
- affect the allocation of resources;
- affect the allocation of time and space;
- can be used by individual teachers to review their own practice;
- lead to staff development;
- provide a coherent explanation of practice for parents, governors, inspectors and visitors.

An English policy is a document that deals with the learning, use, teaching and assessment of speaking, listening, reading and writing. It may also consider the role of language in other areas of the curriculum and the contribution that work in subjects such as ICT can make to children's developing competence as language users. Policies usually contain:

- a statement of principles which inform the teaching of English;
- a statement of aims for development in English;
- a summary of key points;
- curriculum guidelines for each area of language;
- sections indicating how learning develops within each language area;
- implications for classroom organisation and management;
- a section on record-keeping and assessment;
- links with other policies including equal opportunities and special educational needs;

- examples of successful practice;
- a resources and reading list;
- an indication of how the policy is to be monitored and evaluated;
- examples of children's work;
- a definition of the subject leader's role.

Writing a policy

One of the subject leader's main responsibilities is to write an English policy or to keep an existing policy up to date as the policy guides teachers' planning, teaching and assessment. The best policies are discussed and agreed by all staff. They should reflect the needs of the children and the school's approach to teaching and learning. Each policy is particular to the school, the staff and the children.

If a new policy is to be written or if the current policy is being reviewed there are a number of stages before, during and after the writing of the policy which will contribute to successful changes. Initially the English subject leader will want to assess the existing situation in school, including the standards, current practice, the approaches that are used, existing resources and any new ideas that might be profitably employed in school. She can include staff in this process by asking them to review their own practice and identify their own issues or concerns. The review and the topics that the teachers have identified can be discussed in staff meetings dedicated to the English policy. The first staff meeting might focus on the positive aspects of the English curriculum in school. Subsequently there might be meetings for staff to discuss topics such as the aims of teaching English, catering for the needs of all children, identifying indicators of progress, the involvement of parents, the record-keeping system, how to interpret the Primary Framework for Literacy or monitoring the effectiveness of the phonics programme. The subject leader can devise discussion sheets to prompt thinking and to encourage the staff to find solutions to problems that have been identified. Completing an audit of existing practice helps staff to identify gaps in provision and to share good practice. A simple prompt sheet for thinking about speaking and listening is shown in Figure 11.1. A similar sheet could be used for all areas of English.

As part of the policy review staff can be asked to examine their own practice in relation to one or more areas of English. They might survey and record the speaking, listening, reading and writing experiences of two pupils over the course of a week in order to undertake a curriculum audit of English and to establish whether there is a balance between the teaching of the four modes of language. The results can reveal the variety of experiences that children receive or the use that is made of resources in the classroom and indicate examples of good practice that can be shared among the staff. It can also highlight areas requiring development.

After investigating the present situation the staff can begin to devise a strategy for change. At this stage, new ideas and approaches can be trialled before they are incorporated into the school's future practice and policy. During this time the

What do we already do to develop speaking and listening?

How?   When?   Why?

What could we do to develop speaking and listening further?

How?   When?   Why?

How do we already assess speaking and listening?

How?   When?   Why?

What could we do to assess speaking and listening?

How?   When?   Why?

Figure 11.1   Prompt sheet for staff meeting

subject leader monitors and supports positive changes in practice. She can ask the staff for feedback and take account of their opinions and needs. She might need to deal with inconsistencies and where necessary provide staff development sessions. As the review continues, the English subject leader can evaluate, sort and catalogue existing resources and think about additional resources that may be needed to support any changes in practice.

All the staff need to be given ownership of the new or revised policy by making a contribution to it. This can be done by organising drafting groups to work on different sections of the policy. Giving the groups guidelines on deadlines, length and headings is useful as is sharing the drafts among the staff. This provides all the staff with the opportunity to review, understand and become committed to the policy.

Once the policy has been written it should be distributed to all the staff who work with the pupils, including students and volunteer helpers. It should also be given to governors and to local authority personnel. The information it contains can be disseminated to parents and carers through open evenings and workshop sessions. Other local schools which contribute or receive pupils from the school should be aware of how the school teaches English and might be given copies of the policy or invited to meetings at the school. A sample English policy is provided in the Appendix to this book.

Innovations in practice are not always easy and the subject leader may have to ensure that the policy is adhered to despite such factors as staff changes, lack of money and parental criticism, particularly in the early stages. Later the policy will become a framework allowing scope for interpretation and flexibility. An effective language policy is not static. It will change in response to classroom practice, teachers' experience, discussion with colleagues and continuing staff development. As teachers implement the policy they will be learning and redefining its guidelines for themselves. As the staff become familiar with the policy and experience for themselves its implications for their role and their management of the children's learning, new needs will be identified.

Monitoring the effectiveness of the policy

The subject leader and the staff may need to maintain a sense of proportion about the successes and failures of the policy. At regular intervals they may need to take a dispassionate look at how it is working and as a result will evaluate, revise and update the policy by sharing and adding to the examples of good practice and the list of resources and reading. They will make sure that the policy is a useful working document which represents an agreed basis for classroom practice, relates to the individual characteristics of the school, enables the best use to be made of expertise, resources, equipment, time and space and is used to plan and implement a successful language and literacy curriculum throughout the school.

Long-term plans

Long-term plans show what each year group is expected to cover during the school year. They concentrate on learning objectives and curriculum content rather than teaching strategies. They also show when links between subjects can occur. When the plans for each year group are put together teachers can check that there are opportunities to develop children's knowledge skills and concepts systematically during the time that they are in the school and that there is continuity and progression across the school.

In many schools the Primary Framework for Literacy (DfES, 2006a) and the Practice Guidance for the Early Years Foundation Stage (DfES, 2007a) have replaced the need to write individual school long-term plans. In each of these documents there are year-long plans of the objectives to be covered by each year group and the supporting material contains examples of curriculum content.

Medium-term plans

The Foundation Stage

All early-years children need opportunities to play, talk, interact, experience and investigate at their own pace as they learn. These are some of the characteristics of good early years provision. Children in nursery or reception classes will be expected to do less recording and will engage in more play and oral activities than older children. For very young children there will be more opportunities to engage in large-scale, imaginative and construction activities outdoors, more emphasis on role play, greater exploration of materials and collections associated with themes and topics and more involvement in collaborative activities. The teacher will do most of the recording in the form of shared writing to produce large books for the class, although the children will also have the opportunity to write as part of their play and in their individual books. Implementing the curriculum for the Foundation Stage is different in pace and contains a different balance of activities from that designed for children in Key Stage 1.

The Primary National Strategy (PNS) has produced planning guidance for teachers working with children in nursery and reception classes which is available at http://www.standards.dfes.gov.uk/primaryframework/foundation/ cll/. This builds on the material in the Practice Guidance for the Early Years Foundation Stage (DfES, 2007a) and the objectives for reception classes in the Primary Framework for Literacy (DfES, 2006a). It includes a number of sample plans which follow the format shown in Figure 11.2. The plans on the Primary National Strategy website could form the basis of both medium- and short-term plans for the Foundation Stage.

Plans for the Foundation Stage are usually constructed around a theme that is selected for its appeal to young children. Medium-term plans show activities for all the six areas of learning including communication, language and literacy, and objectives from more than one area of learning might be linked to each activity.

The classroom example which follows shows a medium-term plan for a nursery class in action. It shows how, in the Foundation Stage, activities which allow children to practise or extend their communication, language and literacy abilities and understanding arise in all curriculum areas and occur continuously. For this reason medium-term plans take a different format to that used at Key Stage 1.

What we want children to learn (development matters)

A list of objectives, including the Early Learning Goals

Related Early Learning Goals

ELGs from other areas that relate to and underpin this learning in communication, language and literacy

Possible contexts

Contexts in which teaching and learning may take place

Outline of activity – effective practice

Examples of adult-led and child-initiated activities that provide opportunities for children to explore and apply their learning

Look, listen and note

Examples to support observation to aid planning for next steps

Assessment opportunities

Examples to support observation for assessment

Related profile scale points

Foundation Stage profile scale points that these learning contexts might support

---

Figure 11.2 Format for sample plans on the PNS website

Classroom example: nursery children working on the theme of 'Homes'

The following description is taken from a week's work for the nursery on the theme of 'Homes'. The focus for the week is to be moving home. The children have heard the stories *Moving Molly* (Hughes, 1991) and *Moving* (Rosen, 1995) and looked at the book *Our New Home* (Bennett, 1990), and some of them have shared their own experiences of moving with the class. The stories will be read to the whole class again.

The teacher wants the children to consider how the nursery home corner can be moved from its present position to a new location in the classroom. All the furniture and inhabitants of the home will actually be moved later in the week. What jobs will have to be done and how should the move happen? These are the issues for the children to think about, discuss and solve. The children move on to the other activities in the nursery, drawing an item from the collection of building materials, providing a written label for their previously painted home picture, sharing the book *Moving Molly*, making a collection of items for the kitchen using pictures cut from catalogues, engaging in imaginative play outdoors in an area that has been resourced as a building site and playing a lotto game which asks children to match different sorts of homes. All these activities are supported by discussion between the children and the available adults. The teacher positions herself in the writing area with a small group of children and asks them to think about how the class will move the home corner. Suggestions from the children might include wrapping up some of the small items in newspaper, taking the dolls to the new home in the prams, making sure the dolls have access to milk, moving the large items in a truck. As the children make their suggestions the teacher writes them on a flip chart. She will repeat this activity with all the children in the class over the next two days and using the flip chart share each group's ideas with the class. In their home-corner play it has been suggested to the children that they incorporate activities such as writing notes and making phone calls in preparation for the move. On the day of the move the classroom assistant takes photographs of the children packing, moving the dolls and animals and packing the truck. More photographs are taken as the children arrive at the new home. These will later be used to make a large book written by the teacher to record the event. Before the new house is furnished the teacher intends to discuss how the new area can be made into an attractive home. Does it need decorating? Where will the kitchen be? Can we make a separate bedroom for the dolls? The suggestions made by the children will be incorporated into activities on subsequent days.

Key Stage 1

At Key Stage 1 medium-term plans record the teaching and learning that will occur over a half term or a term. They contain coherent units of work which are organised around a number of learning objectives and their outcomes. The units of work at Key Stage 1 are organised around the three major genres of texts: narrative, non-fiction and poetry. The Primary National Strategy website contains a number of helpful resources to support teachers' medium-term planning, including an overview of what should be taught during each year (see Figure 11.3).

The website also contains sample medium-term plans for each unit of work. These suggest the sequence of teaching and learning, activities, resources, cross-curricular links and assessment opportunities. The PNS plans show how learning can be blocked and linked. Blocked work focuses on a coherent set of skills or knowledge which can be taught within a specific amount of time. So Unit 1 in Figure 11.4 focuses on a set of objectives that can be learned in the context of reading stories with familiar settings. Linked work is that which can be developed or applied in different subject areas. If, for example, the children were learning to read and write instructions, they could practise this in science sessions where they were conducting experiments or investigations.

The advantage of identifying opportunities for linked work is that it provides children with additional opportunities to practise and consolidate their skills and understanding and to see the relevance of English in a number of situations. Linking language and literacy with other curriculum areas is vital if children are to make good progress. 'Literacy should be at the heart of curriculum planning so that the subject matter from other curriculum areas is available as content or stimulus for speaking, listening, reading and writing. Equally, skills acquired in the literacy lesson should be applied during the rest of the school day' (DfES, 2006b: 15).

The PNS plans do not show continuous work. Continuous work is that which needs regular attention over long periods of time. For example, children need frequent opportunities to use the 'look, cover, write, check' strategy for spelling. They also need practice at consolidating their recognition of the high-frequency words so these skills are taught continuously during the year. Continuous work may also relate to a skill or concept that the children in a particular school or class have found difficult. As a result the school may have set year group or class targets that will need to be addressed throughout a term or year.

Short-term plans

Short-term plans show the work that will take place in a subject during the course of a week or a day. They translate the objectives on the medium-term plan into a workable plan for each teaching session. Short-term plans are written almost immediately before they are due to be used and so allow the teacher to organise activities and the children in ways which take account of the most recent assessments of children's learning.

Beginning with the objectives listed on the medium-term plan the teacher decides on activities which will allow her to address them and enable children to learn them. The activities that are planned should link directly with learning objectives. Short-term plans should specify how each activity will be organised. They will show which activities are to be undertaken by the whole class, groups and individuals, how the children are to be grouped and the

Year 1
Total number of Units: 12
Total number of exemplified Units: 10
Total number of weeks covered: 34–35

Narrative 16–17 weeks	UNIT1 **Stories with familiar settings** (4 weeks or 2 × 2 weeks) Y1N1	UNIT 2 **Stories from a range of cultures/Stories with predictable and patterned language** (4 weeks or 2 x 2 weeks) Y1N2	UNIT 3 **Traditional and fairy tales (includes plays)** (4–5 weeks or 2–3 + 2 weeks) Y1N3	UNIT 4 **Stories about fantasy worlds** (4 weeks or 2 × 2 weeks) Y1N4
Non-fiction 12 weeks	UNIT1 **Labels, lists and captions** (1 week) Y1NF1	UNIT 2 **Instructions** (2 weeks) Y1NF2	UNIT 3 **Recounts, dictionary** Y1NF3 (2 weeks)	UNIT 4 **Information texts** (5 weeks) Y1NF4	UNIT 5 **Recount (fact and fiction)** (2 weeks) Y1NF5
Poetry 6 weeks	UNIT1 **Using the senses** (2 weeks) Y1P1	UNIT 2 **Pattern and rhyme** (2 weeks)	UNIT 3 **Poems on a theme** (2 weeks)	

Source: http://www.standards.dfes.gov.uk/primaryframework/downloads/PDF/Planning_in_Y1_page.pdf.

Figure 11.3 Overview of units of work in year 1

Unit: 1 Stories with familiar settings (phase 1)   Date: **Year group: 1**

Key Learning Objectives:
Identify the main events and characters in stories, and find specific information in simple texts.
Visualise and comment on events, characters and ideas, making imaginative links to own experiences.
Create short, simple texts on paper and on screen that combine words with images (and sounds).

Learning Outcome for unit (phase 1):
Children can identify the main character and setting in a story using evidence from the illustrations and text.

Session	Shared learning and teaching	Independent learning	Plenary	Assessment criteria	Guided learning
	Read a story based around incidents and settings that are familiar to the children. Demonstrate how to apply word reading skills and strategies and involve children in using these strategies themselves.	Make a character card for one of the characters in the book listing their name, words in the text that describe them and what you think of them.	Children read out their speech or thought bubbles.		Guided writing with one group as they work on one of the independent activities.
1	At the end of the story, identify who is involved. Introduce the word *character*. Involve children in identifying characters by finding names and illustrations in the text and talking about what they do.	Write a list of what the main character likes and dislikes.	The class comment and suggest additions or changes.		
		Write speech or thought bubbles for characters at different stages in the story			
	Reread the story. Demonstrate how to apply word reading skills and strategies and involve children in using these strategies themselves.	Make a chart to describe the setting using the headings *where, when* and *atmosphere*.	Children display setting posters.		Guided writing with one group as they work on one of the independent activities.

(Continued)

(Continued)

Session	Shared learning and teaching	Independent learning	Plenary	Assessment criteria	Guided learning
2	At the end of the story, identify where it takes place. Introduce the word *setting*. Ask children to look for details about the setting using the illustrations and reread descriptive words or phrases with them. Talk about what is familiar or unfamiliar in the setting.	Draw a scene from the book and label different elements of the setting. Draw and label a story map of the setting (paired activity).	Class comment and add words using sticky notes.		
3	Read a description of the setting. Demonstrate how to apply word reading skills and strategies and involve children in using these strategies themselves. At the end of the reading identify key words related to the setting. Demonstrate how changing these words alters the setting.	Complete a cloze text describing the setting but with key words omitted (paired activity).	Children read some of the completed cloze passages. Ask for comments from the class about effective words or phrases.	Identify the main character and setting in a story using evidence from the illustrations and text (teacher observation, discussion).	Guided reading with one group.

Figure 11.4 Short-term planning sheet

support that will be given. This allows the teacher to think about how to cater for all the class, to differentiate work and to make good use of her own time and that of any other adults who work in the class.

Many schools make use of the planning pro formas on the PNS literacy website as a way of recording their short-term plans for Key Stage 1. An example of a short-term planning sheet is shown in Figure 11.4. The work on this plan relates to the objectives for unit 1, phase 1 shown on the medium-term plan in Figure 11.3.

The planning sheets on the PNS literacy website provide a useful format for recording objectives and activities for each literacy session but they do not cover all the opportunities for English that teachers might want to make use of during a day or a week. They do not remind teachers to make use of the library or see story sessions as an important daily teaching time. Work in addition to that in the literacy hour will include reading to the class, pupils' independent reading and writing in other curriculum areas. When planning for the short term it might be useful to consider the following questions to ensure that all available opportunities for language and literacy are being used.

- When will individuals read to the teacher or other adults? Can I sometimes plan for this within the literacy hour?
- When will I carry out reading and writing conferences? Can these take place within the literacy hour if I plan one each day at the start of each term?
- When can children read silently for extended periods? Do I want to plan for some silent reading periods at the start of the afternoon?
- When will children be shown how to use the library and to make informed choices about the books they read? Can I make use of other adults to work with small groups in the library?
- Am I covering the requirements for drama as set out in the National Curriculum for English? Can I incorporate some drama activities into my planning for the literacy hour when the children are exploring character or responding to books?
- Am I linking language and literacy to other curriculum areas? Can I use the time spent on other subjects to introduce and reinforce ways of reading and writing a variety of text types? Can I plan for speaking and listening and drama in other curriculum areas?
- When will children have the opportunity to make use of the writing, reading and imaginative play areas to read and write for their own purposes? Can I incorporate the use of these resources into my planning for literacy?
- Is what has been planned flexible enough to incorporate any ideas the children may have or interests they may develop as the work unfolds?
- When will I evaluate the effectiveness of my planning and my teaching and assess the children's learning?

Session planning

Short-term plans usually provide a summary of the activities for each session. Each session consists of a series of linked stages that support learning by introducing, developing and reviewing what is to be learned. The introduction usually consists of adult-led whole-class activities. The development stage includes independent and adult-led group activities. The plenary is when learning is reviewed and can be led by adults or children. Each stage of the session and each activity needs to be thought about in some detail if sessions are to be successful.

Adult-led activities

Adult-led activities include introductions to each session, shared reading, shared writing, guided reading or guided writing. For all adult-led activities the teacher will consider:

- how to capture the children's interest;
- how to model activities;
- how to recap on previous learning;
- how to encourage discussion, thought and interaction;
- how to make use of other adults to support learning;
- how to differentiate the teaching to cater for the abilities and needs of all children.

Independent learning

The tasks that children work on independently need to be carefully selected. Children need to be able to complete them successfully without adult help. This does not mean that they have to be easy. All the work that children do in school should extend their learning so independent work should present children with some degree of challenge. The key is to match the activities to the children's abilities and present them with a challenge that is achievable but not frustrating. For independent activities the teacher will consider:

- planning collaborative and group tasks which allow children to share ideas;
- introducing activities in shared or whole-class sessions so that children know what to do;
- making sure children know what to do when they have finished an activity;
- making sure children check their own work or work with a response partner;
- planning activities for the listening station, writing area and imaginative play area;
- making use of a range of resources such as story props and games;
- making sure children know what to do if they encounter difficulties.

Chapters 1, 2, 3 and 4 contain suggestions about purposeful activities that children can undertake independently. Successful independent activities give the teacher time to work closely with a group of children on guided reading or guided writing and provide opportunities for her to teach throughout the literacy session.

Plenary sessions

Plenary sessions provide children with an opportunity to reflect on their learning and share their learning with others. Plenary sessions need to be planned so that all the class can be involved. The class might provide feedback to the group who are presenting their work. They can ask questions or make suggestions about developing the work further.

Individual variation in planning

The amount of official guidance on planning for English that exists could mean that there is little variation in what is taught and learned across schools in England. This is not the case. Medium- and short-term plans should fit in with the aims, philosophy and practices that are advocated in the school's English policy. For example, the texts that are selected for the children to work with should meet the criteria for selecting texts that have been agreed by the staff.

Individual teachers have a great deal of flexibility in deciding what will be learned in the classroom. Each teacher's expertise and preferred way of working affects what is planned, learned and taught. Teachers adapt, interpret and extend guidelines in line with their own understanding of each curriculum area and their awareness of the previous experiences, achievements, interests and current needs of their pupils. Each teacher's understanding of the principles of planning, knowledge of the locality, use of resources, teaching style and system of classroom organisation and management will affect individual planning for English.

At the end of each day, week and unit of work, teachers evaluate how successful their planning has been. They consider if they can change some activities in order to make learning more productive. During the year they may discover other activities which they would like to use when they teach a unit of work or theme again. Evaluation and professional development will affect future planning and help teachers to mediate the learning objectives for the classes they teach.

Effective planning

In a well organised and productive learning environment children are meaningfully engaged in learning activities which they see as interesting and relevant. They move between a balance of challenging and more straightforward tasks about which they receive and give feedback. The format of the activities and careful thought about differentiation enables all pupils to succeed. In planning the tasks the teacher has taken account of the amount of teacher support that will be required and the availability of resources. She has made her expectations about the activities clear and has deployed other adults well.

Thoughtful planning and careful classroom management combined with an understanding of how young children learn are likely to lead to successful teaching and learning. You may be able to judge your own success at teaching English by seeing how closely or how often your planning and teaching meets the characteristics listed below.

- Planning has clear and realistic short- and long-term aims for pupil learning.
- Use is made of routine times such as registration to foster children's learning.
- Systematic assessment of learning is built into the planning.
- Space inside and outside the classroom is used well.
- The teacher is aware of the needs, interests, attitudes and experiences of the pupils.
- Planning is detailed and includes reference to how and when reading with children will occur each week, when reading conferences will take place and when and with whom specific work on spelling will take place.
- The classroom atmosphere is calm, orderly and quiet.
- All those who work with the class have been involved in the planning and are clear about the aims of the activities and the teacher's approach.
- Plans and teaching are evaluated at the end of each unit of work or theme.
- The teacher sees herself as the biggest resource in the classroom and organises all the other factors which affect learning, such as equipment, people, the children and space, in order to realise her aims.

Summary

When planning for language and literacy we need to:

- make sure that there is progression, balance, coherence and continuity in the curriculum;
- identify opportunities for English in other areas of the curriculum;
- consider the needs of the children;
- make use of teachers' professional knowledge;
- create plans that are the basis for good-quality teaching;
- understand that good planning is the key to making children's learning effective and exciting.

Reflective activities

1. When you are planning for language and literacy do you link topics and sessions to other curriculum areas?
2. Have you read the school's English policy? Is it a fair representation of the school's approach to teaching? Does it influence your teaching?
3. How do your daily assessments of children's learning and evaluations of your own teaching influence your daily and weekly planning?

Suggestions for further reading

Department for Children, Schools and Families (n.d.) Guidance on literacy planning – available at: http://www.standards.dfes.gov.uk/primaryframework/literacy/planning/.

Department for Children, Schools and Families (n.d.) Communication, language and literacy planning – available at: http://www.standards.dfes.gov.uk/primaryframework/foundation/cll/cllplanning/.

The DCSF website provides detailed guidance on planning with plenty of suggestions about activities.

Marsh, J. and Hallett, E. (eds) (2008) *Desirable Literacies,* 2nd edn. London: Sage (1st edn 1999). This book provides an overview of communication, language and literacy and suggests what practitioners need to think about when planning for children in the Foundation Stage.

Appendix

A sample language and literacy policy

Principles

This policy outlines the approach to the teaching and learning of English at ... school. It should be used by all those who contribute to the development of the pupils' language and literacy in school.

We believe that children learn best when they take an active part in their own learning, when they are aware of the reasons for what they are learning and when they are supported in their learning. When young children begin school they will already have learned a great deal about speaking, listening, reading and writing. By using a developmental approach we use the children's previous experiences and their proven capacity to learn in order to devise an English curriculum that meets their needs, extends their learning and enables all pupils to achieve their potential. English is taught in the context of a broad, balanced curriculum and is guided by the statutory requirements of the Practice Guidance for the Foundation Stage and the Primary Framework for Literacy.

All teaching is informed by the general principle that learning should enrich the lives of all learners.

Overall aims for the teaching and learning of English

- To develop pupils' abilities to communicate effectively and confidently in a range of formats including oral and written standard English.
- To develop pupils' capacities to listen with understanding.
- To enable pupils to be enthusiastic, responsive, knowledgeable and critical readers.
- To encompass all aspects of the statutory requirements for communication, language and literacy in the Foundation Stage and English at Key Stage 1.
- To provide opportunities for pupils to use ICT to facilitate and extend their learning in speaking, listening, reading and writing.

A summary of the key points contained in this policy

This policy contains the agreed aims for the teaching of the speaking, listening, reading and writing curriculum at ... school. It outlines the sequence of development in each area of English and makes some suggestions about the classroom organisation, resources and activities that will encourage learning. It contains sections on the school library, work with the under-fives, bilingual learners, children who experience difficulties, equal opportunities, assessment and record-keeping and parental involvement. Lists of resources for language and literacy and examples of good practice are attached to the policy.

Speaking and listening

Aims
All children should:

- feel confident and valued when they express themselves through the spoken word;
- respect and value all languages;
- learn through discussion with others;
- listen to, evaluate and respect the opinions of others;
- become competent listeners and speakers.

The development of speaking and listening
Speaking and listening are important for learning and as a means of communication. All children start school with considerable oral ability but may still lack experience at using language in certain ways. Teachers will build on what children can already do but will extend the children's competence as oral language users by developing their abilities in the following areas:

- taking account of the needs of listeners;
- talking in front of large audiences;
- turn-taking in large groups;
- participating purposefully, using reasoning and discussion techniques, in collaborative classroom tasks;
- using different styles and forms of language appropriate to particular situations such as telling jokes, participating in a debate or giving reasons and step-by-step explanations;
- organising what is said;
- acquiring and using a more extensive vocabulary.

Organisation for speaking and listening

The effectiveness of teachers, and other adults in school, in extending the oral development of young children is related to:

- their own understanding of the value of talk;
- their attitude to talk;
- planning for talk;
- organisation for talk;
- the choice of classroom activities;
- their own use of language.

Talk has equal status with other aspects of the English curriculum and speaking and listening activities should be considered and included when planning schemes of work. Group work is an effective way of encouraging children to listen and to use language for different purposes. The teacher will also need to support children's talk through sensitive and well-timed dialogue and questions. Planning for talk in a range of formal and less formal situations will encourage children to use different dialect forms, including standard English, in appropriate contexts.

Resources for speaking and listening

These include listening areas, story sessions, whole-class discussion times, collaborative group work across the curriculum, role play and drama, games, computer work, the use of story props and reading and writing activities.

Reading

Aims
All children should

- understand the purposes for reading and learning to read;
- develop confidence in their ability to read and to see themselves as readers regardless of attainment;
- become voluntary users of books for pleasure, interest, information and the extension of experience;
- be able to read fluently and competently from a range of material;
- draw upon a variety of reading strategies in order to make sense of print;
- become critical and discerning readers who are able to evaluate the written word.

The development of reading
During their early years at school children are expected to develop from dependence to independence as readers. Independent readers are those who combine fluency and accuracy and who make sense of and respond to what

they read. Children's development as readers will be supported by hearing and sharing books with adults and other children, having time to browse in the book corner, talking about books and practising reading. Learning to write will support learning to read, giving children further experiences with and insights into print. As they engage in all these experiences children should be encouraged to apply a wide range of strategies to their reading and to read a range of book and non-book texts.

Organisation for reading

Opportunities for reading are provided during individual, paired, guided, shared, class and silent-reading sessions in each class both within and outside the literacy hour. The daily organisation of activities should take account of the need to provide opportunities for pupils to have sustained periods of reading every day. The children will also gain practice in reading during shared writing sessions and during activities arising from curriculum areas other than English which require children to read instructions and explanations. Story-reading and story-telling sessions occur each day and provide valuable opportunities to introduce children to the power and use of books. Listening to audio tapes and reading the books which accompany these give children positive experiences with texts. Every class is allocated a weekly session in the library which can be used for sharing books and for borrowing books. Teachers should make sure that as many children as possible take books home each day to share with their parents.

Resources for reading

A well-chosen range of good-quality picture books, poetry, song books, traditional tales, stories, novels, reference books, non-fiction, big books and books made by children and adults in school is available in classrooms and the library. Books are available in English, other languages and dual-language versions. Each class has a collection of core books which are used in conjunction with enlarged texts, audio tapes and group reading sessions. These have been selected to cover the likely reading level of each class and are used to provide a framework for reading.

Audio tapes, story props and computer programs should be used to foster the development of reading. A selection of reading resources is exchanged between classes once a term to ensure that children experience a variety of books and stimuli for reading each year. Books and other resources are regularly updated and added to. It is an important professional responsibility for all teachers to familiarise themselves and keep up to date with books and other resources that are available for children.

The school library

The school has a well stocked library containing a large collection of fiction and information books. It also houses books written by children, additional sets of core books, group readers, audio tapes, story props, language games and pictures. Library resources can be used by the children who should be introduced to the library system and organisation. Resources may also be borrowed for class use by the teacher. Sets of core books may be borrowed to supplement classroom stock. Teachers should plan for the use of the library for book-sharing sessions, to help pupils to learn how to use the library and to give children access to the library resources. At the end of themes which have necessitated borrowing library stock resources should be returned so that they can be used by other classes. Suggestions for additions to library and class resources should be entered in the stock book located in the library.

Writing

Aims

All children should be able to:

- use the knowledge and understanding of writing that they bring to school;
- develop a positive attitude towards writing;
- understand the reasons for writing and for learning to write;
- understand that writing conveys meaning;
- write for a variety of audiences and in a variety of styles;
- become competent and fluent writers.

The development of writing

When children start school they are given opportunities to demonstrate what they know about writing. Teachers work with what the children are able to do. The children are asked to read back what they have written and are given correct models of writing which are compared with their own versions. As the children's writing becomes more readable the teacher may begin to focus on one or two aspects of transcription, for example word spaces or the correct spelling of one or two words. As children grow in competence they are expected to write more and to write and redraft their work, paying greater attention to organisation, use of language, purpose and audience. Transcription is never emphasised at the expense of discussing the choice of words, detail, organisation and structure of what has been written. As a general aim children are expected to progress in writing in accordance with the points in the Early Years Foundation Stage Profile and the National Curriculum assessment focuses for writing. It is unwise to attach levels exactly to particular ages of children, but most seven-year-olds are expected to produce writing that shows achievement at level 2 or above.

Organising for writing

When only one or two groups are engaged in writing at one time, it is easier for the teacher to give support for each child's writing needs. Occasionally there may be times when all the class is writing at the same time, for example during a special book-making project. For some writing activities children may be organised in collaborative mixed-ability groups and pairs. Shared writing with the whole class or with groups of pupils is a useful way of demonstrating all the processes that are used when writing. It can be used to introduce young children to the conventions of print, and older children to ways of planning, drafting and redrafting. The organisation for writing should always complement the nature of the task.

Writing for different purposes and different audiences

Writing at school should always have a purpose that is made clear to the children. Writing activities should cover the range of uses for writing that exist, including personal, factual, expressive and imaginative. Children should be encouraged to make notes when carrying out practical tasks and to produce labels and captions for the classroom. Wherever possible children's writing should have an audience that goes beyond the teacher, for example older and younger children, children in the class, family members and audiences outside the school.

Resources for writing

Writing should be portrayed as a purposeful, everyday activity. In the classroom children should experience a print-rich environment with displays of lists, greeting cards, notes, letters, name labels, self-made books, registers and notices. In order to participate fully in a range of writing activities and become successful and competent writers, children need to use a range of writing implements including crayons, chalks and pastels. Word-processing facilities should also be available for pupils to use. Pupils should learn that different implements are more suitable for particular sorts of writing, for example thick felt pens for writing notices, writing pens for final drafts and pencils for first drafts. Children should be provided with notebooks, class-made books, card, different sorts of paper and first-draft books for writing. These resources should be available in the writing corner, the home corner and alongside interactive displays. As children become more proficient at writing they should be provided with dictionaries and thesauruses and shown how to use them. Final copies of writing should be discussed with the teacher, before being displayed or stored in the children's writing folders. Erasers should not be used when children are writing.

Transcription

Spelling
Spelling is only one part of the writing process. It should not be overemphasised. Children should be encouraged to consider the look of words and to have a go at spelling when they are writing. The teaching of spelling should arise from what children write and be linked to individual children's needs. Spelling is taught during shared writing sessions, through word games and by the 'look, cover, write, check' method. Reception and Year 1 children should have access to simple dictionaries and word banks, while Years 2 and 3 children should begin to use more sophisticated dictionaries and thesauruses.

Handwriting
All children need to learn to write legibly, fluently and with reasonable speed. They need to be shown correct pencil grip and letter formation. Help with handwriting should be given as children write. Not every piece of writing children produce needs to be perfect, but teachers should emphasise attention to good presentation when they are writing final drafts. When demonstrating writing to left-handers, teachers should use their left hand and be alert to the difficulties that left-handed children may have. If necessary, special provision should be made for left-handed writers. Children in Year 2 who are forming their letters correctly should be introduced to a simple from of cursive script. The teacher's own writing should always provide a good model for the children.

Punctuation
The correct use of punctuation is an advanced transcription skill. Children should not be pressed into using punctuation before they understand what it is for. Discussions about punctuation should arise during shared reading and writing sessions. These will help children to recognise its function in writing.

Other issues

Communication, language and literacy in the nursery
In the nursery opportunities for speaking, listening, reading and writing will be planned for children. Indoor and outdoor play, group work and collaborative activities as well as discussion times and adult involvement in activities will provide occasions for the development of speaking and listening. Story sessions using enlarged texts as well as other books should introduce children to the pleasure and purposes of reading and writing.

The nursery has a well-resourced library area which is used by the children for browsing and borrowing. Story tapes and books should be available in the listening area. Imaginative play areas should contain appropriate literacy resources and adults should enter into children's play to provide models of how these resources are used. All children are expected to explore and enjoy reading and writing during their time in the nursery. Close liaison with carers will enable nursery staff to match language and literacy experiences to the children's needs and to extend the knowledge, skills and understanding children already have.

Writing and reading

Good readers are not automatically good writers. However, as children gain more experience of print through reading, it is likely that their writing will improve. As young children gain more experience of print and books they will learn about written language. Attending to the details of print in reading will help children with the transcription elements of writing, such as knowledge about letters, presentation and spelling. Reading will also provide children with ideas for their own compositions as well as awareness of the structure and organisation of writing.

Bilingual learners and English

Wherever possible, children's development as listeners, speakers, readers and writers in community languages should be supported. Tapes and books in home languages should be available in every class. Initial and continuing meetings with parents should provide teachers with information about children's experiences in language and this should be used to guide the teacher's provision for English. Children who are fluent or literate in a language other than English should not be discouraged from speaking, reading or writing in languages that are familiar to them. This will not prevent them from developing as competent users of English. Support teachers may be available to work with bilingual children. All children should be encouraged to value languages other than their own

Children who experience difficulties with English

Children who are making less progress in speaking, listening, reading or writing than one might expect should be brought to the attention of the English subject leader and the headteacher. Support staff may be allocated to work with these children. As far as possible the language and literacy curriculum should be the same for all children and careful attention to differentiation should make this possible. Some children may need to work on intervention programmes or receive individualised teaching.

Equal opportunities and English

Teachers should ensure that the activities they present to children should be appropriate to the needs and interests of girls and boys. Particular attention should be paid to the needs of both sexes as speakers and listeners, to the resources that are used for reading and to one's expectations about the content and presentation of writing.

Assessment and record keeping

Most assessment takes place as the teacher works with and observes the children each day. More formal evidence of assessment forms part of the language and literacy record for each child. Teachers should collect samples of children's reading and writing, and should keep records of observations, conferences and comments from parents and other teachers who work with the children. Wherever possible, children should be involved in assessing their own development. Judgements about children's work may refer to the Literacy Framework and, in Year 2, the assessment focuses for reading and writing, and should include suggestions for future work. The Early Years Foundation Stage Profile is completed towards the end of the Reception year. At the end of Key Stage 1 teachers should make a summary of children's progress in English and use the standard assessment tasks and tests to confirm their judgements.

Parents and language

We value the experiences of language and literacy that children bring with them from their homes and communities. Making links and sharing information between home and school has a beneficial effect on children's learning and to this end parents are encouraged to participate in the work of the school and in their children's language development through:

- parents' evenings and reports;
- regular parent consultations and discussions;
- informal discussions;
- a home–school reading programme;
- curriculum evenings;
- invitations to parents to make contributions to the language curriculum in school.

Support available to implement this policy

Further information and guidance about the teaching of English is available in the first instance from the English subject leader. Other people who may be able to provide support include the assessment coordinator, the special needs coordinator, support teachers, nursery and playgroup coordinators and local authority advisers. A number of other professionals such as speech therapists may be called upon when appropriate.

Monitoring and evaluating the policy

Regular monitoring is undertaken with regard to the school's aims for each area of English. Each year the effectiveness of the provision for English throughout the school is reviewed. A short report written by the subject leader is discussed by the staff and suggestions for future action are agreed. These are used to inform the school development plan. The yearly review will be attached to the reference copy of the policy document.

Areas for future development

This section could refer to areas of known weakness such as building up resources or the need for staff development sessions. It should identify future developments and give an indication of when and how these will be addressed.

Examples of practice

Samples of records and reports, brief accounts of activities, successful schemes of work and ideas gathered from staff development sessions and courses could be included in this section.

Resources and reading list

Lists of core books, dual-language books, big books, computer software as well as the names and telephone numbers of contacts for book weeks or translations might be included in the resources section of the policy. The reading list could include books that were consulted when the policy was written, a list of books about English that are available in the staffroom and other books that teachers might find useful for their teaching.

Examples of children's work

Samples of work illustrating aspects of the National Curriculum level descriptions, demonstrating appropriate teacher intervention or depicting progress over time can be included in this section.

References and further reading

2Simple Software (2004) *Developing Tray.* Available at: http://www.2simple.com.

Adams, D. and Hamm, M. (2000) *Media and Literacy: Learning in an Electronic Age – Issues, Ideas and Teaching Strategies.* Springfield, IL: Charles C. Thomas.

Agard, J. (1983) *I Din Do Nuttin and Other Poems.* London: Bodley Head.

Ahlberg, A. (1981a) *Miss Brick the Builder's Baby.* London: Puffin Books.

Ahlberg, A. (1981b) *Mrs Lather's Laundry.* London: Puffin Books.

Ahlberg, A. (1988) *Mrs Jolly's Joke Shop.* London: Puffin Books.

Ahlberg, J. and Ahlberg, A. (1978) *Each Peach Pear Plum.* London: Kestrel.

Ahlberg, J. and Ahlberg, A. (1982) *The Baby's Catalogue.* London: Puffin Books.

Ahlberg, J. and Ahlberg, A. (1986) *The Jolly Postman.* London: Heinemann.

Alborough, J. (1992) *Where's My Teddy?* London: Walker Books.

Alexander, R. J. (2003) 'Talk in teaching and learning: international perspectives', in QCA, *New Perspectives on Spoken English in the Classroom: Discussion Papers.* London: QCA, pp. 27–37.

Alexander, R. J. (2006). *Towards Dialogic Teaching: Rethinking Classroom Talk,* 3rd edn. York: Dialogos (1st edn, 2004).

Arizpe, E. A. and Styles, M. (2003) *Children Reading Pictures.* Abingdon: RoutledgeFalmer.

Arnold, H. (1982) *Listening to Children Reading.* London: Hodder & Stoughton.

Asher, S. (1980) 'Topic interest and children's reading comprehension', in R. Spiro, B. Bruce and W. Brewer (eds), *Theoretical Issues in Reading Comprehension.* Hillsdale, NJ: Lawrence Erlbaum Associates.

Baker, P. and Eversley, J. (2000) *Multilingual Capital.* London: Battlebridge.

Barnes, E. (1994) 'One collar, two sleeves ...?', *Language and Learning,* June/July, pp. 9–11.

Barrett, T. C. (1968) 'Taxonomy of cognitive and affective dimensions of reading comprehension', in H. M. Robinson (ed.), *Innovation and Change in Reading Instruction.* Chicago, IL: University of Chicago Press.

Barrs, M. and Pigeon, S. (eds) (2002) *Boys and Writing.* London: CLPE.

Barrs, M. and Thomas, A. (eds) (1991) *The Reading Book.* London: CLPE.

Barrs, M., Ellis, S., Hester, H. and Thomas, A. (1988) *The Primary Language Record: Handbook for Teachers.* London: CLPE.

Baxter, J. (2001) *Making Gender Work.* Reading: National Centre for Language and Literacy.

Beck, I. (1993) *Five Little Ducks.* London: Orchard Books.

Bennett, O. (1990) *Our New Home.* London: Evans.

Bereiter, C. and Scardamalia, M. (1985) 'Children's difficulties in learning to compose', in G. Wells and J. Nicholls (eds), *Language and Learning: An International Perspective.* Abingdon: Falmer Press.

BFI Education (2003) *Look Again!* London: DfES.

Bird, V. and Akerman, R. (2005) *Every Which Way We Can: A Literacy and Social Inclusion Position Paper.* London: National Literacy Trust. Available at: http://www.literacytrust.org.uk/ socialinclusion.

Bissex, G. (1984) 'The child as teacher', in H. Goelman, A. Oberg and F. Smith (eds), *Awakening to Literacy (The University of Victoria Symposium on Children's Responses to a Literature Environment: Literacy before Schooling).* London: Heinemann.

Blake, Q. (1968) *Patrick.* London: Picture Lions.

Blake, Q. (1987) *Mrs Armitage on Wheels.* London: Jonathan Cape.

Book Trust (2007) *The Children's Book Week Resource Guide.* Available from: http://www.book-trusted.co.uk/cbw/downloads/ncbwbooklet.pdf.

Bradley, L. and Bryant, P. (1983) 'Categorising sounds and learning to read: a causal connection', *Nature,* 301: 419–21.

Bradman, T. (1986) *Through My Window.* London: Little Mammoth.

Bradman, T. (1988) *Wait and See*. London: Little Mammoth.

Bradman, T. (1990) *In A Minute*. London: Little Mammoth.

Brice-Heath, S. (1983) *Ways with Words: Language, Life and Work in Communities and Classrooms*. Cambridge: Cambridge University Press.

Brierley, L. (1991) 'A climate for frankness in classroom talk with top juniors', *TALK: The Journal of the National Oracy Project*, Summer, 4: 27–31.

British Psychological Society Working Party of the Division of Educational and Child Psychology (1999) *Dyslexia, Literacy and Psychological Assessment*. Leicester: British Psychological Society.

Brooks, G. (2007) *What Works for Pupils with Literacy Difficulties? The Effectiveness of Intervention Programmes*, 3rd edn. London: DCSF.

Brown, E. N. (1990) 'Children with spelling and writing difficulties: an alternative approach', in P. D. Pumphrey and C. D. Elliott (eds), *Children's Difficulties in Reading, Spelling and Writing*. Abingdon: Falmer Press.

Brown, R. (1981) *A Dark, Dark Tale*. London: Scholastic.

Brown, R. and Belugi, U. (1966) 'Three processes in the child's acquisition of syntax', in J. Emig, J. Flemming and H. Popp (eds), *Language and Learning*. New York: Harcourt.

Browne, A. (1984) *Willy the Wimp*. London: Magnet.

Browne, A. (1985) *Willy the Champ*. London: Magnet.

Browne, A. (1986) *Piggybook*. London: Magnet.

Browne, A. (1988) *I Like Books*. London: Julia MacRae Books.

Browne, A. (1999) *Writing at Key Stage 1 and Before*. Cheltenham: Stanley Thornes.

Browne, A. (2007) *Teaching and Learning Communication, Language and Literacy*. London: Paul Chapman Publishing.

Browne, E. (1994) *Handa's Surprise*. London: Walker Books.

Bruner, J. (1984) 'Language, mind and reading', in H. Goelman, A. Oberg and F. Smith (eds), *Awakening to Literacy (The University of Victoria Symposium on Children's Responses to a Literature Environment: Literacy before Schooling)*. London: Heinemann.

Buckingham, D. (1993) *Children Talking Television: The Making of Television Literacy*. Abingdon: Falmer.

Burningham, J. (1978) *Mr Gumpy's Outing*. London: Puffin Books.

Butler, D. (1982) *Babies Need Books*. London: Penguin Books.

Butterworth, N. (1992) *Jasper's Beanstalk*. London: Hodder & Stoughton.

Campbell, R. (1990) *Reading Together*. Buckingham: Open University Press.

Carle, E. (1977) *The Bad-Tempered Ladybird*. London: Picture Puffins.

Cave, K. (1994) *Something Else*. London: Penguin Books.

Cazden, C. B., Cordeiro, P. and Giacobbe, M. E. (1985) 'Young children's learning of punctuation', in G. Wells and J. Nicholls (eds), *Language and Learning: An Interactional Perspective*. Abingdon: Falmer Press.

Chambers, A. (1993) *Tell Me – Children Reading and Talk*. Stroud: Thimble Press.

Child, L. (2001) *I Am Not Sleepy and I Will Not Go to Bed*. London: Orchard Books.

Children's Literature Research Centre (1996) *Young People's Reading at the End of the Century*. London: Roehampton University.

Clark, K. (1960) *Looking at Pictures*. London: John Murray.

Clark, M. M. (1976) *Young Fluent Readers*. London: Heinemann Educational.

Clarke, S. (2008) *Formative Assessment in Action: Weaving the Elements Together*. London: Hodder Arnold.

Clay, M. (1979) *Concepts of Print: The Early Detection of Reading Difficulties*. Auckland: Heinemann Educational.

Clay, M. (1991) *Becoming Literate: The Construction of Inner Control*. Auckland: Heinemann.

CLPE (1999) *Literacy in Practice: A Parent's Guide to Teaching and Learning*. London: CLPE.

Cole, B. (1986) *Princess Smartypants*. London: Picture Lions.

Cole, B. (1987) *Prince Cinders*. Hayes: Magi.

Comber, B. (2007) 'Assembling dynamic repertoires of literacy practices', in E. Bearne and J. Marsh (eds), *Literacy and Social Inclusion: Closing the Gap*. Stoke-on-Trent: Trentham books.

Conteh, J. (ed.) (2006) *Promoting Learning for Bilingual Pupils 3–11: Opening Doors to Success*. London: Paul Chapman Publishing.

Cremin, T., Bearne, E., Mottram, M. and Goodwin, P. (2007) *Teachers as Readers: Phase 1 Research Report for UKLA Web*. Available from: http://www.ukla.org/site/research/research_projects_in_progress/teachers_as_readers_building_communities_of_readers/.

Crystal, D. (1987) *Child Language, Learning and Linguistics*, 2nd edn. London: Arnold.

Cummins, J. (1979) 'Linguistic interdependence and the educational development of bilingual children', *Review of Educational Research*, 49: 222–51.

Cummins, J. (1984) 'Mother tongue maintenance for minority language children: some common misconceptions', *Forum 2* (ILEA, Languages Inspectorate), Spring.

Cummins, J. (2001) *Negotiating Identities: Education for Empowerment in a Diverse Society*, 2nd edn. Ontario, CA: California Association for Bilingual Education.

Dale, P. (1987) *Bet You Can't!* London: Walker Books.

DCSF (2007a) *Early Literacy Support*. London: DCSF.

DCSF (2007b) *Year 3 Literacy Support: Materials for Teachers Working in Partnership with Teaching Assistants*. London: DCSF.

DCSF (26 June 2007) *SFR20/2007: Special Educational Needs in England, 2007*. Retrieved 28 April 2008 from DCSF at: http://www.dcsf.gov.uk/rsgateway/DB/SFR/s000732/index.shtml.

DCFS (30 August 2007) *National Curriculum Assessments at Key Stage 1 in England, 2007*. Retrieved 21 April 2008 from DCSF at: http://www.dcsf.gov.uk/rsgateway/DB/SFR/s000740/index.shtml.

DCSF (1 May 2008) *Schools and Pupils in England, January 2007 (Final)*. Retrieved 3 May 2008 from DCSF at: http://www.dfes.gov.uk/rsgateway/DB/SFR/s000744/UPDATEDSFR30_2007.pdf.

DES (1967) *Children and Their Primary Schools* (The Plowden Report). London: HMSO.

DES (1975) *A Language for Life* (The Bullock Report). London: HMSO.

DES (1988a) *Report of the Inquiry into the Teaching of the English Language* (The Kingman Report). London: HMSO, Chapter 3.

DES (1988b) *National Curriculum Proposals for English for Ages 5 to 11* (The Cox Committee Report, Part 1). London: HMSO.

Deshpande, C. (1988) *Five Stones and Knuckle Bones*. London: A. & C. Black.

Development Education Centre (1989) *Working Now*. Birmingham: DEC.

DfE (1995) *English in the National Curriculum*. London: HMSO.

DfEE (1998) *National Literacy Strategy Framework for Teaching*. London: DfEE.

DfEE (2000) *Reading and Writing Together*. Sudbury: DfEE Publications.

DfEE (2001) *Developing Early Writing*. London: DfEE.

DfEE/QCA (1999a) *English in the National Curriculum*. London: DfEE.

DfEE/QCA (1999b) *Information and Communication Technology in the National Curriculum*. London: DfEE.

DfEE/QCA (1999c) *The National Curriculum Handbook for Primary Teachers in England*. London: DfEE.

DfES (2003) *Speaking, Listening, Learning: Working with Children in Key Stages 1 and 2*. London: DfES.

DfES (2004) *Excellence and Enjoyment: Learning and Teaching in the Primary Years*. London: DfES.

DfES (2005a) *Higher Standards: Better Schools for All*, White Paper. London: DfES.

DfES (2005b) *Speaking, Listening, Learning: Working with Children with Special Educational Needs*. London: DfES.

DfES (2005c) *Raising Standards in Reading – Achieving Children's Targets*. London DfES.

DfES (2006a) *Primary Framework for Literacy and Mathematics*. London: DfES.

DfES (2006b) *Excellence and Enjoyment: Learning and Teaching for Bilingual Children in the Primary Years*. London: DfES.

DfES (2006c) *Learning and Teaching for Dyslexic Children*. London: DfES, Chapter 8.

DfES (2007a) *The Early Years Foundation Stage: Setting the Standards for Learning, Development and Care for Children from Birth to Five*. London: DfES.

DfES (2007b) *Letters and Sounds: Principles and Practice of High Quality Phonics*. London: DfES.

Dombey, H. (2006) 'Phonics and English orthography', in M. Lewis and S. Ellis (eds), *Phonics: Practice, Research and Policy* . London: Paul Chapman Publishing, pp. 95–104.

Ellis, S. and Barrs, M. (1996) *The Core Book*. London: CLPE.

Ervin-Tripp, S. M. (1978) 'Is second language learning like the first?', in E. M. Hatch (ed.), *Second Language Acquisition*. Rowley, MA: Newbury House.

Essen, J. and Welch, J. (1990) *Survey of Provision for Able and Talented Children*. Northampton: NAGC.

Evans, J. (2001) *The Writing Classroom: Aspects of Writing and the Primary Child 3–11*. London: David Fulton.

Fernald, G. M. (1943) *Remedial Techniques in Basic School Subjects*. New York: McGraw-Hill.

Ferreiro, E. (1986) *Literacy Development: Psychogenesis*. Paper presented at World Congress on Reading, London.

Ferreiro, E. and Teberosky, A. (1983) *Literacy before Schooling*. Portsmouth, NH: Heinemann Educational.

Flint, D. (1993) *China*. London: Simon & Schuster Young Books.

Flynn, N. and Stainthorp, R. (2006) *The Learning and Teaching of Reading and Writing*. Chichester: Wiley.

Fraser, B. and Chapman, E. (1983) 'Children with sensory defects in schools', *Special Education: Forward Trends*, 1 (4): 37–41.

French, F. (1991) *Anancy and Mr Dry-Bone*. London: Frances Lincoln.

French, F. (1999) *Jamil's Clever Cat*. London: Frances Lincoln.

Furchgott, T. and Dawson, L. (1977) *Phoebe and the Hot Water Bottles*. London: Fontana.

Gamble, N. and Yates, S. (2008) *Exploring Children's Literature: Teaching the Language and Reading of Fiction*, 2nd edn. London: Sage (1st edn, 2002).

Gentry, J. R. (1982) 'An analysis of developmental spelling in GNYS AT WORK', *The Reading Teacher*, 36: 192–200.

Goodman, K. and Goodman, Y. M. (1977) 'Learning about psycholinguistic processes by analyzing oral reading', *Harvard Educational Review*, 47 (3): 317–33.

Goodman, Y. and Burke, C. (1972) *Reading Miscue Inventory*. New York: Macmillan.

Gorman, T., White, J., Brooks, G. and English, F. (1989) *Language for Learning: A Summary Report on the 1988 APU Surveys of Language Performance*. London: HMSO.

Goswami, U. (2003) 'Orthography, phonology and reading development: a cross-linguistic perspective', in M. Joshi (ed.), *Linguistic Relativity of Orthographic and Phonological Structures*. Dordrecht, NL: Kluwer.

Goswami, U. and Bryant, P. (1990) *Phonological Skills and Learning to Read*. Hove: Lawrence Erlbaum Associates.

Graves, D. (198 3) *Writing: Teachers and Children at Work*. London: Heinemann Educational.

Gregory, E. (2008) *Learning to Read in a New Language: Making Sense of Words and Worlds*, 2nd edn. London: Sage (1st edn, 1996).

Gross, J. (2002) *Special Educational Needs in the Primary School*, 3rd edn. Buckingham: Open University Press (1st edn, 1993).

Guppy, P. and Hughes M. (1999) *The Development of Independent Reading*. Buckingham: Open University Press.

Hall, K. (2003) *Listening to Stephen Read: Multiple Perspectives on Literacy*. Buckingham: Open University Press.

Hall, N. and Robinson, A. (eds) (1996) *Learning about Punctuation*. Clevedon: Multilingual Matters.

Hall, N., Hemming, G., Hann, H. and Crawford, L. (1989) *Parental Views on Writing and the Teaching of Writing*. Manchester: Department of Education Studies, Manchester Polytechnic.

Halliday, M. A. K. and Hassan, R. (1985) *Language, Context and Text*. Oxford: Oxford University Press.

Hancock, R. (1995) 'Hackney PACT, home reading programmes and family literacy', in B. Raban-Bisby, G. Brooks and S. Wolfendale (eds), *Developing Language and Literacy*. Stoke-on-Trent: Trentham Books.

Hannon, P. (1989) 'How should parental involvement in the teaching of reading be evaluated?', *British Journal of Educational Research*, 15 (1): 33–40.

Hannon, P. (1995) *Literacy, Home and School: Research and Practice in Teaching Literacy with Parents*. Abingdon: Falmer Press.

Harrison, C. and Coles, M. (eds) (2001) *The Reading for Real Handbook*, 2nd edn. Abingdon: Routledge (1st edn, 1992).

Harrison, J. (n.d.) *Opposites*. London: Health Education Authority.

Harste, J., Burke, C. and Woodward, V. A. (1994) 'Children's languages and world: initial encounters with print', in R.B. Ruddell, M.R. Ruddell and H. Singer (eds), *Theoretical Models and Processes of Reading*, 4th edn. Newark, DE: International Reading Association, pp. 48–69.

Herbert, G. (n.d) *Selected Poetry of George Herbert* (1593–1633). Toronto: University of Totonto Press. http://rpo.library.utoronto.ca/poet/159.html (accessed June 2008).

Hester, H. (1983) *Stories in the Multilingual Classroom*. London: Harcourt Brace Jovanovich.

Hewison, J. and Tizard, J. (1980) 'Parental involvement and reading attainment', *British Journal of Educational Psychology*, 50 (3): 209–15.

Hill, E. (1980) *Where's Spot?* London: Puffin Books.

HMI (1990) *The Teaching and Learning of Language and Literacy*. London: HMSO.

HMI (1993) *The HMI Report on the Implementation of the Curricular Requirements of the Education Reform Act English Key Stages 1, 2 and 3: Third Year, 1991–92*. London: HMSO.

HMI (2004) *Reading for Purpose and Pleasure: An Evaluation of the Teaching of Reading in Primary Schools*. London: Ofsted.

HMI (2005). *English 2000–05: A Review of Inspection Evidence*. London: Ofsted.

Hodgeon, J. (1984) *A Woman's World?* Manchester: Cleveland Education Authority and Equal Opportunities Commission.

Hoffman, M. (1991) *Amazing Grace*. London: Frances Lincoln.

Hoffman, M. (1993) *Henry's Baby*. London: Dorling Kindersley.

Holdaway, D. (1979) *The Foundations of Literacy*. London: Ashton Scholastic.

Hughes, S. (1991) *Moving Molly*. London: Red Fox.

Hulme, K. (1985) *The Bone People*. London: Hodder & Stoughton.

Hutchins, P. (1970) *Rosie's Walk*. London: Bodley Head.

Hutchins, P. (1971) *Titch*. London: Puffin Books.

Hutchins, P. (1976) *Don't Forget the Bacon!* London: Puffin Books.

ILEA (1990a) *Language and Power*. London: Harcourt Brace Jovanovich.

ILEA (1990b) *Reading Experience of Pupils: Validation Survey of Reading. Scale 2 from the Primary Language Record*, RS 1285/90. London: ILEA, Research and Statistics Branch.

Jackson, A. and Hannon, P. (1981) *The Belfield Reading Project*. Rochdale: Belfield Community Council.

Jarman, C. (1993) *The Development of Handwriting Skills*, 2nd edn. London: Simon & Schuster Education.

Jarmany, K. (1991) 'Considering gender differences', *TALK: The Journal of the National Oracy Project*, Summer, 4: 23–6.

Kenner, C. (2004) *Becoming Biliterate: Young Children Learning Different Writing Systems*. Stoke-on-Trent: Trentham Books.

Kiefer, B. (1995) *The Potential of Picture Books: From Visual Literacy to Aesthetic Understanding*. Englewood Cliffs, NJ: Merrill.

Klein, G. (1986) 'Resources for multicultural education', in R. Aora and C. Duncan (eds), *Multicultural Education: Towards Good Practice*. Abingdon: Routledge.

Krashen, S. D. and Terell, T. D. (1983) *The National Approach: Language Acquisition in the Classroom*. Oxford: Pergamon.

Lakoff, R. (1975) *Language and a Woman's Place*. London: Harper & Row.

Lazim, A. (2008) *The Core Booklist*. London: CLPE.

Lewis, M. (2001) 'From reading to writing: using picture books as models', in J. Evans (ed.), *The Writing Classroom: Aspects of Writing and the Primary Child 3–11*. London: David Fulton, pp. 66–78.

Lewis, M. and Ellis, S. (eds) (2006) *Phonics*. London: Paul Chapman Publishing.

Literacy Trust (n.d.) *The Reading Connects Family Involvement Toolkit*. Retrieved 1 May 2008 from Literacy Trust at: http://www.literacytrust.org.uk/readingconnects/Family_Involvement_Toolkit.pdf.

Loban, W. (1976) *Language Development: Kindergarten through Grade 12*. Urbana, IL: NCTE.

Lunzer, E. and Gardner, K. (1979) *The Effective Use of Reading*. London: Heinemann.

McCracken, R. A. (1971) 'Initiating sustained silent reading', *Journal of Reading*, 14 (8): 521–83.

McNaughton, C. (1991) *Have You Seen Who's Just Moved in Next Door to Us?* London: Walker Books.

McNaughton, C. (1994) *Suddenly!* London: HarperCollins.

Mallet, M. (1992) *Making Facts Matter: Reading Non-Fiction 5–11*. London: Paul Chapman Publishing.

Marsh, J. and Hallett, E. (eds) (2008) *Desirable Literacies*, 2nd edn. London: Sage (1st edn, 1999).

Meek, M. (1982) *Learning to Read*. London: Bodley Head.

Meek, M. (1988) *How Texts Teach What Children Learn*. Stroud: Thimble Press.

Melser, J. and Cowley, J. (1980) *Mrs Wishy Washy*, Story Chest Large Read Together Books. Walton-on-Thames: E. J. Arnold.

Merchant, G. (2001) 'Supporting readers for whom English is a second language', in C. Harrison and M. Coles (eds), *The Reading for Real Handbook*, 2nd edn. Abingdon: Routledge (1st edn, 1992).

Merchant, G. and Thomas, H. (1999) *Picture Books for the Literacy Hour*. London: David Fulton.

Merchant, G. and Thomas, H. (2001) *Non-fiction for the Literacy Hour*. London: David Fulton.

Millard, E. (2001) 'Aspects of gender', in J. Evans (ed.), *The Writing Classroom: Aspects of Writing and the Primary Child*. London: David Fulton.

Mills, J. (1993) 'Language activities in a multilingual school', in R. W. Mills and J. Mills (eds), *Bilingualism in the Primary School*. Abingdon: Routledge.

Minns, H. (1990) *Read It To Me Now!* London: Virago.

Minns, H. (1991) *Language, Literacy and Gender*. London: Hodder & Stoughton.

Montgomery, M. (1986) *An Introduction to Language and Society*. Abingdon: Routledge.

Moon, C. (1988) 'Reading: where are we now?', in M. Meek and C. Mills (eds), *Language and Literacy in the Primary School*. Abingdon: Falmer Press.

Moore, I. (1990) *Six Dinner Sid*. London: Hodder Headline.

Moseley, D. V. (1990) 'Suggestions for helping children with spelling problems', in P. D. Pumphrey and C. D. Elliott (eds), *Children's Difficulties in Reading, Spelling and Writing*. Abingdon: Falmer Press.

Moss, G. (2007) *Literacy and Gender: Researching Texts, Contexts and Readers*. Abingdon: Routledge.

Moyles, J., Hargreaves, L. and Merry, R. (2001) *The Development of Primary Teachers' Understanding and Use of Interactive Teaching. End of Award Report* (ROOO 238200). Swindon: Economic and Social Research Council.

Mroz, M., Hardman, F. and Smith, F. (2000) 'The discourse of the literacy hour', *Cambridge Journal of Education*, 30 (3): 379–90.

Mullis, V. S., Martin, M. O., Kennedy, A. M. and Foy, P. (2007) *IEA's Progress in International Reading Literacy Study in Primary Schools in 40 Countries*. Chestnut Hill, MA: TIMSS & PIRLS International Study Center, Boston College.

Munsch, R. N. (1980) *The Paper Bag Princess*. London: Scholastic.

Murphy, J. (1980) *Peace at Last*. London: Picturemac.

Murphy, J. (1984) *On the Way Home*. London: Picturemac.

National Writing Project (1989) *Responding to and Assessing Writing*. Cheltenham: Nelson.

National Writing Project (1990) *Perceptions of Writing*. Cheltenham: Nelson.

NCC (1989) *English Non-Statutory Guidance*. York: NCC.

NCC (1993) *National Curriculum Council Consultation Report: English in the National Curriculum*. York: NCC.

Norman, K. (1990) *Teaching Talking and Learning in Key Stage 1*. York: National Curriculum Council.

Nutbrown, C., Hannon, P. and Morgan, A. (2005) *Early Literacy Work with Families: Policy, Practice and Research*. London: Sage.

O'Sullivan, O. and Thomas, A. (2007) *Understanding Spelling*. Abingdon: Routledge.

Ofsted (2007) *Poetry in Schools: A Survey of Practice, 2006–7*. London: Ofsted.

Perera, K. (1987) *Understanding Language*. Manchester: National Association of Advisers in English and the University of Manchester.

Peters, M. L. (1985) *Spelling: Caught or Taught? A New Look*. Abingdon: Routledge.

Peters, M. L. and Cripps, C. (1980) *Catchwords: Ideas for Teaching Spelling.* London: Harcourt Brace Jovanovich.

Polacco, P. (1998) *Thank You, Mr Falker.* New York: Philomel Books.

Porter, L. (2005) *Gifted Young Children: A Guide for Teachers and Parents,* 2nd edn. Buckingham: Open University Press (1st edn, 1999).

QCA (1998) *Science at Key Stages 1 and 2.* London: QCA. Available online at: http://www. standards.dfes.gov.uk/schemes2/science/?view=get.

QCA (2000a) *A Language in Common: Assessing English as an Additional Language.* London: QCA.

QCA (2000b) *Standards at Key Stage 1 English and Mathematics: Report on the 1999 National Curriculum Assessments for 7-Year-Olds.* London: QCA.

QCA (2001) *Assessment for Learning: Feedback.* Available online at: http://www.qca.org.uk/ca/5–14/afl/feedback.asp.

QCA (2003) *Foundation Stage Profile.* London: QCA.

Raynor, K. and Pollatsek, A. (1989) *The Psychology of Reading.* Englewood Cliffs, NJ: Prentice-Hall.

Read, C. (1986) *Children's Creative Spelling.* Abingdon: Routledge & Kegan Paul.

Redfern, A. (1993) *Practical Ways to Teach Spelling.* Reading: University of Reading, Reading and Language Information Centre.

Roberts, R. (2001) *PEEP Voices: A Five Year Diary.* Oxford: PEEP.

Rose, J. (2006) *Independent Review of the Teaching of Early Reading – Final Report.* London: DfES.

Rosen, M. (1993) *We're Going on a Bear Hunt!* London: Walker Books.

Rosen, M. (1995) *Moving.* London: Penguin Books.

Sassoon, R. (2003). *Handwriting: The Way to Teach It,* 2nd edn. London: Paul Chapman Publishing (1st edn, 1990).

SCAA (1995) *Planning the Curriculum at Key Stages 1 and 2.* London: SCAA Publications.

Schermbrucker, R. (1992) *Charlie's House.* London: Walker Books.

Seuss, Dr (1963) *Dr Seuss's ABC.* Glasgow: Collins.

Shook, S., Marrion, L. and Ollila, L. (1989) 'Primary children's concepts about writing', *Journal of Educational Research,* 82 (3): 133–8.

Smith, B. (1994) *Through Writing to Reading: Classroom Strategies for Supporting Literacy.* Abingdon: Routledge.

Smith, F. (1971) *Understanding Reading.* New York: Holt, Rinehart & Winston.

Smith, F. (1983) *Essays into Literacy.* London: Heinemann Educational.

Smith, J. and Alcock, A. (1990) *Revisiting Literacy: Helping Readers and Writers.* Buckingham: Open University Press.

Somerfield, M., Torbe, M. and Ward, C. (1983) *A Framework for Reading: Creating a Policy in the Primary School.* London: Heinemann.

Southgate, V., Arnold, H. and Johnson, S. (1981) *Extending Beginning Reading.* London: Heinemann Educational.

Stanovich, K. (1980) 'Towards an interactive-compensatory model of individual reading differences in the development of reading fluency', *Reading Research Quarterly,* 16 (1): 32–71.

Stebbing, J. and Raban, B. (1982) 'Reading for meaning: an investigation of the effect of narrative in two reading books for seven year olds', *Reading,* 16 (3): 153–61.

Strickland, R. (1962) *The Language of Elementary School Children: Its Relationship to the Language of Reading,* Bulletin. Bloomington, IN: Indiana University.

Sutton, E. (1973) *My Cat Likes to Hide in Boxes.* London: Puffin Books.

Swann, J. (1992) *Girls, Boys and Language.* Oxford: Blackwell.

Swann, J. and Graddol, D. (1988) 'Gender inequalities in classroom talk', *English in Education,* 22 (1): 48–65.

Tilbrook, B. and Grayson, B. (1990) 'What are writers made of?', in National Writing Project, *What Are Writers Made Of? Issues of Gender.* Cheltenham: Nelson.

Tizard, B. and Hughes, M. (2002) *Young Children Learning: Talking and Thinking at Home and at School,* 2nd edn. Oxford: Blackwell (1st edn, 1984).

Treiman, R. and Zukowski, A. (1996) 'Children's sensitivity to syllables, onsets, rimes and phonemes', *Journal of Experimental Psychology,* 61: 193–215.

Trelease, J. (2006) *The New Read-Aloud Handbook*, 6th edn. London: Penguin Books (1st edn, 1982).

Trudgill, P. (1974) *Sociolinguistics*. London: Penguin Books.

Verma, G. K. (1984) *Papers on Biliteracy and Bilingualism*. London: National Council for Mother Tongue Teaching.

Voake, C. (1998) *Ginger*. London: Walker Books.

Vygotsky, L. S. (1962) *Thought and Language*. Cambridge, MA: MIT Press.

Waddell, M. (1992) *Owl Babies*. London: Walker Books.

Waddell, M. (1994) *When the Teddy Bears Came*. London: Walker Books.

Wade, B. (1984) *Story at Home and School*, Educational Review Occasional Publication 10. Birmingham: University of Birmingham.

Wade, B. and Moore, M. (1987) *Special Children ... Special Needs: Provision in the Ordinary Classroom*. London: Robert Royce.

Watanabe, S. (1977) *How Do I Put It On?* London: Puffin Books.

Waterland, L. (1988) *Read With Me: An Apprenticeship Approach to Reading*, 2nd edn. Stroud: Thimble Press.

Weinberger, J. (1996) *Literacy Goes to School*. London: Paul Chapman Publishing.

Wells, G. (1982) *Language, Learning and Education*. Bristol: Bristol Centre for the Study of Language and Communication, University of Bristol.

Wells, G. (1984) *Language Development in the Pre-School Years*. Cambridge: Cambridge University Press.

Wells, G. (1986) *The Meaning Makers*. Portsmouth, NH: Heinemann Educational.

Whitehead, M. (2004) *Language and Literacy in the Early Years*, 3rd edn. London: Sage (1st edn, 1990).

Wilson, A. (ed.) (1998) *The Poetry Book for Primary Schools*. London: Poetry Society.

Wood, D. J., Bruner, J. S. and Ross, G. (1976) 'The role of tutoring in problem solving', *Journal of Child Psychology and Psychiatry*, 17: 89–100.

Wray, D. (1994) *Literacy and Awareness*. London: Hodder & Stoughton.

Wray, D., Bloom, W. and Hall, N. (1989) *Literacy in Action*. Abingdon: Falmer Press.

Wright, K. (1989) *Cat Among the Pigeons*. London: Puffin Books.

Wyse, D. and Jones, R. (2001) *Teaching English, Language and Literacy*. Abingdon: Routledge-Falmer.

Zolotow, C. (1972) *William's Doll*. London: Harper & Row.

Companion website

This website contains additional resources which are intended to be of use to students and lecturers. The resources are organised under the chapter headings used in *Developing Language and Literacy 3–8* (3rd edition).

There are three categories of resources:

Activities

Here I have included activities which can be used in lectures, seminars and workshops. I have also included activities which students can undertake in their study time or in school.

Websites

Here there are direct links to sites that are of particular relevance to the topics in each chapter.

Links to on-line reading

This section contains links to articles and reports that are available on the internet. The readings are intended to develop students' thinking about teaching English. They could be used as background reading for assignments or presentations.

The internet websites and web links to which I refer were consulted during the period February to June 2008. Addresses and details were correct at the dates of consultation but may have been subject to subsequent change.

Index

accent *see* received pronunciation
assessment
  by children 269
  of bilingual children 179–80
  of reading 250–60, 272–3, 274
  of speaking and listening 247–50, 274
  of writing 261–70, 273–4
audience 93, 94–5

bilingual learners
  teaching 164–6, 167–9, 171–2
book
  promotion 66–7
  selection 64–6, 172–3
books
  big books 63
  caption 60–1
  longer narratives 61–2
  non-fiction 62
  picture books 38–9, 61, 62
  plays 63
  poetry 62–3
  reading scheme 63–4, 172
  wordless 60

collaborative activities 14–5
  also see group work
comprehension 34–5
  activities 71–81, 169
contextual knowledge 32–4
critical literacy 38, 40–1, 79–81

dialect *see* standard English
drafting 96–7, 138–9
drama 15–9, 103
dyslexia 220–1

fiction 58–9
  value of 58–9

gifted and talented 224–6
grammatical awareness 31–2
graphic knowledge 30–1
group reading 49
group work 4–5, 6, 11–2, 14–5,
  20, 164–5
guided reading 47–9, 172, 252
guided writing 98, 111

handwriting 141–6
  across the curriculum 145–6
  difficulties 217–18
  teaching 142–6
hearing loss 205–6

ICT 46, 71, 88–9, 139, 146
individual reading 52–4

language and learning 4–5, 7–8, 161, 166
language project 20–1, 156–7, 177–9,
  197–9
layout 153–4
listening area 45
literature circles 51
look, cover, write check 98, 137–8

media literacy 38–40
miscue analysis 255–60

non-fiction 57–8, 62, 65–6
  reading 82–9
  value of 82, 88

oral language development 1–4, 160–1
organisation for speaking and listening 6–7,
  8–9, 9–15

paired reading 52
phonics 27–9, 132, 133–4, 170
phonological awareness 26–7
plans
  long term 280
  medium term 280–3
  short term 283–7
plenary sessions 11
poetry 59–60
  reading 81–2
  the value of 59–60
policy for English 292–301
punctuation 146–53
  development of 148–9
  difficulties 218
  teaching 149–53

reading
  activities 69–81, 83–9, 169, 172, 211–12
  area 45

reading *cont.*
  at home 230, 234–5, 242
  conferences 254
  difficulties 183, 188–9, 207–13
  environment 43–6
  gender differences 188–90
  individual 52–4, 251
  purposes for 37–8
  schemes 63–4, 172
  strategies 25–35, 170–1
  teaching methods 46–55
received pronunciation 23
response partners 112, 125, 269
role play 14, 16, 44–5, 72,
    102–3, 139

scribing 111, 214
self esteem 222–4
shared reading 46–7, 172
shared writing 54–5, 98, 109–10
silent reading 49–51
speaking and listening
  across the curriculum 18, 19–20,
  activities 168–9
  difficulties 203–7
  gender differences 184–8
  organising for 9–15
speech disorders 206–7
spelling 131–40
  development 132–4
  difficulties 216–17
  teaching 132, 135–40

standard English 22–3, 156–7
story reading 10, 67–9

talk partners 10–11
testing 270–4
text types 94–5, 124

visual literacy 38–40, 153–4

word recognition 29–30
  activities 69–71
writing
  across the curriculum 103
  activities 113–23, 125–8, 177, 214–16
  area 45–6, 99–101
  conferences 111–12, 264–5
  developmental approach 104–8,
    174–7, 266–8
  difficulties 213–20
  environment 99–103
  fiction 113–21
  gender differences 190–6
  independent 103–9
  non-fiction 123–8
  organisation for 99–103
  outcomes for 95–6
  poetry 121–3, 192–3
  reasons for 91–2
  resources for 99–103
  samples 265–8
  teaching 103–13, 269–70
  traditional approach 108